LIBRARY OF HEBREW BIBLE/
OLD TESTAMENT STUDIES

# 567

*Formerly Journal for the Study of the Old Testament Supplement Series*

*Editors*
Claudia V. Camp, Texas Christian University
Andrew Mein, Westcott House, Cambridge

*Founding Editors*
David J. A. Clines, Philip R. Davies and David M. Gunn

*Editorial Board*
Alan Cooper, John Goldingay, Robert P. Gordon,
Norman K. Gottwald, James Harding, John Jarick, Carol Meyers,
Patrick D. Miller, Francesca Stavrakopoulou,
Daniel L. Smith-Christopher

PLAYING THE TEXTS

# 17

*Editor*
George Aichele, Adrian College, Michigan

# THE UNCHAINED BIBLE

## Cultural Appropriations of Biblical Texts

Hugh S. Pyper

BLOOMSBURY
LONDON • NEW DELHI • NEW YORK • SYDNEY

Bloomsbury T&T Clark
An imprint of Bloomsbury Publishing Plc

50 Bedford Square
London
WC1B 3DP
UK

1385 Broadway
New York
NY 10018
USA

www.bloomsbury.com

**Bloomsbury is a registered trade mark of Bloomsbury Publishing Plc**

First published 2012
Paperback edition first published 2014

© Hugh S. Pyper, 2012

All rights reserved. No part of this publication may be reproduced or transmitted in any form or by any means, electronic or mechanical, including photocopying, recording, or any information storage or retrieval system, without prior permission in writing from the publishers.

Hugh S. Pyper has asserted his right under the Copyright, Designs and Patents Act, 1988, to be identified as Author of this work.

No responsibility for loss caused to any individual or organization acting on or refraining from action as a result of the material in this publication can be accepted by Bloomsbury or the author.

**British Library Cataloguing-in-Publication Data**
A catalogue record for this book is available from the British Library.

ISBN: HB: 978-0-567-16690-6
PB: 978-0-567-65254-6

**Library of Congress Cataloging-in-Publication Data**
A catalog record for this book is available from the Library of Congress.

Typeset by Forthcoming Publications Ltd (www.forthpub.com)

## Contents

Acknowledgments — vii

Chapter 1
INTRODUCTION — 1

Chapter 2
THE OFFENSIVENESS OF SCRIPTURE — 13

### Part I
### MAKING SENSE OF THE BIBLE

Chapter 3
THE BEGINNINGS OF THE BIBLE — 35

Chapter 4
BIBLICAL NONSENSE — 45

### Part II
### THE RESISTANT BIBLE

CHAPTER 5
RELIGION AGAINST THE BIBLE — 53

Chapter 6
THE BIBLE IN THE METROPOLIS — 61

### Part III
### THE BIBLE AS GUIDEBOOK

Chapter 7
BIBLICAL TOURISM:
EÇA DE QUEIROS AND MARK TWAIN IN PALESTINE — 79

Chapter 8
*THE BOOK OF DAVE* VERSUS THE BIBLE — 85

## Part IV
### THE BIBLE, MUSIC AND NATIONALISM

Chapter 9
WHEN JESUS WAS (NEARLY) A SCOT — 101

Chapter 10
JONAH IN ESTONIA, JOSEPH IN LATVIA — 109

Chapter 11
BRUCKNERIAN TRANSPOSITIONS — 123

## Part V
### ANIMAL BIBLE

Chapter 12
THE LION KING — 133

Chapter 13
CONVERSATIONS WITH DONKEYS — 141

## Part VI
### THE SPORTING BIBLE

Chapter 14
WRESTLING THE BIBLE — 151

Chapter 15
THE NASCAR BIBLE — 157

## Part VII
### THE SURVIVAL OF THE BIBLE

Chapter 16
DISPELLING DELUSIONS:
DAWKINS, DENNETT AND BIBLICAL STUDIES — 167

EPILOGUE — 180

Bibliography — 182
Index of References — 188
Index of Authors — 190

# Acknowledgments

I am particularly grateful in presenting this collection of essays to those who had the temerity to invite me to give talks and seminar papers, many of which became the basis for the present form of these essays. The audiences made their contribution too; their attention and their questions prompted me to rethink and rewrite a number of points. I am also indebted to my colleagues and students in the Department of Biblical Studies at the University of Sheffield; they have provided opportunities for conversation and have allowed me to travel to conferences and to take the periods of study leave which have been necessary for these pages to be written. I am also grateful to Dominic Mattos and his colleagues for their support and encouragement in bringing this book to press, and to George Aichele, editor of the Playing the Texts sub-series.

My principal acknowledgment must be for my father, Jock Pyper, who died as this book was being prepared. He was a dedicated critic of the Bible, who nevertheless appreciated its beauty and its power. Many of the views in this book have their roots in the ongoing discussion between us on the role of the Bible. Without him, I would never have ended up thinking and writing in the way that I do. I dedicate this book to his memory.

Chapter 1

## INTRODUCTION

"It is a good thing we did not all live in the time when the Bibles were chained up in the churches," said Bumpus. "It would have been so lonely."

"Well, but it is a good thing to read the Bible," said Francis.

"Of course it is the most beautiful book," said Emily. "And now we are modern, and only read about wickedness, it is so nice to have it unchained, isn't it? It really ought to be chained, I think."

"Ah, you try to get at us, Miss Herrick," said Francis, not quite checking a laugh.

"Ah, there is much warning in it for us," said Miss Lydia.

"In all great pictures," said Francis, firmly pulling himself together, and finding the effort inspiring, "we are shown the dreadful as well as the beautiful. We are surely not given only one side of the lesson."[1]

This volume explores a number of instances of unexpected readings of the Bible in popular culture, literature, film, music and politics. The argument that connects them all is that the Bible continues to have effects on contemporary culture in ways that may surprise and sometimes dismay both religious and secular groups. The title "Unchained Bible" comes from the epigraph above where an avowedly irreligious novelist, Ivy Compton-Burnett, nevertheless stages a conversation about the Bible in her first acknowledged novel. Rigidly atheistic in her beliefs, Compton-Burnett inevitably knew her Bible, as did any educated Englishwoman of her generation. Her own inimitably aphoristic style of conversational novel owes more than a little in its cadences and in its structures to biblical models. Her capacity to offer the "dreadful" as well as the beautiful in the spaces between the carefully modulated set-pieces of her novels is unmatched and so her characters' appreciation in dialogue above of the importance of the "dreadful" in the Bible is particularly apposite.

1. Ivy Compton-Burnett, *Pastors and Masters* (London: Gollancz, 1972 [1925]), 93-94.

That the Bible was at one time chained in English churches is true, although the ostensible reason was to preserve and protect this valuable and controversial text from thieves and those who would mishandle it. The subversive misreading of this enchainment as a symbol of a book in captivity to the established church is hard to suppress, however. Yet, once released from these chains, the Bible proves to be a text that gets everywhere and which undergoes surprising and sometimes contradictory metamorphoses. Rather like the rabbits introduced to an unsuspecting Australia, the Bible proves that it is unexpectedly adaptable to unfamiliar landscapes and can spread to unpredictable places and survive and reproduce there. Some of what it gives rise to is beautiful, much is dreadful and at times the two coincide.

As Emily Herrick rather mischievously suggests in the extract above, the Bible is at once revered as the most beautiful book, the high point of English prose (in the Authorized Version), and yet is a book which, read with a salacious or irreverent eye, proves to be full of "wickedness." The pious advocates of making the Bible accessible who sought to free it from the churches' chains may then be the very people who then decry some of the results when the Bible is free to roam.

A delightful example of these unintended consequences comes from the memoirs of the celebrated African American novelist Zora Neale Hurston. She recalls:

> I came to start reading the Bible through my mother. She gave me a licking one afternoon for repeating something I had overheard a neighbour telling her. She locked me in her room after the whipping and the Bible was the only thing in there for me to read. I happened to open to the place where David was doing some mighty smiting, and I got interested. David went here and he went there, and no matter where he went, he smote 'em hip and thigh. Then he sung songs to his harp awhile, and went out and smote some more. Not one time did David stop and preach about sins and things. All David wanted to know from God was who to kill and when. He took care of the other details himself. Never a quiet moment. I liked him a lot. So I read a great deal more in the Bible, hunting for some more active people like David. Except for the beautiful language of Luke and Paul, the New Testament still plays a poor second to the Old Testament for me. The Jews had a God who laid about Him when they needed Him. I could see no use waiting till Judgment Day to see a man who was just crying for a good killing to be told to go and roast. My idea was to give him a good killing first, and then if he got roasted later, so much the better.
>
> In searching for more Davids, I came across Leviticus. There were exciting things in there to a child eager to know the facts of life. I told Carrie Roberts about it, and we spent long afternoons reading what Moses

told the Hebrews not to do in Leviticus. In that way I found out a number of things the old folks would not have told me. Not knowing what we were actually reading, we got a lot of praise from our elders for our devotion to the Bible.[2]

Here in a nutshell Hurston lays out most of the issues that are explored in the following chapters. Once out of the hands of the adult guide, the Bible, given to a child, proves to be an eye-opener in many ways. It is both punishment and reward. What the young Hurston recognizes in it is the violence and the vengeance but also the vitality that seems to go against the grain of what she has been taught in a subversive and liberating fashion. The Bible gives a unique form of licensed transgression. As Hurston tells us, she and her friend were praised for reading the Bible, but no-one seems to have asked what they were reading and what their reading was teaching them. The "unchained Bible" becomes a first manual of sex education and a justification for a crude but clear moral order where the just would get their deserts. Again, Hurston testifies to what her pious elder relatives would no doubt have found a scandalous preference for the Old Testament as against the New because it speaks in a more lively way to her youthful desires and predilections.

The unique and privileged position of the Bible, then, allows it to become a book of "unsuspected subversion," to borrow a phrase from the poet Edmond Jabès.[3] As another American author, Annie Dillard, put it in her memoirs,

> The Bible's was an unlikely, movie-set world alongside our world. Light-shot and translucent in the pallid Sunday-school watercolors on the walls, stormy and opaque in the dense and staggering texts they read us placidly, sweet-mouthed and earnest, week after week, this world interleaved our waking world like dream.
>
> The adult members of society adverted to the Bible unreasonably often. What arcana! Why did they spread this scandalous document before our eyes? If they had read it, I thought, they would have hid it. They didn't recognize the vivid danger that we would, through repeated exposure, catch a case of its wild opposition to its world. Instead, they bade us study great chunks of it, and think about those chunks, and commit them to memory, and ignore them.[4]

---

2. Zora Neale Hurston, *Dust Tracks on a Road* (London Virago, 1986 [1942]), 54-55.
3. The phrase appears in the title of his volume *The Little Book of Unsuspected Subversion* (trans. Rosemary Waldrop; Stanford: Stanford University Press, 1996)
4. Annie Dillard, *An American Childhood* (San Francisco: HarperPerennial, 1998), 134–35.

This strange mixture of enforced memory and forgetting, the biblical texts diligently learnt by heart and then ignored, is another facet of the unchained Bible's peculiar influence. It can operate "hidden in plain sight," to coin a phrase. In some ways, it becomes too familiar to be recognized. That, however, does not mean that it is not at work, however. It means that its effects are not noticed and that it can effectively operate at an unconscious level in society. Indeed, as Hélène Cixous would argue, the biblical texts are peculiarly adept as this as, according to her, they already partake in the qualities of the unconscious: "The light that bathes the Bible has the same crude and shameless color as the light that reigns over the unconscious," she writes.[5] Once again, that gives the Bible particular power, but with unpredictable consequences.

It also means, however, that readings and misreadings of the Bible may propagate unchecked within our culture, just because no one recognizes them and therefore calls them to account.

Both Hurston and Dillard testify to the profound shaping effect the Bible had on their growing sensibilities as writers. Meeting the unchained Bible as children, they found it both exciting and alarming. No less a writer than Graham Greene reinforces the idea that such encounters have lasting effects:

> Perhaps it is only in childhood that books have any deep influence on our lives. In childhood all books are divination, telling us about the future, and like the fortune-teller who sees a long journey in the cards or death by water they influence the future. I suppose that is why books excited us so much. What do we ever get nowadays from reading to equal the excitement and the revelation in those first fourteen years?[6]

The after-effects of such reading can, however, be unpredictable. As Ruth Bottigheimer, the premier scholar of children's Bibles, has reminded us, the seventeenth-century child exposed to the Bible was protected to an extent from some of its most alarming portrayals of sexuality and violence by being inducted into reading traditions of types and figures.[7] The Bible was still "chained" to its ecclesiastical roots, although for many such child readers the theological emphasis on hell and punishment, a dimension that the church read into the Old Testament texts, carried its own terrors which left a lasting and sometimes very damaging impression.

5. Hélène Cixous, *Three Steps on the Ladder of Writing* (trans S. Cornell, S. Sellers; New York: Columbia University Press, 1993).
6. Graham Greene, *Collected Essays* (London: Vintage, 1999), 13.
7. Ruth B. Bottigheimer, *The Bible for Children: From the Age of Gutenberg to the Present* (New Haven: Yale University Press, 1996).

The fact, however, that for many generations children not only had access to the Bible, often as one of only a few books that were available, but were actively encouraged to read and to memorize it, cannot avoid having cultural consequences. More recent generations, however, grow up in a cultural heritage shaped by conscious and unconscious memories of the Bible but are themselves not exposed to the Bible, which adds another layer of complication. Unaware of the roots of the attitudes and actions that their society instills in them, they may find themselves unwittingly embracing dangerous or half-understood ideas based on past readings of the Bible without any tools of critical analysis to examine, question and counter them.

The essays collected in the present volume do not presume to expose all the ramifications of the unchanged Bible, or to provide the tools for an adequate assessment, critique and response to its influence. What they do, however, is trace some of the places where the Bible and its readings have unexpected influence and to suggest what a more conscious engagement with these influences might entail, both in terms of contemporary and historical cultural critique and as an important element in biblical reception and interpretation.

The chapters that follow fall into a number of clusters that deal with different aspects of the question of the Bibles influence. The volume begins with a consideration of the "offensiveness" of Scripture. It arose out of an invitation to give a presentation on that topic to the Society for the Study of Theology in the UK, a rather flattering one for a biblical scholar, but also a rather daunting if intriguing assignment. It allowed for a direct engagement with the perceived danger of the unchained Bible. The basic argument is that offensiveness is necessary if any text is to survive and to gain and retain the kind of cultural significance that the Bible as Scripture has maintained for some two thousand years at least. This is a development of the idea of the Bible as "unsuitable book" that I pursued in an earlier collection.[8] It also allowed for an exploration of the nature of offence itself. What is it to be "offended" and what are the psychological and biological roots of the response? Again, it turns out that the capacity to be offended is as old as life itself, and that any living system, by its very nature, generates material that is offensive to itself. A Scripture, then, that avoids offence is avoiding a fundamental part of what allows human organisms, and beyond that, human societies, to survive. Much of the material in the following chapters explores in more detail particular sources of offence in the Bible and in its interpretative

---

8. Hugh S. Pyper, *An Unsuitable Book: The Bible as Scandalous Text* (Sheffield: Sheffield Phoenix, 2005).

legacy, and the consequences of the ways in which communities shaped by the Bible seek to mitigate or repress the offensiveness of Scripture.

The following part of the book consists of two essays that deal with the linguistic and literary structure of the Bible itself under the general heading of "Making Sense of the Bible." One immediate source of offence for a reader is to be confronted with a text that does not seem to make sense, and the response has tended to be for the reader then to make sense of the text. How readers go about this, however, can be more revealing about them than is about the text, as their conscious and unconscious assumptions about what is comprehensible and what is not are enacted in their readings. The first essay, "The Beginnings of the Bible," examines the assumptions that lie behind the seemingly obvious fact that the Bible begins "In the beginning." The essay argues that there is nothing obvious or necessary about this and indeed that it is the fact that the Bible begins with the beginning that has made Western culture and scholarship take this as axiomatic. This is explored in dialogue with A. D. Nuttall's study of narrative beginnings, where he sets out a contrast between the Greek interest in formal beginnings and the Hebrew interest in natural beginnings. Through an examination of Augustine on the one hand and Rashi on the other, the argument is made that the idea of the natural beginning is in fact Platonic, and that the Hebrew tradition is interested in what is important, rather than what is chronologically prior. Indeed, the theological notion of "the beginning" derives from the Greek philosophical tradition rather than from the Bible. This may lead us to question whether "In the beginning" is in fact the best translation of the first words of the Bible and how far cultural norms framed by re-readings of the Bible then become reimported into the interpretation of the text.

This is then followed by an essay on "Biblical Nonsense." Following on from the previous chapter's questioning of the "obvious" translation of Gen 1:1, this chapter problematizes the matter further. Translators typically see their job as "making sense" of the biblical text in the receptor language. Yet a translation of the Bible into Klingon, the speech of one of the alien races in Star Trek, is available online. What sense does a Klingon translation make? This problem is compounded if the text that is being translated is expressly about the lack of meaning. Isaiah 28:3 is a text that seems to be representing the "nonsense" of foreign speech. Should a translator make sense out of what is nonsense? In investigating the various ways in which translators have dealt with this verse, and in particular the Klingon translation, the complexity of the idea of "making sense" of the Bible in contemporary culture is revealed, as is the fact that the Bible has made its way into interstellar space.

## 1. Introduction

The second part combines two essays that deal with the general issue of "The Resistant Bible." The first, entitled "Religion Despite the Bible," draws on Ernst Bloch's work *Atheism in Christianity* and indeed began as a contribution to a symposium on Bloch and Religion held at the University of Sheffield. Bloch's book is a remarkable work that uncovers the politically radical voice of the Bible that, in his view, is repressed by the official editors of the corpus but with only partial success. The liberative potential of the Exodus tradition is stifled by a conservative creation theology but not defeated. Bloch's commitment to "materialist" reading has had an important influence on liberation and postcolonial biblical readings and he is an engaging reader whose interest is in "unchaining the Bible" in order to make explicit the subversive potential of the text. In this chapter, however, the view is put forward that Bloch is not materialist enough because he is not theological enough in his reading. The Exodus story is tied inescapably to the Conquest narrative and what is liberation for one group may well be oppression for another. Bloch's materialist hope for utopia founders on the material inescapability of death. The creation narratives, as read by Paul and the Greek Fathers, are more radical in their account of the contingency of matter itself and their vision of a fully material, not spiritual, redeemed cosmos. Bloch's hope may, in Kierkegaardian terms, turn out to be defiant despair. The biblical vision is at once darker and more hopeful.

The next essay in this part is "The Bible in the Metropolis." An earlier form of this was delivered as the Ethel M. Woods lecture in Kings College, London, and so this provided the impetus to explore how the Bible is at work, consciously and unconsciously, in the way in which a great metropolitan city, once the capital of an Empire and still a major commercial and cultural centre is conceived of. In particular, the chapter explores the relationship between the biblical view of the city and late Victorian views of London and how these affect both the city's inhabitants and those who look on it with admiration and envy from the outside. At the height of empire, images of the evanescence and eventual destruction of the city in terms based on biblical passages are surprisingly prevalent, even to the point of being denounced as clichéd. This brings out the ambivalence of biblical imagery of the city both as the "new Jerusalem," the object of hope and desire, and Babylon, the alluring but dangerous enemy destined for destruction. Both in biblical prophecy and in Victorian and later postcolonial literature, the city becomes a site of longing and of mourning, and Jerusalem and Babylon become overlaid in complex ways in a "vertical" rather than "horizontal" account of their relationships. The city of Revelation is a new Jerusalem that looks remarkably like Babylon, in an eschatological version of what postcolonial theorists would call "mimicry." The Bible then finds a new relevance as a text that can speak into the mixture of mourning and celebration that immigrant and native populations share as they cope with living in an ever-changing metropolis.

Following on from this, the third part, "The Bible as Guidebook" explores the odd consequences of the turn to historical reading of Bible and how it becomes assimilated to tourist literature and the guidebook, with interesting effects. Again, there are two essays in this part. The first, "Biblical Tourism: Portuguese Novelists and the Life of Christ," charts the way the rise of "biblical tourism" in the nineteenth century leads to a rereading of the Bible. Once tours to Palestine became a possibility, politically and financially, the interest in mapping the book onto the land increases but so does the realization that this is less easy than might be expected. Out of this mismatch between text and reality there arises a new kind of satirical literature that subjects the historical claims of the gospel to a new scrutiny. No longer a pious pilgrim, the traveler to the Holy Land becomes a critical tourist. One important example of this is the Portuguese writer Eça de Queirós's novel *The Relic*. Through the adventures of his cynical hero, Eça critiques the credulity of Portuguese society, but is also drawing on the work of writers such as Renan on the one hand and Mark Twain on the other. The importance of such works for the popular perception of the Bible on one hand, and of the people and politics of Israel/Palestine on the other has often been underestimated and raises questions about the potential dangers of what could be another form of "biblical tourism" when cultural commentators make brief excursions into the text to reinforce existing cultural prejudices.

The metaphor of the guidebook underlies the use of the Bible in Will Self's novel *The Book of Dave* that is the focus of the second essay. The title refers the novel by Will Self but it is also the title of the book that its protagonist writes in the novel itself. Dave is a London taxi driver whose viciously misogynist diaries chronicling his divorce and his obsession with the taxi driver's "knowledge" are rediscovered many centuries later and become the scriptures of a future society. Self is satirizing contemporary fundamentalism, but in various interviews has put forward the view that any book could become scripture, in the right circumstances. This chapter challenges that assumption, arguing that only a particular sort of text can generate the kind of community that would propagate it. In fact, the development of the kind of novel that Self is writing is itself a product of the particular sort of text that the Bible models. As it turns out, within the novel itself, Self shows a much more nuanced understanding of the factors that might lead to a text acquiring sacred status.

However, in the end he sidesteps the crucial question as to how and why within the novel his character's *Book of Dave* is adopted by its readers in this way. I then argue further that in re-writing the Bible as "The Book of Dave," Self is himself revealing the importance of rewriting and rereading in the development of a scriptural text. The Bible is already rewritten, with layers of interpretation and juxtaposition, and this is at least part of what allows it to support the multiple interpretations later readers place on it.

Part IV moves to a consideration of another form of cultural appropriation of the Bible, its place in the development of nationalism in Europe and the role of biblically based music and drama in defining and reinforcing national identities. The first case study "When Jesus was (nearly) a Scot" examines an intriguing moment at the end of the eighteenth century when German-speaking scholars began to seek for a way of asserting a coherent German identity in the newly emerging Europe of nation states. A key figure is Johann Gottlieb Herder, who sought to ground the common identity of a nation in its language, folklore and poetry. This is aligned with the displacement of the Hebrew Scriptures in Lutheran culture. Herder called for the German people to find a new basis for their identity, rather than borrowing a Jewish text. For a brief moment, the Scottish writer James MacPherson's *Poems of Ossian*, purporting to be the ancient epic cycle of the Celtic peoples, seemed to provide an alternative source of ancient, song-based, cultural identity. This moment quickly passed with the allegations that MacPherson was a forger and, more importantly, the discovery of the cultural links between German and Sanskrit. This led to the development of a new myth of Indo-European culture, based on sacred books even more ancient than the Semitic corpus, which could bolster claims to the antiquity, unity and superiority of Germanic cultures in Europe, where Jewish culture now seemed a later, narrower and fundamentally alien intrusion. The disastrous political and religious consequences of this ideology in the nineteenth and twentieth centuries hardly need to be described.

The remaining two essays in this part look at case studies of the way that this works itself out particular cases. First is a comparison of two rather different works based on biblical stories have become iconic in the national struggle of two of the Baltic countries. In Estonia, the long-lost oratorio *Das Jonas Sendung* by Tobias was hailed as a masterpiece when it was premiered in Tallinn in 1990. This chapter explores why and how Tobias reworked the Jonah story and how his adoption of the oratorio form in German demonstrates the dilemmas around hybridity and mimicry that beset the attempt to assert a minority national identity. Indeed, Tobias' reworking of Jonah sheds light on the way that the writer of Jonah and other biblical writers reworked texts from their tradition in order to comment on issues of identity. The Latvian playwright Rainis opts for the Joseph tradition in his play "Joseph and his Brothers," an important work in the reassertion of Latvian identity. This work shows a number of contrasts with that of Tobias. By writing in Latvian, Rainis falls on the other side of the dilemma of how a community with a minority language can assert its identity internationally. Rainis also demonstrates issues that are taken up in a later essay in the unfortunate consequences that an unconscious tendency to assert national identities in terms of the Christian assertion of independence from Judaism has for the political life of twentieth-century Europe.

Political issues are also, perhaps surprisingly, at work in the second essay, which is based on the complex history of the critical reception editing and publishing of Bruckner's symphonies. What it reveal is that even in what might be supposed to be a matter of rather arcane scholarship, the political and cultural environment has powerful effects and the publication of the collected edition has important propaganda value for the National Socialists. The parallels to the issues surrounding the development of critical biblical scholarship at the end of the nineteenth and early twentieth century are clear and striking and even articulated by musicologists. Not only does the comparison reveal the political elements in what is presented as dispassionate scholarship, but it also makes clear that some of the same issues about the nature of repetition and the problems of creating coherent large-scale musical and literary structures are to be found in both critical enterprises. If the assumptions of some source-critical scholars were applied to Bruckner's works, there would be a plethora of Bruckners. Here I suggest that there may be fruitful ways to apply musical understandings of structure in biblical studies that take the study of the Bible and music beyond investigating the setting of biblical texts by composers.

Quite another field of cultural activity is explored in Part V, "The Sporting Bible." The first of two essays on different aspects of American popular culture is "Wrestling the Bible" and examines a complex interaction between Bible, politics, media and popular entertainment. World Wrestling Entertainment is a multi-million dollar corporation whose products reach over sixty countries. Its writers and marketers have to have a shrewd understanding of their core audience. Biblical themes and allusions are found in the most unlikely forms in their programmes. The chapter investigates the way in which a particular American audience responds to a kind of biblical shorthand in order to set up personal but also political tensions, especially around the engagement of the US with the Middle East. An extraordinary match when the General Manager and his son actually call out God into the ring for the showdown shows the way in which biblical images are used as powerful incitements to emotional involvement. It also reveals an intriguing structural similarity between the positions of the General Manager of the WWE and the God of Genesis, which can shed light on the dynamics of the biblical text itself.

Another sport that is now one of the top spectacles on American television and which has an international fan base of millions is the form of motor racing known as NASCAR. The publication of an edition of the Bible for NASCAR fans is an intriguing example of the synergy between evangelical groups who are seeking a new outlet for mission and a corporation which is seeking to expand beyond its traditional base in the Southern States and so wishes to appear "American" in the broader sense. The adoption of NASCAR drivers almost as secular saints, complete with pilgrimage sites is one manifestation of this. The Bible performs an intriguing double function as a marker of Southernness (hence the Bible Belt) but also as a symbol that can be promoted as fundamental to American family values. The chapter argues that the Bible has been an important and useful symbol in effecting the cultural changes that many commentators have described as the "southernization" of the US at the end of the twentieth and early twenty-first century.

In the wider development of cultural studies, the role of animals has become an increasingly important topic. This is reflected in the two essays that follow in Part VI. The first traces the way in which the Hebrew Bible delimits the human through the double deployment of the figure of Yahweh as both sovereign and beast, a device most clearly demonstrated in the way that the lion is used as metaphor and as narrative element in biblical texts. Derrida's series of seminars published as "The Beast and the Sovereign" offer a rich vein of reflection on the way that the limits of the human are marked out both "above" and "below" in the exceptional categories of "sovereign" and "beast." This particular conflation of beast and sovereign informs subsequent political theology in the Western tradition in ways that have unexpected and underappreciated contemporary consequences for political life.

In contrast, the second essay turns to donkeys. "One does not say foolish things to a donkey" writes Hélène Cixous in her essay "Conversation with the Donkey," alluding to the donkey that accompanied Abraham. This chapter follows her lead and stages a number of conversations with biblical and other donkeys. After all, Balaam's ass is the only animal that carries out a conversation in the biblical corpus, apart from the serpent.

The donkey is also, surprisingly, the animal of choice when the opponents of both Jews and Christians in the ancient world are seeking a term of abuse. The donkey carries a confusing range of symbolic freight. Discussing his film *Au Hasard Balthazar*, where a donkey is the main character, Robert Bresson points out that the donkey is not only a symbol of patience and submissiveness, but also an important sexual symbol. On the other hand it is also the symbol of stubbornness. The donkey often literally carries the biblical story, but it also brings an element of wilfulness to the biblical narrative connected with the untamableness of sexuality. Cixous uses the donkey to reflect on her writing, and in this essay, the interaction between human and donkey will be used to reflect further on the unpredictable aspects of biblical narrative.

The final chapter comes under the heading of "The Survival of the Bible." Under the title "Dispelling Delusions: Dawkins, Dennett and Biblical Studies" it argues that the debate over the Bible and evolution is, as popularly presented, quite misconceived. Some evolutionary theorists, particularly Richard Dawkins and Daniel Dennett, have produced more or less sophisticated reductive accounts of religion in terms of memetics and the evolution of cultural forms. In this discussion, the suggestion is made that the tables can be turned. The writings and arguments of these two scholars can be read, in their own terms, as proof of the power of biblical memes. In his polemics against organized religion, Dawkins is in a direct literary and rhetorical line from the denunciation of idols in Isaiah. Dennett's more subtle investigations of cognitive science are direct descendents of the sceptical inquiry into how we know what we know that is at the heart of Ecclesiastes' thought-experiment. Biblical scholarship, I suggest, need not be defensive in this debate. Indeed, embracing the insights of Darwin in terms of understanding the Bible as a cultural replicator which evolves under selective pressure over time is an under-explored heuristic device. At the same time, writers of popular science could learn much from seeing their own work in a similar evolutionary perspective, where the Bible is an inescapable and still important part of their literary inheritance.

Chapter 2

## THE OFFENSIVENESS OF SCRIPTURE

On November 21, 1905, Mark Twain wrote to Asa Don Dickinson, a young librarian who had asked his confidential advice on how to counter a move by the Brooklyn Public Library system to have Twain's *Adventures of Huckleberry Finn* removed from its children's sections. Twain's reply contains the following remarkable passage:

> The mind that becomes soiled in youth can never again be washed clean; I know this by my own experience, and to this day I cherish an unappeasable bitterness against the unfaithful guardians of my young life, who not only permitted but compelled me to read an unexpurgated Bible through before I was 15 years old. None can do that and ever draw a clean sweet breath again this side of the grave.[1]

Semi-jokingly, he suggested to Asa Dickinson that he hoped his book indeed *would* be removed if the children's department contained an unexpurgated Bible, as poor Huck's character would be corrupted if he were left in the same room.

Twain is out to makes his point by causing offence through claiming that he is offended by the Bible. For our discussion of the offensiveness of Scripture, we can already glean some important questions from this letter. Is offensiveness intrinsic to the offending object, or does it rather reflect a particular response to the object? Is that reaction innate or learned? Whichever is the case, in any particular instance we can also ask if the offender intends offence to be taken or whether he or she unintentionally triggers offence in the offended party. We are also made aware that another's reaction of offence may well be in itself offensive and, furthermore, that such reactions can be manipulated for rhetorical

---

1. Dickinson asked Twain to keep his correspondence confidential, a request Twain respected. Dickinson himself published this letter and others relevant to the controversy thirty years later in his article "Huckleberry Finn is Fifty Years Old—But is He Respectable?," *Wilson Bulletin for Librarians* 1 (1935): 80–85 (82).

effect. Twain is offended by the reaction to his book and turns the tables by claiming to be offended by the Bible. Other writings of his certainly indicate that this reflects a genuine reaction on his part, but here he is surely consciously playing on the rhetorical effect of counter-offence, if we may put it that way. This passage is sometimes quoted as expressing his considered verdict on the Bible, but that misses the context within which it is found.

It is also notable that Twain uses metaphors of dirt, washing and cleanliness to express his revulsion. His complaint is over an ineradicable soiling of his mind and a corruption of innocence, something that cannot be expunged or cancelled. The Bible he was exposed to and which he fears for Huck's sake is "unexpurgated," itself a term that expresses the need for the Bible to be "purged." In the Bible itself, there is that which needs to be removed in a way that suggests not just external cleansing but elimination and excretion of something intrinsic. In Twain's letter, we also have a way into an examination of the metaphorical language in which offence is described and discussed.

In this discussion, then, I want to use these questions and insights to explore the notion of the offensiveness of Scripture. Even to juxtapose these two words might already raise hackles in some quarters. At this stage, my response is simply to ask: "Would it be any less disturbing if this contribution was entitled 'The *Inoffensiveness* of Scripture'?" I am not sure that any of the Bible's champions would pick "inoffensive" as their adjective of choice to describe the text, and indeed might take offence at the suggestion.

Such a claim to inoffensiveness, in my view, is among the many flaws with the philosopher A. C. Grayling's recent attempt to produce an alternative secular Bible for humanists and atheists. The "Epistle to the Reader" which introduces *The Good Book*, as he entitles it, contains the following paragraph:

> All who read this book, therefore, if they read with care, may come to be more than they were before. This is not praise of the work itself, but of its attentive reader, for the worth to be found in it will come from their minds. If there is anyone who learns nothing from this book, that will not be attributable to faults in it, but to that reader's excellence [*sic*: presumably *lack* of excellence is what is implied]. If readers judge candidly, none among them can be harmed or offended by what it asks them to consider. Yet all who come hungry to these granaries of the harvest made by their fellows and forebears, will find nourishment here.[2]

---

2. *The Good Book: A Secular Bible* (London: Bloomsbury, 2011), v.

There is something peculiarly offensive about the claim that any offence the book might cause can only be the fault of the reader, who has clearly failed to "judge candidly" (whatever that might mean; is candour really the point at issue?). Already the reader's freedom and right to react negatively to the book is denied in a work that trumpets the values of intellectual freedom and the vices of dogmatism. In actual fact, it is not hard to find material in the book that could well be judged offensive by many readers.

Take, for instance, Chapter 11 of Grayling's "Genesis" (*The Good Book* is set out as a collection of "books," the titles of which consciously echo the biblical tradition, and these are printed complete with double columns and chapter and verse numbers). This chapter is a celebration of sexuality, a conscious counter, one presumes, to a long tradition of the religious repression and denigration of sexuality, which many, including Grayling, find offensive. Yet the way that this chapter sets about doing this is really rather troubling. Those who condemn sexuality are seen as foolishly resisting the bounty of nature "who" has linked affection and procreation (note the seemingly unavoidable personification here). When two individuals "of the same species and of a different sex" (Gen 11:19) are presented with each other, "Sight is troubled, delirium is born, reason, the slave of instinct, limits itself to serving the latter, and nature is satisfied." Anyone who has a problem with this has earlier been directed to consider his [and it is "his"!] own mother: "Do you believe your own mother would have imperilled her own life to give you yours if there were not inexpressible charms in the embrace of her husband? Be quiet, unhappy man, and consider that it was this pleasure that pulled you out of nothingness and gave you life" (11:14–15).

It is hard to know where to start here. Tell that to the children of the victims of tactical military rape in Bosnia and the Congo. Tell that to the children of women throughout the centuries who bore children out of duty or under coercion to further a dynastic or communal imperative. And why is the address only to the "unhappy *man*"?[3] Furthermore, such a passage seems to lend itself to the invocation of natural law in the condemnation of homosexuality better than anything in Paul. Sex is related to procreation in a way entirely consonant with Catholic teaching, although marriage does not figure. However, neither does any sense of discrimination. At any time that two beings of opposite sexes meet together, delirium ensues and so does procreation. This is empirically bad biology. Leaving aside asexual reproduction and those species which are hermaphrodite, it ignores the fact that humans are very much the

---

3. My italics.

exception in the natural world in not having a clear mating season. Most of the year, encounters between males and females do not lead to any delirium.

It also leads us to an exegetical problem. Grayling's Gen 4:10 states unequivocally, "Nothing comes from nothing: all things have their origins in nature's laws, and by their edicts reach the shores of life." Yet here, the unhappy man is told that he "was pulled out of nothingness" and given life. Grayling will have to get used to the fact that biblical readers are attuned to contradiction and be ready to be on the receiving end of the kind of hair-splitting textual analysis that the Bible has had to endure. How telling, we might say, that it is precisely at the point of the coming into being of the unique human person that the text invokes the otherwise forbidden category of *origo de nihilo*. The individual is pulled out of nothing by the pleasure of his mother.

It is also very hard to know where to start with the book labelled *Histories* which could not be more upfront in declaring the agenda that it is promoting, which is "to give account of the great war between East and West, on which the hinge of history turned." What he calls "the free hearts of the fathers of the West" (*Hist.* 1.5), although always numerically and politically weaker, kept the East at bay with its "indifference to liberty" (*Hist.* 1.4). This theme runs throughout the book, which is a retelling of the ancient Greek resistance to Persia.

Such Eurocentrism also reveals itself in the list of (unwitting) contributors. The majority are classical authors, Greek and Latin. The next largest group are French, mostly from the Enlightenment, and English. There are few Germans and very few other Europeans. Americans are not well represented, but there are a number of classical Chinese poets. There are three Arabic names, Abulfazi, Hafiz and Rumi, and two Indians, Carvaka and Kautilya. The great secular traditions, then, are the Greek tradition and to a lesser extent Confucianism. Any other traditions are represented, if at all, by poets rather than philosophers. More to the point, in the list of sources at the end of the book, which is reduced to an alphabetical catalogue of the authors most commonly referred to, I can only spot one woman among the hundred or so names: Sappho.

Even the Bible can boast more women poets than that (Miriam; Hannah; Mary) and even the Bible is more generous in citing its sources. Above all, the Bible knows that it is offensive and knows why that is important. As we shall see later, even internally, the Bible contains books and voices which take great offence at each other, and knows that often enough to offend others or to take offence is the mark of "candid judgment," rather than the blandly offensive attempt to ignore or belittle offence.

## 2. *The Offensiveness of Scripture*         17

Enough, however, of Grayling. The business of this chapter is to examine more closely the nature and consequences of the offensiveness of the Bible. In order to do this, I propose to begin by looking at the biological and cultural basis of the reaction of offence, drawing principally on the work of Darwin, William Miller and Martha Nussbaum, and then to look at the way in which this fundamental human response shapes and is dealt with within the biblical text. We will discover that this is a pervasive motif and that the text itself is witness to all the complications of intended, unintended and rhetorically manipulated offence and counter-offence that we might imagine—and possibly more. This is true both internally, in the interactions between characters, between strands of biblical tradition and between the Testaments, but also externally, in the relationship between the text and its readers. By tracing an unexpected link between Ezekiel, Peter and Jesus, we will be led, with some help from Kierkegaard, to suggest what is at the heart of the offensiveness of Scripture, and why the offensiveness of the Bible is intrinsic to its function.

### *The Biology of Offence*

The capacity to take offence is a fundamental characteristic of what it is to be alive. Nothing is more basic to any living system than the ability to discriminate between what can be assimilated and what should be rejected. A cell differentiates itself from its environment by such selectivity. It is not simply a matter of accepting and rejecting what the cell encounters in its surrounding, essential though that is. The very chemical reactions that undergird the processes of life within the cell itself generate by-products that are potentially harmful and have to be eliminated. Any metabolism of proteins, the building materials of life, for instance, will inevitably generate poisonous nitrogenous chemicals that, if allowed to accumulate, can fatally interfere with the workings of the cell.

The point is worth emphasizing. It is not simply that any living system needs to avoid or expel toxic material that it encounters in the environment; any living system intrinsically generates toxins that must be identified and expelled if life is to continue. At every level, then, living systems only keep living by identifying, expelling and, if possible, avoiding potential toxins. There is, however, no ideal environment free from any harmful elements that could provide a refuge for life to flourish. Life as a process itself generates the potential for its own destruction. Every living thing, intrinsically, exists by producing what could kill it if retained. When, for instance, yeast is introduced to a sugar solution, it will thrive by generating energy from converting the sugar to alcohol.

Sooner or later, fermentation stops as the yeast is poisoned by the alcohol it produces. In higher animals, the problem is solved by the evolution of the remarkable selective filtering capacities of the kidney and the lining of the gut.

All this suggests that the capacity for offence is in with the bricks of life, so to speak. It is as deeply built in to what it is to be a living being as could be conceived. It is intrinsic to maintaining the integrity and identity of the living being, but also betrays the fact that no entity can be living which is sealed off from its environment. Integrity and identity need constant maintenance so that the living organism does not merely dissolve into the environment nor die through the accumulation of its own waste products. To live is to be capable of being offended, of detecting and rejecting the potentially harmful, but also, always, of producing the potentially harmful.

The word "potentially" is significant too. The stakes are too high to wait until the harm is done. It is vital, literally, to be able to detect and reject the harmful before it is ingested if at all possible and in any case as soon as possible. If that means that, on occasion, something innocuous is needlessly rejected, that is a small price to pay. That means that even at the level of the cell there is a vested interest in being able to pick up cues that may warn of potential danger, so that something not in itself dangerous becomes the signal for avoidance. That, of course, immediately introduces the possibility of error and miscategorization; any cue can be misleading or misread, but the drawbacks of rejecting the harmless are outweighed by the need to avoid potential harm. The role of disgust in the development of semiotics and language, with all the dangers this can bring, is one that needs further reflection.

## The Culture of Offence

In this regard, Charles Darwin's *The Expression of the Emotions in Man and Animals*, first published in 1872, is a pioneering and characteristically meticulous investigation of the expression of disgust.[4] Darwin not only discusses the way in which this is related to taste and to the rejection of food, but also the way it is linked to other senses: smell, most obviously, but also vision and touch, and, to a lesser extent, hearing. He is struck, for instance, that soup, which, in itself, is attractive and

---

4. Charles Darwin, *The Expression of the Emotions in Man and Animals* (London: John Murray, 1872). The discussion of disgust is found in Chapter 11, pp. 254–77.

tasty, can revolt us when we see it on the tie of the diner opposite us. Equally, he discusses the well-known phenomenon by which someone who has happily finished a dish of meat only to be told that it is dog or monkey can be struck with what seems to be involuntary vomiting, although what was eaten has not changed.

This example shows that disgust is not directly related to taste or even to harmful chemicals, but to a complex learned set of reactions that can clearly vary between different cultural groups. What would revolt one group may appear appetizing to others.

The corollary of this is that as children mature they are inducted into a complex culture of signs that help to distinguish the acceptable from the unacceptable. It is important to note at this point that this cultural induction leads as much to overcoming as to extending their instinctive reactions. Any adult who eats olives or drinks beer has had to overcome an initial aversion, and indeed that overcoming can be seen as a marker of maturity. By the same token, children are taught that other things that seem appetizing are to be avoided, as in the British cultural, but not rational, aversion to horsemeat but acceptance of beef.

Darwin's research through correspondence with friends around the world led him to conclude that the facial expression of disgust—screwing up the face, raising the upper lip, protrusion of the tongue—runs across cultures, a conclusion that has been borne out by subsequent research. Human beings universally share the reaction and the facial expression of disgust, but can vary, or even flatly contradict each other, in what triggers that reaction. Disgust is thus both universal and particular, instinctive and learned, in a way that has intriguing consequences for the development of communities and cultures.

It is this complex interaction between nature and nurture in the reaction of disgust that is taken up by William Ian Miller in his wide-ranging study *The Anatomy of Disgust*.[5] He broadens the issue by arguing that culture can to a large extent be measured by the refinement of the sense of disgust. He reminds us that the relationship between disgust and other emotions such as contempt, shame and moral outrage is undoubtedly complex and to reduce them all to one phenomenon is misleading. We might add to this the category of offensiveness.

Nevertheless, he argues that the visceral energy of disgust is a major component in maintaining cultural structures:

---

5. William Ian Miller, *The Anatomy of Disgust* (Cambridge, Mass.: Harvard University Press, 1997).

> Disgust seems intimately related to the creation of culture; it is so peculiarly human that, like the capacity for language, it seems to bear a necessary connection to the kinds of social and moral possibility we have. If you were casually to enumerate the norms and values, aesthetic and moral, whose breach prompts disgust, you would see just how crucial the emotion is to keeping us in line and minimally presentable.[6]

The relationship between disgust and the body, and especially sexuality, is a particularly complex but inextricable one, he argues, basing much of his analysis of endemic misogyny in our culture on male disgust at semen and its excretory associations. He sees the idea of contamination as at the heart of the extension of the primary notion of disgust, and this links it immediately with the idea of cleanliness and the horror of the slimy and the sticky, that which cannot easily be washed off.

Martha Nussbaum takes issue with Miller, while acknowledging her debt to him, in her study *Hiding from Humanity: Disgust, Shame and the Law*.[7] Whereas Miller implies that the sign of a culture's advancement is the ever-growing sophistication and refinement of what it deems disgusting, she argues that justice depends on overcoming the sense of disgust. Allowing our sense of revulsion free rein to decide who is or is not acceptable to our society will lead, she argues, to manifest injustice. This is clear when a society turns against the sick or the foreigner. Disgust at the victim is no defence for a murderer, for instance.

Yet Nussbaum sees a similar defect at work in forms of liberalism that rely on shame to police the social order. Disgust may equally mislead in dealing with the whole complex of legal issues around the definition and regulation of pornography, for instance, in such a way that it obscures the real harms that are being perpetrated. She particularly questions an assertion she attributes to Miller that disgust is a necessary bulwark against cruelty; too often, she argues, it leads to cruelty against the weak, although, to be fair to him, this is a point Miller makes too. For Nussbaum, advancement depends on overcoming reactions based on disgust in favour of rational considerations. Both agree, however, that disgust and offence are essential sources of what we might call moral energy that then needs to be tempered by reflection if it is not to be simplistic or misdirected.[8]

---

6. Ibid., 18.
7. Martha C. Nussbaum, *Hiding from Humanity: Disgust, Shame and the Law* (Princeton: Princeton University Press, 2004).
8. Psychological studies bear out this link between the physiological and the moral aspects of disgust: see, for example, P. Rozin, J. Haidt and K. Fincher, "From Oral to Moral," *Science* 323 (2009): 1179–80, and the bibliography cited there.

We can sum this up by arguing that offence and disgust are fundamental physical and emotional reactions to a perceived threat to the integrity of the body that can also be extended to the integrity of a person or a group. The paradox is that the model of integrity that depends on maintaining the boundaries between inside and outside, self and other, deconstructs around the necessity for permeability between the two and the fact that the threat is at least in part self-generated.

## Biblical Offence

Nussbaum, interestingly, does not cite the Bible at any point in her discussion. Miller devotes a couple of paragraphs to a passing mention of the Levitical food restrictions. Yet the individual, social, sexual and political dimensions of disgust, its relevance to law, to the relationship between the biological and the cultural and its foundational place in the understanding and self-understanding of any living organism and its integrity relate intimately to the concerns not only of the biblical text itself but of the communities that base their life upon it.

The anxiety about contamination has obvious resonances with the concern for purity in the Hebrew Bible. Less obviously, but more significantly, it underlies the text's wider concern with maintaining the identity of Israel in distinction from the cultures that surround the community and are perceived as a threat, but from which it cannot entirely separate itself if it is to survive. The mechanisms of disgust and offence serve to detect and regulate this. At the same time, Israel cannot avoid generating its own legacy of impurity that has to be eliminated if it is not to disrupt the life of the community. Just as every human body in Israel generates waste to eliminate, so too does the community. The Bible is part of this process. To carry the metaphor even further, the Bible is part of the elaborate excretory mechanism of Israel, the communal equivalent of the kidney that filters out the body's waste products from its blood in ways we will develop below.

For a reader such as Mark Twain, however, it is the Bible itself that needs expurgation. For all that his tongue is in his cheek in the quotation with which we started, he declares not only that the Bible needs its own internal purging of a poisonous accretion of antiquated offensiveness, but that the culture within which he operates in its turn needs to be purged of the influence of the Bible. In what follows, we will turn to look at the way in which the tensions of the offensive are negotiated in the Bible itself before examining the way in which the Bible itself offends its readers.

What singles the biblical texts out in this regard is that they know these tensions. Biblical writers are offended by the Bible. The writer of Jonah does not like Nahum. Chronicles and Kings hardly get on. Job is not keen on Proverbs and the Wisdom of Solomon cannot be doing with the likes of Ecclesiastes. James and Paul have their problems in coexisting in the New Testament, and we could multiply this as we look at the battling voices within texts. Psalm 37 and Ps 73 glare at each other, for instance. Psalm 37 cannot abide the defeatism that gives up on God's care for the faithful, whereas Ps 73 is explicitly offended by the naïve or wilful blindness that seeks to deny the sufferings of the faithful.

It is clearly not possible to analyze exhaustively all the instances and dimensions of the offensive in the whole of the Bible. In order to keep this discussion within bounds, we must be more selective. One way that suggests itself would be to ask the following question: Which is the most offensive verse in Scripture? That might be at least a starting point for research into the scope of the offensive in the text.

As soon as we ask that question, we realize that the answer will tell us as much if not more about the respondent than about the text. It will reveal something about the norms against which the respondent thinks Scripture should be judged and the boundaries that the respondent finds it most threatening to have put in doubt. The verse that offends one reader may be a favourite of another who will find the fact that the first reader is offended itself offensive. Women may be offended by Paul's ruling that women should keep silent in church. LGBT readers may be offended by Lev 20:13. Jewish readers may be offended by Matt 27:25. In each case, there are those who are equally offended by their reaction. It would be an instructive if unorthodox exercise to collate the answers to the question of which verse is the most offensive and to make them the basis of a theology of Scripture. Once again, however, this would take us beyond the limitations of the present study.

We may get further, then, by asking a related but less subjective question: Which of its own verses does the biblical text label as offensive, either by the explicit claim of the author or character who utters the verse, or through the reaction of its hearers? Here we might find just the kind of exposure of the reactions and assumptions of readers within the text that will enable us to gauge how we as readers outside the text are being educated in offence as part of the text's endeavour to enlist us in the community of readers that will lead to its propagation through time. To fall into a convenient, though risky, shorthand of intentionality, the text uses offence to dismiss those readers who will not take it seriously enough to ensure its survival.

## 2. *The Offensiveness of Scripture*

Once again, an exhaustive study is beyond our scope. Instead, I shall concentrate on a very few notable examples of offence within the text, acknowledging that this is a preliminary foray which could bear much further refinement and correction.

### *Offending Ezekiel*

The best approach with such a topic may be to jump in at the deep end. The prophetic literature makes a point of being offensive, to the point that the term "pornoprophetics" has been coined by those who find the treatment of women and sexuality in these books particularly repugnant.[9] Ezekiel is the past master of this rhetorical plot and the mixture of disgust and voyeurism in the graphic accounts of the rape and degradation of Jerusalem in Ezek 16 and of Oholah and Oholibah in ch. 23 has offended many. Ezekiel's rhetorical ploy in describing the depth of Yahweh's disgust at his people's unfaithfulness draws on what he appears to assume will be his audience's shared disgust at the flaunting of women's sexuality, an assumption in its turn deeply offensive to many contemporary readers.

Yet even Ezekiel reaches his limits when the Lord commands him in 4:9–15 to enact the consequences of a siege by lying on his side and cooking a Spartan diet. Having given him the measures of his food, the Lord instructs him, "You shall eat it as a barley-cake, baking it in their sight on human dung" (4:12), explaining that this is to show how the Israelites will eat their bread once they have been driven out of the land.

This seems to be the last straw for Ezekiel, who has faithfully carried out a number of increasingly bizarre and arduous commands up to this point. He breaks out, "Ah, Lord God! I have never defiled myself; from my youth up until now I have never eaten what died of itself or was torn by animals, not has carrion flesh come into my mouth" (4:14). God, perhaps surprisingly, concedes a point: "See, I will let you have cow's dung instead of human dung" (4:15). It is, when one thinks of it, interesting that this exchange is recorded at all. Why is it important that we are exposed to the initial extremity of the divine command, the prophet's protest and the divine concession, instead of just learning that Ezekiel cooked his food on cow dung?

I think this exchange is rather revealing. Ezekiel's reaction seems to imply that the taboo against contact with human excrement is a given

---

9. For discussions of this term and its implications, see Athalya Brenner, ed., *A Feminist Companion to the Latter Prophets* (Sheffield: Sheffield Academic, 1995), especially Section 2.

within his culture. In that case, we might expect to find elsewhere in Scripture a complex code of law regulating this aspect of life, given that it is an inescapable part of being human. After all, the dietary laws of Leviticus show that ingestion was a subject of intense interest.

In actual fact, excretion and excrement are rarely mentioned at all in the Hebrew Scriptures. This might indicate that the writers were unconcerned about the matter, although Ezekiel would seem to give the lie to that. Conversely, it could be that they had such a horror of the subject that they prefer to gloss it over. There is only one discreet passage that contains a law on excretion: Deut 23:12–14 enjoins every Israelite to have a trowel so that they can go to a designated place to dig a hole and cover their excrement, the reason for this being that God travels with the camp and the sight of something offensive might cause him to desert the people. A God who is squeamish about the inescapable consequences of his own creation has only himself to blame, you might think, but that is another matter.

What this passage does indicate, however, is that the way to deal with the inescapable cause of offence is, literally, to bury it. The offensive is hidden. The lack of mention elsewhere, then, is of a piece with this stratagem. Yet this can add an extra dimension to offence. To bite into what seems a sound piece of fruit and encounter the mushiness and mustiness of decay, or, worse, a writhing maggot (or, in the old joke, worst of all, half a maggot) triggers a powerful reaction in most of us. At some level, we have been fooled into a potentially harmful act. The apple that looks rotten may disgust us but as long as we do not touch it, cannot be a source of immediate harm. In the case of an apple that we have already bitten into, the harm may already be done. A person or social group that deals with offence by concealment risks causing even more offence if the offence then comes to light. The exchange in Ezekiel reveals that effort at concealment; even Ezekiel cannot deal with a God who demands his exposure to something that, according to Deuteronomy, is intolerable to his sight.

In a remarkable paper entitled "Prophetic Scatology: Prophecy and the Art of Sensation," Yvonne Sherwood traces the tangled history of the ways that commentators have sought to evade the blood, excrement, pus and putrefaction that seep from the pages of the prophets in order to wrest a noble and poetic meaning from these books.[10] At the same time, she reflects on the evidence of her own squeamishness even as she writes

---

10. Yvonne Sherwood, "Prophetic Scatology: Prophecy and the Art of Sensation," in *In Search of the Present: The Bible through Cultural Studies* (ed. Stephen D. Moore; Semeia 82; Atlanta: SBL, 2008), 183–224.

## 2. The Offensiveness of Scripture

the article: her use of Latinate or other euphemisms, of inverted commas, of irony and cultural allusion to avoid the blunt offensiveness of Anglo-Saxon terms. Even the most fervent literalist may baulk at reproducing the force of prophetic language at some points, where prophetic writers seek to shock their hearers into sharing some inkling of God's disgust at the people and institutions of Israel. It is a matter of register; translators settle somewhere on a spectrum from unclean things through dirt, filth, ordure, dung, faecal matter, excrement, stool to shit, although there is little to suggest that the prophetic writers themselves were pulling their punches rhetorically or linguistically. Hebrew, especially, offers few get-outs in this way and its vocabulary consists, if not of four-letter words, of three-letter ones. What happens in such prophetic texts is not a simple confrontation with the threat of death, but the threat of dissolution, of decay and of dismemberment. That which the body rejects, excrement and menstrual blood, in order to live, or that which signals the onset of bodily decay, bleeding, pus and rottenness, are thrust into our vision. Of course there is a risk, too, in the other direction, in a childish seeking out of the sexual and other crudities of the Bible. Any implication, however, that the use of such language by biblical writers is a forgivable sign of the lack of literary sophistication or cultivated taste by its authors is both patronizing and misleading. That is not an excuse that could or would be proffered for James Joyce or D. H. Lawrence, for instance.

Yet it is not enough simply to explain this as a rhetoric of shock. As we all know, such rhetoric tends to be self-defeating, leading to diminishing returns. Sherwood finds the most disturbing and offensive aspect in the abjection of the prophetic voice itself through physical and mental abuse until it rails and wails its way to silence. By "rubbing our noses in it," or, as Sherwood puts it,

> By taking their language and the human body to the edge, the prophetic texts have practically guaranteed the strange critical/liturgical reflex whereby they are extolled, but not read, commented on, but not too closely, and diluted as the work of gentlemen, the stuff of fairytale. The paradox is that this story of rejection is also in some strange way the story of prophecy's legitimation.[11]

The very effort to shock the audience into listening may stop them listening, or prevent them from hearing. Yet this is exactly the charge that the prophets appear at times to have: to speak to the people "lest they hear" or to predict to them the inevitability that they will not listen.

---

11. Ibid., 215.

Offence, as we suggested above, selects readers and reading strategies. We may take offence at Ezekiel, or we may, with our exegetical and theological trowels to hand, find ways of covering up the offensive material in such scriptures, thereby running the risk that the next generation of intelligent readers, such as Twain, uncover the carefully hidden offence and are then doubly offended by the hypocrisy.

## *Offending Peter*

An intriguing parallel to this passage to Ezekiel is to be found in Acts 10:9–16. It is the account of Peter's vision of the great sheet coming down from heaven containing every kind of four-footed creature, creeping thing and birds. From his reaction, it is clear that, for him at least, one of the most offensive verses in the New Testament is Acts 10:13: "Get up, Peter, kill and eat." His response is a shocked refusal. In almost the same words as Ezekiel he replies, "By no means, Lord: for I have never eaten anything that is profane or unclean." Like Ezekiel, he draws the line at eating what is forbidden and is prepared to go against a direct command from heaven. To a devout Jew, Acts 10:13 is such an offensive statement that, even if comes from a heavenly source, only the manifestation of the Spirit can justify acting on it. Peter is being asked to go against not only a verbal command but, quite literally, his gut feeling of the uncleanness of the food and the indelible effect on the criteria for his identity.

The incident is repeated three times and we get no indication that Peter's answer is any different the third time. The story then moves on to Peter's encounter with the centurion Cornelius, where Peter does seem to have taken on board something from his earlier vision in that he overcomes his initial reluctance to have any contact with this Gentile, even though he is God-fearing and well spoken of by other Jews. This is reinforced by the descent of the Holy Spirit on Cornelius and his household that seems to convince Peter to the extent that he stays with Cornelius and presumably eats with him. His actions get him in trouble with the "circumcised" in Jerusalem, and he repeats the whole story in ch. 11 in self-justification.

When we read Galatians, of course, we seem to get another twist on this story (Gal 2:11–22). Paul tells us that he had to confront Peter in Antioch when, under the influence of the disciples of James, he had apparently changed his mind about eating with Gentiles. He and the rest of the Jews draw apart. The relationship between Peter in Acts and Peter in Galatians is a complex literary question, but the point is made of the depth of the reluctance to eat what is unclean. This is not simply a cerebral decision or an act of will, but relates to a deeply ingrained sense of cleanliness, contamination and disgust, and an assault on the integrity of Peter's identity, both as an individual human body and in terms of the cultural structures he inhabits and which give him meaning. In this case, it takes Paul's reconfiguration of the boundaries of what constitutes the identity of both Jew and Gentile to change his mind.

## *Offending Jesus*

It is no wonder, then, that the apparent breach of the most basic dietary taboo, cannibalism, is a matter of the gravest offence. The fact that the body as a metonym of identity and integrity can be dismembered, that we are confronted with the fact that we are not only flesh, but meat, that hands and limbs and tongue and guts conspire to reduce human bodies to what can be ingested, digested and excreted, is a key site of the reflex of disgust not only on the body consumed but also on the one who consumes.

Throughout the Hebrew Scriptures, the resort to cannibalism represents the nadir of human experience. Yet a passage such as Deut 28 does not simply warn against cannibalism as a possibility, but predicts it as the inevitable outcome of Israel's disobedience: "In the desperate straits to which the enemy siege reduces you, you will eat the fruit of your womb, the flesh of your own sons and daughters whom the Lord your God has given you" (28:53). This is not an awful warning of what may happen if the people fail to repent, but a prediction of what will happen when the people inevitably fail to repent. The passage goes on to hammer home the point that even the most refined of men and women will refuse to share with anyone else, even their own spouses and children, the flesh of the children they are reduced to eating. This passage finds some fulfilment in the story of the quarrelling cannibal mothers in 2 Kgs 6:24–32, squabbling over a child that has been hidden. Their behaviour is an outrage to the king. The disintegration of the city and the nation is embodied in the breaking down of the barrier between human flesh and meat, the reversal of the mother's role as nurse to her child to feeding upon it, and the dismemberment of the vulnerable body that she has given shape to.

All this lends background to our understanding of the one explicit time that Jesus asks his disciples "Does this offend you?" (John 6:61). Unsurprisingly, they recoil from his teaching that only by eating the flesh and drinking the blood of the Son of Man will they have life. "This teaching is difficult," they murmur; "who can accept it?" (6:60)

Jesus contrasts his flesh as bread with "the bread from heaven" that their ancestors ate, an allusion to the description of the manna in the wilderness in Exod 16:4. This gave life for a while, but those who ate it died eventually. Though this further detail is not explicitly recalled in John, one of the characteristics of manna in Exodus is its swift decay, as recounted in Exod 16:20: "Some left part of it until morning, and it bred worms and become foul." This is an unusually explicit reference to the possibility of decay, even of a divine gift. It is in John also, in the story of Lazarus, that we get the most explicit admission of the corruptibility of human flesh when Martha protests against Jesus' instruction that the stone at the mouth of Lazarus' tomb should be rolled back: "Lord, already there is a stench because he has been dead for four days" (11:39).

As we have explored above, here the examination of offence and disgust may unexpectedly contribute to the complex debates about the nature of signs that coalesce around the theology of the Eucharist and the relationship between the bread and the body. Disgust, as we have seen, depends not on what we eat, necessarily, but on what we think we are eating. It is not a matter of complex metaphysical analysis of what we ingest or advanced semiotics but of gut reactions and atavistic responses and how we deal with those. This is well beyond my area of competence, but I simply ask how far theologies of the Eucharist get beyond various strategies of hiding the offence rather than confronting it. What we may find, if we confront it, is that it puts in question the basis of the integrity of the person and the community through the breach of the boundaries of body and not-body, food and not-food, Israel and not-Israel in such a way that these cannot be redefined by simply altering the scope of the categories.

Would it be too shocking to suggest that what happens in the trial and rejection of Jesus is a concerted act of attempted excretion, where Greek, Roman and Jewish social bodies seek to displace that which threatens their integrity, but which is intrinsic to their integrity? Jesus, after all, demonstrates a surprisingly frank and matter-of-fact attitude to the whole business in another passage in Mark where he manages to offend his hearers. Confronted by those who are offended by his disciples' failure to observe the rules of handwashing, he argues, "Do you not see that whatever goes into a person from outside cannot defile, since it enters not the heart but the stomach and goes out into the sewer?" (Mark 7:18).

It is not what one ingests that causes uncleanness, as that passes out into the sewer. It is what is generated from within that causes uncleanness. In terms of a modern understanding of the digestive processes, this distinction is less clear. What passes into the sewer is not simply food material that has remained undigested, but a whole slew of waste products of the body and dead human cells, together with a rich fauna of commensal bacteria and protists.

Taken further, however, this raises the question with which we started. Given that all living cells only exist through a perpetual exchange with their environment, and that on the level of the organisms, the same principle applies, what is in or of the body and what is outside it is not so simple to describe. Is what is in the gut "in" the body? What about what is in the bloodstream rather than the cell? What Jesus does point to, however, is the fundamental paradox that uncleanliness and the source of offence is not and cannot be made extrinsic to the human person. It is part and parcel of the odd relational entity that we identify as the person that it will be offensive to others and to itself. The theological conundrum of the incarnation is that instead of sloughing off this intrinsically unstable structure of flesh in relation, which is the perfectly understandably Gnostic answer to this, Christianity presents the paradox of a God entering into this world of drains and excrement, of flesh that decays and rots.

## An Offensive Conclusion

The Scriptures of a community exist to exclude as well as to include, to offend as well as to seduce. What is peculiarly obvious in the Jewish and Christian Scriptures is that this struggle is enacted within the form of the text. Books and voices within books are still struggling to eradicate each other, offended by each other's presence within the canon, frozen in a moment of suspended expulsion. At the same time, readers are caught up in this dynamic of assimilation and exclusion. At different points, they stumble on passages that seek to repel or expel them, and have to decide, individually and communally whether they will resist, ignore or cover over these points of repulsion. The texts themselves enact this long process of offence and concealment and uncovering a history of hidden offence may itself compound the offence to the reader. What cannot be done, except by such a hermeneutic of concealment, is to establish secure bounds of personal and communal integrity on the basis of such texts. Their offensiveness is such that all such attempts at reification fail.

But what are we to do in the face of this? Are we to remain in Twain's unenviable state of an unredeemable sense of defilement? Let me finish with two responses that are at least suggestive.

The first comes from Pascal Mercier's novel *Night Train to Lisbon*. The main character, an elderly Swiss teacher, has become intrigued by the life and writings of a little-known Portuguese writer, Amadeu do Prado, and travels to Lisbon to find out what he can from those who remember him. Amadeu's old school teacher tells him the story of the remarkable graduation speech the 17-year-old gave (in Latin) at his school, which took the Bible as its topic. The following is a striking quotation from the speech:

> I revere the word of God for I love its poetic force. I loathe the word of God for I hate its cruelty... The poetry of the divine words is so overwhelming that it silences everything and every protest becomes wretched yapping. That is why you can't just *put* away the Bible, but must *throw* it away when you have enough of its unreasonable demands and of the slavery it inflicts on us.[12]

His former teacher, Father Bartholomeu, recalls, that at the end of the speech, there was silence:

> But then something happened that seemed to everyone in the hall like a joking proof of God's existence: a dog started barking outside. At first, it was a short dry bark, that scolded us for our petty humourless silence; then it turned into a long-drawn-out wail as if echoing the misery of the whole occasion.
>
> Jorge O'Kelly burst out laughing, and after a second of fear, others followed him. I think that Amadeu was taken aback for a moment; humour was the last thing he had counted on. But it was Jorge who had started, so it had to be all right.[13]

Offended by the Bible, Amadeu urges us not to ignore it but to throw it away. The unexpected juxtaposition of the dog barking, enacting the "wretched yapping" of any protest, sparks off laughter. Here we are in the world of the great poet of offence in Scripture, Søren Kierkegaard. He would have applauded, in so far as they go, both responses. For him, the opposite of offence is not faith, but spiritlessness.[14] To throw away

---

12. Pascal Mercier, *Night Train to Lisbon* (trans. Barbara Harshav; London: Atlantic, 2009), 168, 169.

13. Ibid., 163.

14. Kierkegaard's pseudonym Anti-Climacus explains this in *The Sickness Unto Death*: "The Jews had a perfect right to be offended by Christ because he claimed to forgive sins. It takes a singularly high degree of spiritlessness (that is, as ordinarily found in Christendom), if one is not a believer (and if one is a believer, one does believe that Christ was God), not to be offended at someone's claim to forgive sins. And in the next place, it takes an equally singular spiritlessness not to be offended at the very idea that sin can be forgiven. For the human understanding, this is most impossible—but I do not therefore laud as genius the inability to believe it, for it *shall* be believed" (Søren Kierkegaard, *The Sickness Unto Death: A Christian Psychological Exposition for Upbuilding and Awakening* [ed. and trans. Howard V. Hong and Edna H. Hong; Princeton: Princeton University Press, 1980], 116).

the Bible is a response that at least acknowledges and responds to its offensiveness and takes action on an ethical level. Beyond that ethical response, for Kierkegaard, however, is humour, which sees the absurdity and vanity of setting oneself up as an individual human to embody the ethical. What we would hurl away in discarding the Bible is something intrinsic in the whole fabric of individual and collective existence. We would discard ourselves in the process.

Yet for Kierkegaard, humour is not the final resting point. Beyond the realization of absurdity and impossibility and incommensurability that it represents is his great claim that "God is that all things are possible." That includes the impossible things as well.

What is really at stake, in his view of offence, is the impossible possibility of forgiveness. That is the other way of dealing with offence. Yet, for Kierkegaard, "Your sins are forgiven you" is the most offensive verse in Scripture, and understandably so. The offensiveness of Scripture is a reminder of how offensive that offer of forgiveness is, in the way it undermines our notions of what it is to construct and defend individual and collective integrity. In terms of Christian theology, the heart of the matter of the offensiveness of Scripture may come down to the fact that it poses what comes to be an unavoidable but unacceptable question: Can we forgive God for his audacity in forgiving us?

Part I

MAKING SENSE OF THE BIBLE

Chapter 3

THE BEGINNINGS OF THE BIBLE

So, to begin: but wait a minute—have I not already begun? Can I really begin again, having begun before I begin? This kind of mock-Derridean flourish, I realize, can quickly become very irritating. So enough; let's begin again.

The title of this chapter, "The Beginnings of the Bible," is, not undesignedly, ambiguous. I wonder what you are expecting to read. Indeed, it crossed my mind that the chapter could be constructed on the basis of that curse of modern communication, the call-centre menu. There are a number of options that we could follow. Press 1 if you want to read a discussion of which are the earliest pieces of tradition or writing in the Bible, 2 if you would prefer to inquire into the first moments at which the concept of a biblical canon began to emerge, 3 if you are interested in a discussion of the earliest events referred to in the narrative world of the Bible, 4 for a treatise on the variety of creation myths within the canon and 0 to abandon the whole enterprise.

Of course I am not fool enough to offer you all these options. On the other hand, the first four, at least, would be viable topics. What I want to do, however, is none of these. Indeed, the beginnings of this investigation were, I am happy to say, a result of my teaching, which is where most good research questions arise. Charged with providing an overview of the Hebrew Bible from Creation to Revelation, I began to wonder about the oddity that the Bible begins with beginning and indeed with the very word "beginning" (ברשית, *bereshit*), the kind of oddity that seems so natural that it must be viewed with suspicion.

*The Beginnings of Scriptures*

A canon of Scripture does not have to begin with the beginning. Other traditions manage very well without doing this. Two examples of well-known canons illustrate this point. The Quran begins first with a prayer to Allah and then with the Sura entitled "The Cow":

*[The Opening]*
In the name of Allah, the Beneficent, the Merciful.
All praise is due to Allah, the Lord of the Worlds.
The Beneficent, the Merciful.
Master of the Day of Judgment.
Thee do we serve and Thee do we beseech for help.
Keep us on the right path.
The path of those upon whom Thou hast bestowed favors.
Not (the path) of those upon whom Thy wrath is brought down, nor of those who go astray.

*The Cow*
In the name of Allah, the Beneficent, the Merciful.
Alif Lam Mim.
This Book, there is no doubt in it, is a guide to those who guard (against evil),
Those who believe in the unseen and keep up prayer and spend out of what We have given them,
And who believe in that which has been revealed to you and that which was revealed before you and they are sure of the hereafter.
These are on a right course from their Lord and these it is that shall be successful.
Surely those who disbelieve, it being alike to them whether you warn them, or do not warn them, will not believe.[1]

The Quran begins, then, with an authoritative statement in the first person by Allah as to the nature and the purpose of the book. It is an infallible guide, guaranteed by its divine author, which in itself will provide the test that will distinguish believers from the unbelievers. That, surely, is quite a helpful way to begin. At least its readers are clear what they are engaging with and what the appropriate response, in the book's terms, might be.

By contrast, the Tao Te Ching, not uncharacteristically, refuses the whole question of beginnings and the temporal ordering that narrative imposes on experience. Indeed, it begins by questioning the usefulness of language and the appropriateness, or even the possibility, of the kind of authoritative guidance that the Quran sets out to offer:

As for the Way, the Way that can be spoken of is not the constant Way;
As for names, the name that can be named is not the constant name.[2]

---

1. The translation is from M. M. Pickthall, *The Meaning of the Glorious Qur'an* (Hyderabad: Government Central, 1938).
2. Lao-Tzu, *Te-tao Ching* (trans. Robert G. Henricks; New York: The Modern Library, 1993).

These two examples demonstrate that there are quite legitimate other ways of beginning a scripture than with a narrative account of the beginnings of creation. Indeed, beginning in the way that the Hebrew Scriptures and the book of Genesis do leaves important questions unanswered about the purpose and scope of what we are about to read.

In turn, this puts in question the interest that biblical scholars have so often had in origins and beginnings. For two centuries at least, much scholarship has pursued the intriguing literary issue of how and where the texts had their beginning and the status of this privileged moment in the life of the text. It also set me thinking about the number of beginnings in the Bible. Each biblical book, each chapter, begins in that it has a first word, but do they all begin in the same sense? Is the beginning of a prophetic book, of Lamentations, of Psalms, a beginning in the same sense as the beginning of Joshua or Ruth? In a broader sweep, the Bible seems to be full of new beginnings, or beginning again. The whole story told in the Torah and the Deuteronomistic history begins again in Chronicles, for instance. But if we have to begin again, did we ever really begin in the first place?

This then leads me to wonder if there is not something at work in our culture that makes the fact that the Bible begins at the beginning seem like a tautology, whereas it is only one option among many. This has some resemblance to the so-called anthropic principle in cosmology.[3] Briefly put, the anthropic principle argues that we need not get too excited about the vanishingly small probability that all the conditions for life should be met on this planet. If, for instance, the earth's distance from the sun, the melting point of ice, or any number of apparently arbitrary constants had been different, life would not have existed. The fact is that we can only observe the kind of universe that sustains us as observers. We are bound to look out and see a universe that sustains human life, because any other sort of universe we would not be here to see. The application of this to the question of the beginning of the Bible is that we might argue that our intellectual culture has developed in a context permeated by the Bible and its apparent interest in beginnings. We are the product of a Bible-reading culture, so that we see it as both natural and important to inquire into the beginnings of things, to seek origins and the original. By the same token, the fact that the Bible begins with a beginning seems obvious and the obvious question to address to it is to

---

3. For a full discussion of the variety of understandings of this concept and its consequences, see John Barrow and Frank Tipler, *The Anthropic Cosmological Principle* (Oxford: Oxford University Press, 1988).

inquire into its origins. Yet it may be the Bible itself, or the way that it has been read, that has made this seem natural.

## *Narrative Beginnings*

This sense is heightened once one examines the literature concerning beginnings in literature. This is surprisingly sparse, given the importance that people give to the first lines of novels and poems, perhaps because the whole issue seems too obvious. The standard study, one of only a handful, devoted to the way narratives begin is A. D. Nuttall's learned and readable *Openings: Narrative Beginnings from the Epic to the Novel*.[4] One of Nuttall's avowed intentions in this work is to row back against the tide of what he calls formalist theory and to explore the literary tension between the undoubted freedom of an author to begin his or her work wherever he or she likes on the one hand and the continuing sense that there are natural beginnings, "echoes," as he puts it, "more or less remote, of an original creative act." He sums up the tension as between "*in medias res*, as against 'In the beginning.'"[5] The allusion to Genesis is quite deliberate, and here is set against Horace's well-known advice in his *De Arte Poetica* that aspiring poets should follow Homer's example and begin, not "*ab ovo*" [from the egg], but "*in medias res*" [in the midst of things]:

> Nor does he begin Diomedes' return from the death of Meleager from the [twin] egg[s]; ever he hastens to the issue and hurries the hearer to the midst of things as if already known and what he fears he cannot make attractive with his touch he abandons…[6]

Homer's concern is not with chronology or origins, Horace explains, but, in the rather charming phrasing of Francis's verse translation, "to the grand event he speeds his course" [*ad eventu festinat*]. His priority is what is important, not what is merely temporally prior. This contrasts with Genesis and its interest in strict chronological sequence.

For biblical scholars, however, there is in such a way of putting things a familiar but always questionable binary divide between two entities broadly labelled Greek and Hebrew culture. Nuttall makes this explicit

---

4. A. D. Nuttall, *Openings; Narrative Beginnings from the Epic to the Novel* (Oxford: Clarendon, 1992).

5. Ibid., viii.

6. Horace, *Satires, Epistles and Ars Poetica* (trans. and ed. H. R. Fairclough; LCL 194; Cambridge, Mass.: Harvard University Press, 1926), 463.

when he expands on this opposition as follows: "We begin to sense in the history of European literature enormous tension between (say) 'In the beginning God created the heaven and the earth' and 'Hardly out of sight of Sicilian soil they were joyfully setting sail,' that is between a natural and a formal beginning."[7] Horace, so Nuttall contends, is adopting a Greek priority of form over matter into Roman culture in a way that counters the natural sense of order in Roman—and, he explicitly adds, Hebraic—culture. This opens the way, once theology's dead hand is weakened, for the great experiment of Western literature that exploits this tension.

Nuttall's way of putting this, however, should raise questions for scholars of the Hebrew Bible. Such binary oppositions between Hellenic and Semitic cultures come and go in biblical scholarship, but the story usually turns out to be more complicated than the stark contrast implied. Nuttall himself sees an instability in this opposition when he turns to Virgil. His way of beginning the *Aeneid* is a classic example of starting "*in medias res*" and yet Nuttall detects in Virgil a nostalgia for a natural beginning. This, he contends, is seen in the constant hints in the *Aeneid* that point towards an overarching shape of history within which the action unfolds. Nuttall, again, labels such a sense "Hebraic," although there is no suggestion that there is any traceable Hebrew influence on Virgil.[8]

On the other hand, Nuttall also alludes to what he calls "a strange tremor in the Hebrew"[9] in the notorious ambiguity of *bereshit* and the contested grammar of the first verse of Genesis. Space does not allow us to rehearse all the arguments that have broken out over the lack of an article on this first word and its apparent construct form, let alone definitively to settle them; the point is that centuries of interpreters have seen an issue here. The apparent contrast between the "natural" beginning in Genesis and the "formal" beginning of the *Aeneid* seems to be breaking down on both sides.

## The Anxiety of Beginnings

I want to seize, unfairly perhaps, on Nuttall's diagnosis of this "tremor" as a way into the discussion of what I will call the "anxiety of beginning" in the Hebrew Bible. This is a term and a concept drawn from the work

---

7. Nuttall, *Openings*, 27.
8. Ibid., 28.
9. Ibid., 210.

of the philosopher Gillian Rose.[10] Far from presenting beginnings as "natural," the poetics of the Hebrew Bible are characterized by an evasion of beginnings. This anxiety manifests itself not only in the leap *"in medias res,"* but also the reiteration of beginnings, in the plural. After all, when we have to begin again, that suggests that the previous beginning was not truly the beginning, in that it did not lead to the outcome that was expected. Yet by the very fact that we have to begin again, the new beginning is not now truly a beginning either, but a continuation.

The equation of the Hebraic with the natural and the sequential in Nuttall's argument belies the diversity of the many beginnings of the Hebrew Bible and their formalism. Indeed, I want to go further and suggest that, far from being natural, "beginning" in the Bible is the antithesis of the "natural." It may in fact be the way in which the literary structures of the Bible betray this positive "anxiety of beginning," rather than any adherence to natural beginnings, that is their bequest to the subsequent development of European literature and culture.

Furthermore, I shall suggest that the apparent obsession with natural beginnings in biblical scholarship, as in the wider culture, is not "biblical," and particularly not characteristic of the Hebrew Scriptures, but theological. The roots of that theological interest are at least as much to be found in the Greek, and indeed Latin, traditions as in the so-called Hebraic world. In lieu of a review of the whole of the classical, biblical and Christian theological traditions and the two-thousand-year history of their reception, I shall point to some key evidence that suggests that another understanding of the biblical concept of "beginning" is possible.

The Jewish tradition, after all, has a continuing strand that questions this interest in origins and, indeed, the beginning with a beginning. Rashi, for instance, is clear in his discussion of Gen 1:1 that this is not a programme of origins, and indeed is not the natural beginning of Torah:

> Said Rabbi Isaac: It was not necessary to begin the Torah except from "This month is to you," (Exod. 12:2) which is the first commandment that the Israelites were commanded. Now for what reason did He commence with "In the beginning?" Because of [the verse] "The strength of His works He related to His people, to give them the inheritance of the nations" (Ps. 111:6). For if the nations of the world should say to Israel, "You are robbers, for you conquered by force the lands of the seven nations [of Canaan]," they will reply, "The entire earth belongs to the Holy One, blessed be He; He created it (this we learn from the story of

---

10. See her *The Broken Middle: Out of Our Ancient Society* (Oxford: Blackwell, 1992), and in particular Chapter 3, "Anxiety of Beginning: Kierkegaard, Lacan, Freud."

the Creation) and gave it to whomever He deemed proper When He wished, He gave it to them, and when He wished, He took it away from them and gave it to us."

For Rashi, the "natural" start would be Exod 12:2, with the first command given to Moses, which as he indicates is itself a command about which month is to be the first month of the year: "This month shall mark for you the beginning of months; it shall be for you the first month of the year." The objection may be made that this is indeed a story of beginnings, but this is a beginning of the most formal kind. The year does not naturally begin on any day; that is a purely formal decision. Choosing to begin the year on this day is the result of a divine command, not a reflection of a natural point of origin.

Indeed, the story of cosmic origins to be found in Genesis is, in Rashi's view, something that the nations need, not Israel. It is the question of those outside Israel and the story is only necessary to counter the animosity of those who think that Israel's claim to land is based on conquest rather than being part of the order set out by God. Israel is not interested in its origins in that sense. Indeed, Rashi goes further and denies that the story of Gen 1 is setting out some kind of systematic record of creation.

Of course, we could argue that Rashi is himself set within a polemical context where the Christian interest in origins is something he needs to counter, but this line goes back much further. Take the book of *Jubilees*, for instance. It begins with a short summary of its purpose as a record of the divisions of the Jubilee, but the first event it records is God summoning Moses to the mountain to give him the law, with a specific date: the sixteenth day of the third month of the first year of the Exodus. The story of creation is thus told in retrospect, although interestingly what *Jubilees* records is what the angel of the presence told Moses to write about the creation, not what Moses himself wrote. The point of the telling, however, is not to reflect on the metaphysics of being, but to provide the grounding for the periodicity of the Sabbath and the Jubilee. Here it seems that both Rashi and *Jubilees* show a distinct preference for beginning "*in medias res*," which I want to suggest is actually the default for the Hebrew Bible, which "speeds its course to the grand event." For *Jubilees* and Rashi, the grand event is the giving of the Law, not the coming into being of the universe.

So where does the prevalent idea in Western culture of the impossible quest for the natural beginning come from? As with so much else, I would contend, it is to be laid at the door of Plato as mediated by Augustine of Hippo. In his *Timaeus*, Plato makes the case for the importance of natural origins far more explicitly than any biblical author when he discusses the reason for believing that the universe has a beginning, rather than existing eternally, principally on the grounds of its changeability. Furthermore, Timaeus regards it as axiomatic that this cosmic hypothesis has literary and rhetorical consequences:

> Now in every subject it is of utmost importance to begin at the natural beginning, and so, on the subject of an image and its model, we must make the following specification: the accounts we give of things have the same character as the subjects they set forth. So accounts of what is stable and fixed and transparent to understanding are themselves stable and unshifting. We must do our very best to make these accounts as irrefutable and invincible as any account may be. On the other hand, accounts we give of that which has been formed to be like that reality, since they are accounts of what is a likeness, are themselves likely and stand in proportion to the previous accounts; i.e. what being is to be becoming, truth is to convincingness.[11]

Here, not in the Bible, is talk of "natural beginnings" and their fundamental importance for the understanding and discussion of any subject. The idea of natural beginning not only is the point to begin a discussion, but also provides the model for the discussion of the subject. Plato, through Timaeus, demonstrates the way in which literary form has to reflect the nature of what is being discussed. This is not a biblical idea.

When Augustine then goes on to his fascinating discussion of the nature of creation and of beginning in ch. 11 of the *Confessions*, his model is one drawn from the Platonic tradition in which he was schooled. Furthermore, it is shaped by the grammar and syntax of the Latin that was his familiar language. He is quite frank about this. Addressing God in his usual way, he prays:

> May I hear and understand how in the beginning you made heaven and earth. Moses wrote this… He is not now before me, but if he were I would clasp him and ask him and through you beg him to explain to me the creation… If he spoke in Hebrew, he would in vain make an impact on my sense of hearing for the sounds would not touch my mind at all. If he spoke Latin, I would know what he meant.[12]

Actually, that final sentence points to the heart of the problem of the relationship between the biblical and the Platonic traditions: the issue of translation. There is an immediate difference between the first words of any Latin version of Genesis and of the Hebrew; the anomalous lack of the article in *bereshit*, however we explain it, becomes invisible in an anarthrous language like Latin. *In principio* means both "in the beginning" and "in a beginning." Our cultural fixation on the search for natural

---

11. Plato, *Timaeus* 29c.
12. Augustine, *Confessions* XI iii (5).

beginnings is not a biblical one, but a consequence of the genius of Augustine and the oddities of translating Greek Platonism into Latin, where "a beginning" and "the beginning" can so easily elide into one another. Augustine's Latin Bible permits him to read the Platonic interest in origins into the biblical text with long consequences, as I have argued. Indeed, in the end, these interests come to be characterized, illegitimately, as themselves biblical.

A most revealing comment that shows how pervasive this identification is comes from Gerhard von Rad. In his Genesis commentary, he dismisses the possibility that *bereshit* can be taken as some kind of dependent clause, giving a reading such as "At the beginning, when God created…," with the following assertion: "Syntactically, perhaps, both translations are possible, but not theologically."[13] "Theologically" is not "biblically"—and whose theology?

My contention is that we can turn the tables on Augustine and Nuttall; after all, if we are going to take on anyone, we should take on the best, given that we are modestly endeavouring to account for the history of Western civilization in this brief compass. Given the consequences of rendering Genesis into Latin, we could reverse the process: How would the Latin of Horace's *in medias res* be rendered in Hebrew? Would it not come out something like *betokh devarim*—or *hadevarim*: "in the midst of things/deeds/words"?

What seems to me interesting in the beginnings of the Bible is that this first word of Genesis begins in the middle of God's action. I am not even convinced that the translation "beginning" for *reshit* is necessary, given that it comes with such post-Augustinian theological freight. How about "first of all" as an alternative, or even, "most importantly"? The Hebrew root takes us into different senses of priority. It could be construed in terms of order or importance quite as easily as priority in genetic or temporal terms. The important point is that with this first word we are literally taken into the midst of things, of deeds and of words in Genesis. No time is spared for the metaphysical questions of origin as to why things came to be. What is clear is that creation in Genesis is emphatically *not* natural. Things did not come about through some natural process, but through the unmotivated speech and action of an unexplained God. In fact, one could argue that the whole point of the text is to declare that there is nothing natural about this beginning. There is no process that could traced back to a further origin, no intrinsic quality in matter or in space/time that explicably gave rise to whatever is.

13. Gerhard von Rad, *Genesis* (rev. ed.; OTL; London: SCM, 1972), 48.

## Unnatural Beginnings

All I have offered here is a beginning. It seems to be that there is more to be done in looking at the way in which biblical books begin—or do not begin. One of the consequences of the way that Augustine frames things is that the question of beginning comes into biblical scholarship itself in the quest for the point of origin, both as manuscript and meaning. That quest has now been problematized, but the counter to it, the recovery of the literary and the narrative structures of the Bible, suffers its own obsessions with origins. Narratives begin, but anthologies do not. The assimilation of the Bible itself to a narrative conception of order is something that itself can be skewed and has theological roots and consequences. Every book has a first word, but not every book has a beginning in narrative terms, and I think we are still caught up on a narrative paradigm as we seek to interpret biblical material. Did anyone ever start reading at the beginning of Jeremiah and read all the way through in Ancient Israel, or did they search the text for the thing that mattered to them—"hastening to the issue"? In point of fact, the Bible itself more resembles a prophetic book like Isaiah, with its mixture of genres, its stops and starts, its endlessly deferred anxiety over the impossible possibility of beginning again.

As Edward Said warns us in his study *Beginnings: Intention and Method*, "There is always the danger of too much reflection on beginnings."[14] You may well feel that this point has already been amply demonstrated in the present discussion. The biblical writings both know and betray that anxiety, however, and have bequeathed it to us. As the writers of the commentary to Gen 1:1 in the Jewish Publication Society's *Etz Hayim* put it, "The Torah begins with *bet*, the second letter of the Hebrew alphabet, so summons us to begin even if we cannot begin at the very beginning"[15]—or perhaps, to realize that, having always already begun, beginning is not such an ordeal after all.

---

14. Edward Said, *Beginnings: Intention and Method* (London: Granta, 1997), 76.
15. The Rabbinical Assembly, *Etz Hayim: Torah and Commentary* (New York: The Jewish Publication Society, 2001), 3.

Chapter 4

BIBLICAL NONSENSE

I begin with the following epigraph, perhaps all too predictably:

> The Red Queen shook her head. "You may call it 'nonsense' if you like," she said, "but *I've* heard nonsense compared with which that would be as sensible as a dictionary!"[1]

How sensible dictionaries actually are may be one question we should bear in mind as we proceed with this topic. But first a clarification. *Biblical Nonsense* is already the title of a book by Jason Long Ph.D. that sets out to show that the world was not created in seven days, Noah could not have housed all the animals in the ark and Jonah could not survive in a whale.[2] That is not what the point here. What I want to look at is the presence of nonsense words in versions of the Bible, why they exist and what we might be able to deduce from their existence. In the course of the discussion, I hope to show that there are several sorts of nonsense, and that biblical readers and biblical translators may reveal more than they realize about themselves by the way that they deal with making sense of these; "*Making* sense—out of what?," we may ask.

The very fact that translating nonsense is a problem is intriguing. If something is completely devoid of sense, why would it need translation, even supposing that a translation would be possible? The need for translation surely indicates that nonsense, at least some kinds of nonsense, is predicated on sense. Of course, there is an almost too easy deconstructionist move tempting us here, suggesting the reverse argument that it is the possibility of nonsense that makes sense of making sense. We might go that way, but we might not. Wait and see.

Enough already. I want to start with the following text:

---

1. Lewis Carroll, *The Annotated Alice* (ed. Martin Gardner; London: Penguin, 2000), 171
2. Jason H. Long Ph.D., *Biblical Nonsense: A Review of the Bible for Doubting Christians* (New York: iUniverse, 2005).

vaj the mu' vo' joH'a' DIchDaq taH Daq chaH precept Daq precept,
precept Daq precept; tlhegh Daq tlhegh, tlhegh Daq tlhegh; naDev
a mach, pa' a mach; vetlh chaH may jaH, pum DoH, taH ghorta', taH
snared, je taH tlhappu'.

Only the geeks among my readers, who are no doubt thin on the ground, will realize that this is the Klingon Language Version of the Bible, a product of the Klingon Language Project. Who in the world needs a Klingon Bible? In a blog entry on Klingonword.org, the online begetter of this version, one Joel Anderson, who is, you may be surprised to hear, a software engineer, argues that there is a virtue to this enterprise. A project such as this both stretches and expands the resources of the language and gives it a literature, as well as being a spiritual exercise for the translator. Klingon, after all, has a complete grammar and a growing vocabulary, being the creation of Marc Okrand, a linguist commissioned by Gene Roddenberry to flesh out the language once a few words had been uttered in various episodes of *Star Trek*.

So, is this text nonsense? Well, there are Klingon speakers who could, if asked, independently produce a recognizable English version of it. However, the real geeks among you will have spotted that the extract quoted above is not in fact in classical Klingon. It is actually generated by a computer and represents what Anderson calls a kind of pidgin Klingon, where English grammar underlies a mixed Klingon and English vocabulary. To a native Klingon speaker (where am I going with this?), quite apart from the disrupted syntax and grammar, there is indeed a nonsense word in this text—the word "precept," which occurs four times in this short passage. Klingon, even when transliterated, contains no letter equivalent to "c." The programme has simply repeated the English word. Does that mean that "precept" here is a nonsense word in Klingon?

Well, the plot becomes thicker when we look back to the biblical verse that underlies this particular version. It is Isa 28:13, which is a verse that has generated remarkably different translations. Compare the following:

NKJV:
For precept must be upon precept, precept upon precept, line upon line, line upon line, Here a little, there a little.

NIB:
For it is: Do and do, do and do, rule on rule, rule on rule; a little here, a little there.

NJB:
With his: Sav lasav, sav lasav, kav lakav, kav lakav, zeer sham, zeer sham!

## 4. *Biblical Nonsense* 47

Otto Kaiser:
For he says, "Saw to Saw, Saw to Saw, Qaw to Qaw, Qaw to Qaw; boy, be careful! Boy, be careful!"

TNK:
That same mutter upon mutter, murmur upon murmur, Now here, now there!

NEB:
It is all harsh cries and raucous shouts, "A little more here, a little there!"

REB:
A babble of meaningless noises, mere sounds on every side.

Now there is a range, if ever there was one. They represent in miniature a vast number of options suggested by the interpretative tradition. As Willem Beuken remarks, "…exegetes throughout the centuries have given full range to their imagination and ingenuity in order to find all sorts of hidden meanings and allusions behind the words."

The NKJV follows in an ancient line that was sure that the words must mean something, and thus traced out plausible roots for the otherwise rather inexplicable Hebrew words. But, as Beuken again comments, "If translated in this way, however, the words completely lose their character of stupid language." That is a phrase worth pausing over: "stupid language." What this reveals is that the word "precept" which has crept into our pidgin Klingon version may be incomprehensible to a Klingon and recognisable to an English speaker, but is imposed upon rather than rooted in the Masoretic text. It is a word which makes sense of the word "*zaw*" but it is not in any simple way the sense of "*zaw*."

The more contemporary translations are prepared to reflect not the possible root meaning of the language, but in some sense what we might call a phatic translation, one that reflects not a semantic message in the language but its communicative effect. NJB takes the unusual step of simply transliterating the Hebrew, thus retaining the rhythm and the repetition. Yet, is this the same kind of nonsense in English as it is in its Hebrew context?

Kaiser's version, although it is by no means transparent to the English reader, follows in another lineage, traceable at least to Wellhausen, which latches onto the fact that *tsadeh* precedes *qoph* in the Hebrew alphabet and thus sees in these words a parody of a teacher drilling his pupil with the alphabet. But note that his nonsense words "Saw" and "Qaw" are transliterated from his German spelling, using a "w" in place of a "v." This has the strange result that "sav" becomes "saw," a perfectly defensible if old-fashioned English near-synonym for "precept." In

German of course, it remains a nonsense word. Transliteration here leads to accidental sense.

Intriguingly, J. Wash Watts follows this line too: "Interpreters have understood this to mean everything from speaking tongues to being code-words for great thoughts. But the picture of the drunken teacher is most simple and appropriate."[3] Does he here betray something of his opinion of the general state of the teaching profession, I wonder? But what this line also suggests is the sting in the epigraph from *Alice* we began with. How sensible is the dictionary? Simply to read through a dictionary, or recite the alphabet, does not give rise to coherent meaning, as this verse may be indicating in his translation. Dictionaries may give rise to intriguing or amusing juxtapositions of words, but read sequentially they do not purport to make coherent sense.

The final versions cited above resort entirely to paraphrase, but again not a semantic or conceptual paraphrase, but a writing out of the communicative effect of the words. The TNK reproduces the aural effect of the words, while the final two translations explicitly name the language as meaningless and do not attempt any translation of the individual words. This is not a translation of the Hebrew, but a verdict on it. This is biblical nonsense, the translators tell us, "stupid language" in Beuken's striking phrase.

But what is this nonsense doing here? The problem gets more and more complex, unfortunately, as the surrounding verses in Isa 28 are notoriously hard to disentangle, especially with regard to the all-important issue of who is saying what to whom. Indeed, decisions on those matters depend to a large extent on readers' opinions on who is likely to be using "stupid language" to whom. The passage itself makes clear that, in this verse, the quoted language is the word of the Lord, but conveyed through men with "strange lips and an alien tongue," as the RSV puts it. Yet earlier, in v. 10, where the same nonsense speech occurs, the speakers are very obscure. Who talks nonsense in biblical texts?

The answer most commonly agreed is that they are those whose tongues cannot or do not frame proper Hebrew. Either these are children (hence the teachers who appear in various translations), or those with a speech defect. This may be the result of permanent mental or physical incapacity, or it might refer to those who are temporarily impaired in their speech. This state in turn could either be the result of drunkenness, or of being in some ecstatic state related to prophecy or divination. Finally, those incapable of comprehensible speech could be foreigners. All these groups can be lumped together as being excluded from the

---

3. John D. W. Watts, *Isaiah 1–33* (WBC 24; Waco: Word Books, 1985), 363.

norm of those who speak comprehensible Hebrew rather than nonsense. In that sense, children, prophets, diviners, drunkards, idiots and foreigners form a group.

So what other examples are there of these defective speakers? The Hebrew Bible is on the whole blind to the variety of language. People of all ethnic groups are represented as speaking perfect Hebrew: Egyptian pharaohs, Babylonian kings and Persian satraps among them. There seems to be some kind of universal translator at work in most biblical encounters with people from other language groups. Just occasionally, however, we do get some indication that there are other ways of speaking besides Hebrew. The tower of Babel of course gives us the story of the diversity of languages, but no examples. The characters in Genesis thereafter seem to have no trouble in understanding one another.

Moses in Exod 4:10 uses as his final excuse to avoid taking on the responsibility of acting as spokesman for is people the claim that he is "slow of tongue." One way that this can be understood is as an indication that he was not as fluent in Egyptian as he had been. The same idiom is used in Ezek 3:16 of the peoples of obscure speech and difficult language to whom Ezekiel is *not* being sent. Isaiah has the same attitude to the speakers of other languages when he writes in Isa 33:19, "No longer will you see the insolent people, the people of an obscure speech that you cannot comprehend, stammering in a language you cannot understand," which seems to refer to the Assyrians.

One interesting exception to the usual convention that characters understand each other without problems is the encounter between Joseph and his brothers in Gen 42. The issue of language in this chapter is intriguingly and deliberately complicated. The chapter records the dialogue between Joseph and his brothers without comment and we only learn that there is a linguistic problem when in v. 23 the narrator records, "They did not know that Joseph understood them, since he spoke with them through an interpreter." Up to that point, no mention has been made of any barrier to communication, but it becomes relevant because the plot turns on the fact that the brothers are unaware that Joseph has overheard Reuben's reproach to his brothers. The presence of the interpreter is highlighted at a point where, ironically, no translation is actually required. Joseph is pretending not to understand his brothers in order to maintain the deception that prevents them from recognising him, but in actual fact he shares their language.

Yet, in the passage we have just read, it is in precisely this idiom that the word of the Lord is to be spoken. The point in Isaiah is that it is not the speakers who are at fault if there is no communication—it is the listeners. Isaiah, of course, has his unclean lips seared by the seraph in the temple in ch. 6, yet he is given the paradoxical message that he should instruct the people so that they do not understand. It is not what Isaiah says that is nonsense; the people are unable or unwilling to hear it, so it *might as well* be nonsense, just as in Isa 28:13 God's word might as well be in Assyrian.

The Hebrew Bible on the whole shows no curiosity about the language of others or their culture. What is at stake is the comprehensibility of its own text to its own people. The well-known passage in Neh 8:8, which seems to indicate that at some level, whether via exegesis or perhaps by translation, the people need interpreters to understand the book of the law that Ezra reads to them makes this point. It is abundantly clear in Daniel, which is perhaps the book most interested in language in the Hebrew Bible, unsurprising perhaps in this bilingual text, which almost seems to revel in the borrowed vocabulary of the Persian court and the Greek musicians. Daniel is the only one, apparently, who can read the text on Belshazzar's wall; yet he is also the one who fails to understand the message of the later part of the book.

In 2 Kgs 18:13–36, too, the message seems to be that there is more trouble with foreigners who speak Hebrew than with those who speak their own language. The story of the Tartan, the Rabsaris and the Rabshakeh seems to make a point of the exoticness of these titles, but it is the Rabshakeh's surprising fluency in the language of Judah that is the problem as the people hear his threats against Hezekiah and the leaders of the people and the leaders try to persuade him to speak in Aramaic. It is understanding that is the problem here, not misunderstanding.

The Lord's word, so this verse of Isaiah would seem to suggest, is always nonsense to those who are not destined to hear it. What then would be the point in translating it? Perhaps, after all, the best thing to do with it is to render it into Klingon, the language of the warrior race par excellence, the galactic Assyrians of the Star Trek universe.

Part II

# THE RESISTANT BIBLE

Chapter 5

RELIGION AGAINST THE BIBLE

Why was Ernst Bloch's *Atheism in Christianity* not on my core reading-list as a Biblical Studies student? Why is it so often the case that it is those who are not specialists in Biblical Studies who manage to convey the sense of excitement that these remarkable texts can generate? Bloch's verdict that modern biblical criticism is "one of the most exciting achievements of human acuteness"[1] should be on every departmental website and might surprise Biblical Studies students as they wade through the technicalities of biblical source analysis. It is now on the required reading list for a course I teach on "The Bible and the Postcolonial World."

It is there for two reasons. Firstly, because it gives such a clear and interesting account of how the conflicting strands in the biblical material provide at the same time the tool of oppression in the hands of the ruling classes and the agency for liberation in the hands of the oppressed. Bloch's analysis of the "underground Bible" is crucial to understanding postcolonialism and the Bible's role within it. Secondly, and this time I am more critical, it will be there because it raises the problems of using these texts within and against modernity and in particular as resources in the essentially modern debate about "religion," a word which has no equivalent in either Biblical Hebrew or New Testament Greek.

In all that follows, it will be obvious that I am no more than an interested visitor in the world of Bloch studies and so all I feel able to do as a biblical scholar is to pose some questions to which there may be quite simple answers. Nevertheless, I want to suggest that Bloch is both too theological and not theological enough in his engagement with the Bible, although his awareness of its relevance to addressing the problem of "something missing" in modernity and in the Marxist tradition is startling and never more timely; all the more reason to get the analysis of its influence right, in that case.

---

1. Ernst Bloch, *Atheism in Christianity* (trans. J. T. Swann; London: Verso, 2009), 63.

First, then, he is too theological in that he accepts a particular consensus about the shape and meaning of the biblical canon in theological terms, albeit in order to criticize it. In this verdict I agree with Roland Boer, and am indebted to his discussion of Bloch's work that forms the first chapter of his recent *Criticism of Heaven: On Marxism and Theology*.[2] Bloch's Bible is a modernist Bible.

However, I want to build on Boer's critique to suggest that Bloch is at the same time not theological enough. Bloch's insight into the "cunning" of myth, as he terms it, is remarkable, but I think these biblical myths are even more cunning than he himself seems to allow. I want to bring him into dialogue with a perhaps unlikely conversation partner, the contemporary Orthodox theologian John Zizioulas, and his subtle understanding of the relationship between creation and freedom. Contrary to superficial dismissals, the theological tradition is actually quite adept at outsmarting myths; indeed, that is a theologian's stock-in-trade and one reason why theology, myth and religion cannot be conflated, let alone Biblical Studies. In particular, the opposition between creation and exodus which Bloch sets up can be criticized on his own grounds and undercuts his discussion of utopia and of hope. Zizioulas' work seems to me to reframe the debate over religion, modernity and hope in an intriguing way, worth taking seriously even by those who would find his premises alien.

More specifically, the point of contact between Zizioulas' thought and that of Bloch is in the seriousness with which they take the fact of death. In their dialogue entitled "Something Missing," Bloch and Adorno agree that the real problem for all utopian discussion is the fact of death.[3] It is a proper engagement with death which is the something missing in contemporary political debates. The religious, then, becomes a name for those strategies by which this challenge has been variously evaded or redescribed, as Bloch outlines in detail in his fascinating treatment in volume 3 of *The Principle of Hope*. I think that is right, but also want to suggest that Bloch's use of the biblical tradition in *Atheism in Christianity* fails to recognize adequately the truly radical way in which that tradition gives resources for an uncompromising materialist and utopian engagement with death and sets itself against the forces of religion, as Bloch defines it, in its own world.

---

2. Roland Boer, *Criticism of Heaven: On Marxism and Theology* (Leiden: Brill, 2007).

3. Ernst Bloch and Theodor Adorno, "Something's Missing: A Discussion between Ernst Bloch and Theodor W. Adorno on the Contradictions of Utopian Longing," in *The Utopian Function of Art and Literature: Selected Essays* (trans. J. Zipes and F. Mecklenburg; Cambridge: MIT, 1988), 1–17.

## Bloch and Ecclesiastes

Part of the problem is that Bloch's Bible is itself a theological construction. He reads the texts through the double lens of biblical criticism and the Christian, rather than the Jewish canon. What this does is to privilege the historical, or at least historiographic, elements of the Bible. In a way that is typical of biblical scholarship in the mid-twentieth century, the wisdom traditions and the legal material of the Bible are left to one side, except for Job, and the prophetic books are read as historical commentary. The New Testament, and in particular the book of Revelation, is read back into the Hebrew tradition. There are many ways of reading the Bible, of course, but the trouble is that the critical and theological traditions are so easily conflated. Theological conventions are blended into critical judgments. What this also means is that the full range of conflicting myths and ideologies is not available, which is a pity when Bloch is so adept at dealing with their complexities.

Not unnaturally, Bloch accepts the results of critical scholarship of his day. This posits four sources behind the first five books of the Bible, collectively known as the Pentateuch, which have been conflated and edited together by priestly groups. The revolutionary potential of these sources has been, in Bloch's words, "purposely veiled over by the priests, with their counter-revolutionary religious outlook."[4] Only a few outcrops remain, such as the radical words of Cain, the serpent in paradise and the dialogues of Job. These testify to a subversive "underground Bible" which rejects the domination of the creator God Yahweh. The exciting task of the biblical scholar, in Bloch's view, is the detective work that uncovers these repressed sources. Of course, such a reading of the corpus has a long history in the Gnostic sects of both Judaism and Christianity.

What is interesting, however, is that this particular scholarly construct is itself theologically grounded. The very suspicion of priesthood that such a reading represents is a commonplace of German (Protestant) criticism in the nineteenth and twentieth centuries, and has not a little to do with a long history of anti-Catholic polemic. It does, however, also reflect a negative view of the Jewish priesthood and temple. Bloch himself makes no bones about accusing the leading scholar in this tradition, Julius Wellhausen, of anti-Semitism in his devaluing of the legal and historical aspects of later Judaism without realizing that this same tendency is in evidence in his own accusation that some priestly group suppressed the underground tradition.

4. Bloch, *Atheism*, 67.

The wider point here is that it is very difficult to substantiate anyone's claim to an objective critical approach that can stand against the religious or theological biases of the text as the critical tradition itself is deeply theologically involved. That to an extent is Bloch's own point, but he is less able to extricate himself from this contradiction than he seems to imply.

What Bloch does seek to do is to extricate a radical exodus tradition from the texts. The trouble is, however, that the exodus tradition itself is an intrinsically ambivalent one. The promise of freedom and the establishment of a new community is there, but always at the price of the suppression of some other community. One person's exodus is another person's conquest. The exodus myth as it plays out in African colonial history, for instance, is certainly not a story of universal heroism. In South Africa it undergirds the self-understanding of the Afrikaner with the myth of the Great Trek as a liberation from the British, cast in the role of Egyptians. This movement to the promised land has its consequence in the suppression of the Zulus as the equivalents of the inhabitants of Canaan in the establishment of a new homeland. At the same time, the Exodus myth underlies the establishment of Liberia, where southern plantation owners in the United States were happy to sponsor the ideology of the exodus of Africa of freed slaves to remove their disruptive presence, and where the indigenous Liberians found themselves dispossessed by the newcomers in ways that feed the roots of the recent civil wars. Throughout the prophetic tradition, the celebration of the liberation from Israel is consistently tied to the gift of the land of Canaan and the expropriation of the Canaanites.

Yet even from the point of view of Israel itself, the Exodus is not an easy story. As early as Exod 14:11, before even the Red Sea had been crossed, the people say collectively to Moses, "Is it because there are no graves in Egypt that you have taken us away to die in the wilderness?" They speak more truly than they know, because by the time we get to Num 14:22, God decrees that none of the people who left Egypt will see the land of their fathers, and will indeed, as they suspected, die in the desert. In the words of a mnemonic quasi-limerick I learned at school:

> Joshua the son of Nun
> And Caleb the son of Japhunneh
> Were the only two
> Who ever got through
> To the land of milk and honey.

So much for an easily liberative view of the Exodus tradition. At the same time, the creation tradition, which Bloch represents as priestly propaganda for an overweening demiurge, is one that allows truly allows for liberation. It is true that the particular critical tradition that Bloch is following makes it clear that the creation accounts that begin Genesis are later additions which, remarkably enough, are nowhere referred to in the rest of the Hebrew Bible, although the New Testament writers reuse them creatively. That does not mean, however, *pace* Bloch, that creation is peripheral to the prophetic vision of a new earth and a new heaven. It is precisely the claim that God is creator that enables the expectation of destruction and recreation. Here it is clear that Bloch, and much of the modernist tradition, is led astray by an understanding of creation that is at odds with the biblical and theological tradition, but which is derived from other religious traditions and from a Platonic understanding of the relationship between spirit and matter. It is the biblical tradition that is the truly materialist one in that it, in terms, points to redemption of and through the material, not redemption from or despite it.

It is a pity that, as far as I know, Bloch does not engage with the book of Ecclesiastes. Ecclesiastes is notoriously pessimistic, on some readings, which may account for Bloch's neglect of it, but what the book does express is the sense of the finality of death (3:19-20): "For the fate of the sons of men and the fate of beasts is the same; as one dies, so dies the other. They all have the same breath, and man has no advantage over the beasts; for all is vanity. All go to one place; all are from the dust, and all turn to dust again." It would be hard to imagine a more materialist view of human destiny—dust is dust. That is another element of the underground Bible which Bloch does not acknowledge. The corollary of this strand of the underground tradition is that in such a world, hope—what Bloch, echoing Kierkegaard, calls the hope against hope—must itself be couched in materialist terms. The counter to Ecclesiastes is not some spiritual consolation or abstract principle of hope, but Paul's astonishing claim in Rom 8 that hope resides in the fact that the whole creation waits with eager longing for the revealing of the sons of God, and that human beings too wait for the redemption of their bodies.

The Christian theological tradition underwent a stern internal struggle to save the Old Testament from its dismissal by Marcion, whom Bloch admires as a radical. Among the most important theological reasons for seeking to retain the Old Testament was its insistence of the important of the created order as the instrument of redemption, in contrast to the Gnostic teaching that creation itself was what the human spirit had to be redeemed from. Absurd it may sound, but the doctrine of the resurrection of the body is the theological tradition's answer to the problem of death for materialist utopian thought. Nor should this be thought of as an individual expectation of revival; it is part of a conception of the way things are which places such a high value on the material that only a recreated cosmos is thought worthy as a ground of hope.

This is where the Christian theological tradition parts company from appeal to another non-material form of existence which could be labelled "spiritual" and in this way sets its face against "religion" as popularly conceived. From this theological point of view, the materialist hope for a utopia that has to admit the finitude of death is not hope at all. As Kierkegaard so perceptively points out, it is a form of despair: more specifically the despair that wills despairingly to be itself. If death puts an end to utopian thought, then modernity defiantly wills to operate within the confines of death and chooses to make a virtue of that defiance. All very well, retorts Kierkegaard, but defiance is not hope.

But can the idea of resurrection be anything other than fantasy and can it be taken seriously in the discussion of religion and utopian hope in modernity? Well, if we are to look at Bloch in this regard, it is only fair to point out that he is the one that invokes the biblical tradition with such enthusiasm. The fact is that there are more dimensions to the underground Bible that he seems to acknowledge and there is such a radical materialism to its vision of hope that even Bloch seems to have ducked out of confronting it. His own reading of the Bible is more dependent on a modernist understanding of religion than he seems to be aware, and the critical tradition that he is following is itself blind to some of the intransigencies of the biblical tradition. Bloch's talk of atheism in Christianity is provocative, but the tradition itself is more radical. Bloch rebels against the creator demiurge: Christianity will have no truck with such a conception of deity.

For an example of a radical theology of creation that is more materialist than much atheism, take the recent work of John Zizioulas. In the chapter of his *Communion and Otherness* entitled "'Created' and 'Uncreated': The Existential Significance of Chalcedonian Christology," he opposes the Christian tradition to the Platonic notion of the demiurge as found in the *Timaeus*.[5] Plato's creator is, so Zizioulas contends, merely a kind of interior decorator, giving form to the cosmos rather than giving it existence, because the Greek tradition cannot deal with absolute nothingness. In such cosmological thinking, God and the world are indissolubly linked as creator and created. Matter is either pre-existent or an emanation of the divine.

---

5. John D. Zizioulas, *Communion and Otherness* (ed. Paul McPartlan; London: T&T Clark International, 2006), 250–85.

## 5. Religion Against the Bible

Christian thought, starting from Paul, is not cosmological. What is in question for Paul is not *kosmos* but *ktisis*, the act of bringing something out of *nothing*. The cosmos is not formed of pre-existing matter or from transmutation of some divine substance. Zizioulas reads the Greek fathers as constantly harping on this distinction, precisely because they operate in a Greek philosophical environment. The distinction that matters for them is not that between God and world, spirit and matter, but between created and uncreated. For the Fathers, the material world is founded on absolute freedom and the God who created it cannot be spoken of as a supreme Being. God, again in a phrase of Kierkegaard's, does not exist; he is eternal. Being itself, even the being of God, depends on God as cause.

Seen against this backdrop of nothingness, the absolute contingency of whatever is, is exposed. Whatever is could *not* be. The inescapability of this means that existence is always exposed to death, the reality of non-being. "The whole world," writes Zizioulas, "by the very fact that it is *created*—perishes while existing and exists while perishing: its life and ours are not 'true life'…by space and time, we all commune with one another in weaving together the thread of life; but it is also by time and space that we are divided from one another by the cutting edge of death."[6] In this sense, Zizioulas regards creation as tragic, but the solution is not some kind of pious or intellectual accommodation with death. He demands that we rage against death. For him, the ground of hope is precisely in this radical sense of createdness. Death is natural to creation, but creation itself is radically contingent, not "natural," and it is death that is the paradoxical pointer to this contingency, thereby also pointing to its own inability to say the final word.

For Zizioulas, the final answer is a person, not a principle, celebrated in the Chalcedonian definition that proclaims that in Christ, created and uncreated are united without division and without confusion. Creation can only overcome death through union with the uncreated. The cross and resurrection are not about expiatory sacrifice and some kind of moral victory but are an answer to the problem of death in that the created inherits immortality from the uncreated.

There is a great deal more to Zizioulas' thought. The doctrine of the Trinity is central in all this. Any Marxist materialist reader may well by now have had more Orthodox theology that he or she would like, but the point here is that seen from an Orthodox perspective, Marxist atheism sets itself against modernity as the latest despairing manifestation of the Western obsession with an idea of "being" in the abstract. For Zizioulas,

---

6. Ibid., 257.

person precedes being, and insofar as God can be said to exist, that existence springs out of the Father's relationship to the Son and the Spirit. Again, this may seem extravagant nonsense to those outside this tradition. What is important in this, however, is that theologians have seen and attempted to address the very issue that Bloch and Adorno find so difficult in their discussion of "something missing." Indeed, Adorno in that dialogue remarks at one point to Bloch, "We have come very near to something like the ontological proof of God." Zizioulas would remind us, however, that the very notion of an ontological proof for God is predicated on a certain Western metaphysical tradition that equates God with being, and seeks to think being in the abstract.

Once again, Bloch's trouble is that he is both too theological and not theological enough. He is a brilliant and original expositor of a radical tradition within the fundamentally ontological theological heritage of Western, and Protestant, Europe that rebels against its own essentialism and the purchase that such essentialism gives to oppressive discourses of power. The Bible can be and has been assimilated to this particular tradition, but it can be read differently. Bloch, I think, is not theological enough to see his own theology and to set it in its context as one theology among many. The point here is not to convert anyone to Chalcedonian Orthodoxy, although that does mark the moment, in my view, where the greatest diversity and the greatest unity of theological thought are to be found. Recalling this wider context raises the question of the inherited limitations of utopianism within the Western tradition and whether there are resources that might speak otherwise about the nature of human freedom and the life to be hoped for.

This is something rather different to what is often described as the return to religion, which is also a return to a whole slew of mostly recycled panaceas against the outrage of death. Bloch, admirably, enjoins us to set this at defiance, but I cannot help wondering yet again with Kierkegaard whether such defiance is hope or despair. The true materialist cannot ground hope in anything that does not redeem matter, cosmos and body from what seems and intrinsic liability to revert to futility and nothingness. As the much-maligned apostle Paul puts it, "The creation was subjected to futility, not of its own will but by the will of him who subjected it *in hope* [my emphasis], because the creation itself will be set free from its bondage to decay and obtain the glorious liberty of the children of God" (Rom 8:20–21 RSV). That is materialist utopianism, in full biblical style.

Chapter 6

THE BIBLE IN THE METROPOLIS

I often have the feeling as I deliver a lecture in a hall lined with the portraits of great scholars of the past that the ghosts of that great assembly are sighing collectively, "So it has finally come to this." Biblical Studies, certainly, has changed and is changing, in ways that some of them would have deplored. One thing, for instance, that strikes me as I look at those august portraits, is that there are precious few women, and I have yet to notice an African or Asian face among them. Now that is an easy, some might even say cheap, point to make, and I do not have a leg to stand on, either; after all, I have all the qualifications of the archetypal dead white Anglo-Saxon Protestant male—except the first, and I am working on that.

But in a way that is my point. In particular, this chapter arose out of the honour of being asked to give a lecture in London, the imaginative heartland of white male Protestant Anglo-Saxondom and the imperial seat of the British Empire, to a group of people gathered to listen to a talk on the Bible, a miscellaneous collection of Semitic and Hellenistic texts written thousands of years ago in a different place and indeed a different world. How strange. We do not often remember just how strange that is. If we do keep that in mind, however, whatever our aim, we cannot avoid also learning more about ourselves in the encounter with the otherness of this book. In that process, it becomes less strange, and we become more so, or at least we can learn to recognize how strange we are, and how much of that strangeness is actually biblical in origin.

One key way that Biblical Studies is changing is precisely because of the imperial ambitions of Great Britain and its aftermath. Out of this city, the metropolis of the Empire, the Bible was sent forth in the knapsacks of missionaries and adventurers and the diplomatic bags of ambassadors and colonial administrators. I found a very telling statement of the significance of this in a volume entitled *King's College Lectures on Colonial Problems*, the published version of a series of talks given by distinguished academics and public figures in King's College in May and June of 1913. It makes a fascinating read, with an added piquancy in hindsight because of its date. In his lecture entitled "The Influence of Science on Empire," Sir C. P. Lucas, a former head of the Dominion Department of the Colonial Office, writes this:

> Science and religion, two forces often coupled and often contrasted, have been and are, I should say, two of the strongest and two of the most underrated forces in our Empire. It is idle to minimize the effect of religion. Take religion out of English history and but a skeleton of history would be left. Where would have been our Central African Empire if David Livingston had not lived? I submit that a book is wanted, setting forth the potency of religion in the making and keeping of Empire, setting religion in its right place as a great imperial force.[1]

Any account of the role of religion in the story of Britain's empire inevitably would include a significant reflection on the role of the Bible. As an example, I cannot resist giving you Sir Charles Lucas's interesting opinion in the same essay that the private motor car is a stimulant to democracy. Showing his own biblical knowledge, he quotes from Nahum (verse 2:4, to be precise): "The chariots shall rage in the streets, they shall jostle one against another in the broad ways, they shall seem like torches, they shall run like the lightnings." This, he says, provokes the sense of right and wrong. I quote: "A man who is in constant danger of being run over becomes keenly conscious of his own rights and other people's responsibilities, and this has something to do with modern democracy."[2] Or perhaps it is not such an aside, if you substitute "motor car" with "British imperial armies"; the danger of being run over by the forces of a colonial power can have the same effect in heightening political awareness. The chariots in Nahum, after all, are those of the avenging army that is destroying the great imperial metropolis of Nineveh.

Be that as it may, Lucas's endorsement of the imperial function of the Bible is unfashionable but significant, though in hindsight, again, it has an ironic edge. Now, almost one hundred years later, the Bible is returning to the centre. Echoing the oft-quoted title of one of the pioneering works on postcolonial literary studies, *The Empire Writes Back*,[3] we may say that African, Asian, Latin American, Polynesian biblical readers have been finding their voices and writing back to the European scholarly

---

1. C. P. Lucas, "The Influence of Science on Empire," in *King's College Lectures on Colonial Problems* (ed. F. J. C. Hearnshaw; London: G. Bell & Sons, 1913), 107–41 (128–29).
2. Ibid., 115.
3. Bill Ashcroft, Gareth Griffiths and Helen Tiffin, *The Empire Writes Back* (2d ed.; London: Routledge, 2002).

tradition by developing their own scholarly literature. But where they are writing back to has also changed and is changing. London and Britain are very different in the aftermath of empire and from the city of 1913. Who lives in London, and how they live, has been profoundly shaped by the gain and loss of the Empire. Who reads the Bible and how in London has also been profoundly shaped by that experience.

What I want to explore is the consequence of this for the metropolitan readers of the Bible, if I can put it that way—the people of the old centre. As someone whose salary is paid at least in part by inducing people from impoverished ex-colonial countries to pay overseas fees to a British university to learn from me how to understand the Bible in their own postcolonial context, I am aware of the contradictions and absurdities this involves. Those ironies reinforce what I shall suggest here: that the Bible itself is a more complex and interesting participant in the thinking and rethinking of the metropolis than is often acknowledged, and that Biblical Studies does have an important, if ambivalent, contribution to make to such rethinking, which the current economic and political situation makes all the more relevant. If the Empire is writing back, who is reading what is written, and what are we to make of it? How is our study of the Bible affected by this?

Having begun by invoking the pictures of my distinguished predecessors, I want to use three pictures to structure my further ruminations. The first is of these in a picture that in its day became what the art critic Jan Marsh has called an "icon of the age" and now is in danger of becoming a cliché in postcolonial studies.[4] It was painted by Thomas Jones Barker and exhibited in 1863 under the title of "The Secret of England's Greatness"; the subtitle is "Queen Victoria Presents a Bible in the Audience Chamber of Windsor Castle."

Its iconic significance in the 1860s and the different effect it now has are, I suspect, plain. Yet, as I hope to show, it is a more complex cultural artifact than might at first appear and than it has been read by some postcolonial critics, raising real questions about the Bible in the metropolis. In the picture, the Queen of England is flanked by her consort, Prince Albert, and her then Prime Minister, Lord Palmerston, and Foreign Secretary, Lord John Russell, with, in the background, the faint figure of the Mistress of the Robes, Elizabeth, Duchess of Wellington. Before the queen a kneeling African is stretching out his hands to receive the closed book she is giving him, though her gaze never meets his. As

---

4. Jan Marsh, "Icon of the Age: Victoria and *The Secret of England's Greatness*" in *Black Victorians: Black People in British Art 1800–1900* (ed. Jan Marsh; Aldershot: Lund Humphries, 2006), 57–67.

R. S. Sugirtharajah, the doyen of postcolonial Biblical Studies in Britain and internationally, puts it:

> Queen Victoria…is gifting to the African England's greatest cultural product, the English Bible, possibly the King James Version, a book in which "not a line single line was written, or single thought was conceived by, an Englishman." A collection of books which originated in West Asia, rooted in Mediterranean cultural values, clothed in the everyday imagery of Semitic and Hellenistic peoples, has now been assimilated by the English, reinscribed into their linguistic poetic forms, and turned into a cultural artefact of the English people. From now on, it will be distributed throughout the world as an icon containing civilizing properties. The African, kneeling, represents the heathen foreigner whose moral improvement was seen as the responsibility of the English.[5]

Yet there is more to this than Sugirtharajah suggests. In her essay on the picture in the catalogue for an exhibition she curated entitled "Black Victorians," Jan Marsh points out several interesting pieces of background. The first is the fact that that in 1863, of course, the American Civil War is coming to a head. Victoria, a keen abolitionist, is shown giving away the secret of England's greatness to an African king, whose posture, though subservient, is not necessarily more so than some white supplicants. In addition, it recalls the typical posture of the grateful slave receiving manumission in abolitionist tracts of the time.

Marsh also points out that the particular event depicted never took place. Rather, the painting illustrates a widespread but apocryphal anecdote published in its typical form in the *British Workman* of December 1859. There, it is recounted that the Queen, in response to an ambassador sent by an African king to enquire what the secret of England's greatness was, "did not, like Hezekiah in an evil hour [note the reference to 2 Kgs 20:12–15], show the ambassador her diamonds and her jewels, and her rich ornaments, but handing him a beautifully bound copy of the Bible, she said, 'Tell the Prince that THIS IS THE SECRET OF ENGLAND'S GREATNESS'."[6] The event is mythical, and the location, given so specifically in the title, is pictorially entirely vague, as Barker was refused permission to make sketches of the Audience Chamber.

---

5. R. S. Sugirtharajah, *The Postcolonial Bible* (Sheffield: Sheffield Academic, 1998), 14–15. The embedded quotation is from James Blaikie, *The English Bible and Its Story: Its Growth, Its Translators and Their Adventures* (London: Seeley, Service, 1928), 7.

6. Cited in Jan Marsh, "Icon of the Age," *The British Workman* (December 1859), 1 (capitals original).

But already in this picture, the notion of the gift is unsettled. The traffic is not simply one way. This is shown in the dress of the two leading figures. The spectator might ask: Where did the silk for the queen's dress come from? Where did her jewels originate? Not in England. There are a number of visual echoes between the two main characters, particularly in their headdresses. Both are wearing white feathers. Where, if not from Africa, did the Queen get the ostrich feather she is wearing? Her royal persona is built of the products of the Empire, not of England. Already, in the term that Homi Bhabha has made central to postcolonial studies, her identity is hybrid. In no way does she represent some pure ideal of England before Empire. She is a product of the Empire she rules.

And what then of the Bible, which is so central to this transaction? What language is it in? Who can, or would, read it? The book the queen is holding is closed and is functioning as a symbolic object, rather than a text in the picture. Sugirtharajah presumes, and so would most of the picture's viewers, I suspect, that it is the Authorized Version. How useful would that be to the recipient?

Interestingly, however, in the transaction that most clearly lies behind the myth depicted in the picture, an exchange in 1848 between Queen Victoria and Sagbua Olukemun, the Aleke of Abeokuta, in what is now southern Nigeria, the diversity of the Bible is at least acknowledged. Responding to the Aleke's assurance that he welcomed the missionaries of the Church Missionary Society and was abolishing slavery in his domain, the Queen replied how glad she was, that slavery always failed to prosper and that England prospered through its Christian faith. The message concluded: "To show how much the queen values God's Word, she sends with this, as a present to Sagbua, a copy of this work in two languages—one the Arabic, the other the English."[7] For all we know, the volume in this picture is also an Arabic Bible. If so, it stands in direct rivalry to the great Arabic Scripture, the Quran, and the influence of Islam on the peoples of colonial Africa. But it is a gift that is handed on, one given to, not produced, by the British Empire that hands it on, as Sugirtharajah makes so clear.

Language and literacy aside, both of which are concomitant gifts with the gift of the text, for good or ill, the text she is giving encodes both the liberation of slaves, but also the theological roots for the racism that underlay African slavery and the imperial adventure itself; it both exalts and decries the institution of monarchy and the position of a woman as ruler; it rails against but also mourns the loss of the power of the

---

7. Ibid., 61–62.

metropolis and indeed aspires to that power itself. The Bible is the focus of this picture. As such, however, it underpins but also potentially undermines the relationships that the picture purports to enshrine, and as such also enshrines its own deconstruction.

This is made clearer in a second picture. Without a title, but with the information that this is an engraving by Gustav Doré, the viewer would be forgiven for failing to see what is going on. A tattered figure sits with head bowed beside a river in which the remains of a great stone bridge can be seen. Across the river we see the ruined domes, walls and bridges of what was one clearly a great city. Is this Jeremiah lamenting the destruction of Jerusalem, or of Babylon, or Nahum gloating over the ruins of Nineveh? But on a second glance, the shattered buildings begin to seem familiar. Is that the dome of St Paul's and the stump of the famous clock tower of the Houses of Parliament? The engraving in question is, in fact, the final plate of a guidebook, *London: A Pilgrimage*, produced by Doré and Blanchard Jerrold in 1872.[8] The picture itself is entitled "The New Zealander," somewhat surprisingly, until we learn from David Skilton that the figure of the New Zealander, that most remote and barbaric of colonial subjects, contemplating the ruins of London was a commonplace in Victorian literature, to the point of raising protests in *Punch* at its banal ubiquity.[9]

The probable source of the image was a review by Lord Macaulay, who in the process of warning his readers that the Catholic Church was not the spent force described by many of his contemporaries, prophesied that it "may still exist in undiminished vigour when some traveler from New Zealand shall, in the midst of a vast solitude, take his stand on a broken arch of London Bridge to sketch the ruins of St Paul's."[10] This is precisely the scene Doré seems to have in mind.

The origin and cultural impact of this image is reviewed in an intriguing article by David Skilton, but the picture itself is included as the final plate in Lynda Nead's *Victorian Babylon: People, Streets and Images in Nineteenth-century London*.[11] What her fascinating work

8. Gustave Doré, *London: A Pilgrimage* (London: Grant & Co., 1872).

9. David Skilton, "Contemplating the Ruins of London: Macaulay's New Zealander and Others," n.p. Online: homepages.gold.ac.uk/london-journal/march2004/skilton.html.

10. T. B. Macaulay, Review of Leopold von Ranke, *The Ecclesiastical and Political History of the Popes During the Sixteenth and Seventeenth Centuries* [*Die römische Papste*] (trans. S. Austin; London, 1840), *Edinburgh Review* 72 (October 1840), 227–58 (258, cited by Skilton).

11. Linda Nead, *Victorian Babylon: People, Streets and Images in Nineteenth-century London* (New Haven: Yale University Press, 2000).

emphasizes is the degree to which Babylon, and other biblical cities, shaped the imagination of imperial London, to the extent that the Empire writing back was already, in embryo, described within it. The New Zealander of the picture is the postcolonial subject, par excellence. Even at its heyday, champions of imperialism such as Macaulay and the illustrator of a guidebook such as Doré know that London, like Babylon, or Nineveh, or Rome, is a great city that will fall. That is part of what the imaginary—the *biblical* imaginary—of its status as metropolis implies: the biblical city is built on proleptic lament and mourning. Its destruction is inevitable, but so is the fact that it will be a site of remembrance.

Exactly this point is made by Dante Gabriel Rossetti in his poem "The Burden of Nineveh," which is inspired by the sight of a winged lion statue from Nineveh being installed in the British Museum. Rossetti reflects on all the history, including biblical history, that the statue has seen and then turns to an imagined future, as he puts it:

> When some may question which was first,
>   Of London or of Nineveh.
> For as that Bull-god once did stand
> And watched the burial-clouds of sand,
> Till these at last without a hand
> Rose o'er his eyes, another land,
>   And blinded him with destiny: —
> So may he stand again; till now,
> In ships of unknown sail and prow,
> Some tribe of the Australian plough
> Bear him afar, — a relic now
>   Of London, not of Nineveh![12]

Once again, notice the place of the Antipodean returner, but the striking sense that, in the broad scheme of things, London and Babylon will be indistinguishable. This sense of the proleptic mourning of the great city is caught with inimitable economy by the Japanese poet Bashō in a haiku that runs:

> *Bird of time—*
> *in Kyoto, pining*
> *for Kyoto.*[13]

---

12. Dante Gabriel Rossetti, *Poems* (London: F. S. Ellis, 1870), 28–29.
13. Bashō, *Haiku* (trans. Lucien Stryk; London: Penguin, 1995), 24. In Makoto Ueda, *Bashō and His Interpreters: Selected Hokku with Commentary* (Stanford, Calif.: Stanford University Press, 1992), 294, the Japanese commentator Katō Shūson (b. 1905) is quoted as explaining, "The first Kyoto in the poem is the real city; the second is the city that lives yet in ancient poetry and fiction." This identity

In "Eden, Babylon, New Jerusalem," itself a suggestive title, Jamie Scott and Paul Simpson-Housley develop a taxonomy of writing on the city.[14] Scott and Simpson-Housley see Western writing on the city as being imbued with biblically derived images of the city "as a place in quest of a lost Eden in the form of a New Jerusalem and in flight from the threat of an encroaching Babylon."[15] However, they go on to suggest that this tradition is transcended in the images of the city in postcolonial literatures where this Judaeo-Christian "horizontal" narrative of loss, exile and redemption is replaced by a "vertical" superposition of urban and rural, oppressor and oppressed. This, they argue, reflects a global shift in the condition of the city, in the West as much as in the non-Western world, but one that develops what has always been a truth about the multiplicity, diversity and fluidity of urban life.

Because of this fluidity, writing the city is, in their view, always an ideological act, inevitably privileging one version of the city among the many possible stories. Realistic fictions that purport to describe the city inevitably encode implicit ideological commitments about what the city should be. The point of their argument is that ideological critique only becomes possible when the irony of this mismatch between intention and practice come to the fore. The importance of both postcolonial and biblical writing for this is clear when they end their discussion with this sentence: "In the last analysis, however, we must recognize the ironic, and hence problematic, ideological interpenetration between things Judeo-Christian and western and things otherwise."[16]

In his study *Postcolonial London: Rewriting the Metropolis*,[17] John McLeod makes a comparable point as he charts the emergence of a resistant writing by immigrant writers who become London writers, writing of a city which is itself transformed by the experience of colonialism and postcolonialism. As the capital of Britain, a symbol of enduring English and imperial identity, it is also ever-changing and increasingly and more

in difference, and the mourning of one within the other, are at the heart of the argument of this chapter, although the question as to which Kyoto is which can also be raised.

14. Jamie S. Scott and Paul Simpson-Housley, "Eden, Babylon, New Jerusalem: A Taxonomy for Writing the City," in *"Writing the City": Eden, Babylon and New Jerusalem* (ed. Peter Preston and Paul Simpson-Housley; London: Routledge, 1994), 331–41.

15. Ibid., 339.

16. Ibid., 340.

17. John McLeod, *Postcolonial London: Rewriting the Metropolis* (Abingdon: Routledge, 2004).

volubly diverse, ethnically and culturally. London is the site of the interaction between these identities, sometimes in violently destructive conflict, at other times in creative and transformative ways. But there is another aspect to this. For many of those migrating to Britain in the mid-twentieth century, London was the site of hope, of civilization and opportunity, a city of dreams. Much of the post-war literature produced in Britain by migrant writers reflects the disappointment of those who came to a war-ravaged city, many of whose inhabitants were poor, culturally deprived and ill-educated, and where racism and economic decline meant that the promised jobs never materialized. The loss of the London that epitomized British imperial domination and injustice might be welcome, but the loss of this utopian London, which was never real, was something to be mourned. The metropolis is the object of envy, and sometimes the source of hope, as well as the oppressor and the enemy. London can be lamented as well as berated by those who were the subjects of imperial rule.

The lesson I want to take is that the opposition of New Jerusalem and Babylon is not a stable one and collapses into the superimposed complexity of the real city. Although the trope of the journey from Eden to New Jerusalem which is threatened, but also made possible, by the existence of Babylon, has undeniable roots in the Bible, I would contend that the biblical texts on the city also support their "vertical" view. For one thing, nowhere in the Hebrew Bible is Eden explicitly held out as a model for aspiration by later writers. In fact, it is conspicuous by its absence. In any case, Eden is not an image of primeval wilderness but is derived from the royal garden, of which Babylon's legendary gardens are the prime model. The great city is the prerequisite for Eden, rather than its opposite. Similarly, in Exodus it is clear that, for most of the people Moses is leading into the desert, Egypt is much more obviously the source of aspiration and the model of a viable existence, indeed the Promised Land, than the desert of Sinai and the hostile highlands of Canaan. They mourn the loss of Egypt, as Diana Lipton has lately explored.[18]

The great cities of the ancient Near East as they appear in the Bible are by no means simply the object of contempt. Tyre and Babylon in particular are described with envious wonder. Indeed, one could characterize a good deal of the biblical history of Israel as the attempt to turn Jerusalem into Babylon. The imagery associated with the new Jerusalem makes it

---

18. See Diana Lipton, *Longing for Egypt and Other Unexpected Biblical Tales* (Sheffield: Sheffield Phoenix, 2008).

seem closer to a new Babylon, the great city of temple and power with its glittering jewelled gates and its flowing rivers. In all such biblical writing, the names of the cities encode ideologies as well as actualities.

This is a complex interaction, as the colonial cities of the British Empire show. British imperial architecture is a monumental style that harks back to emulations of French and Italian architecture, themselves modelled on Roman styles, adapted from Greece. Indeed, the ruins of London in Doré's picture recall ruined Rome. The influence runs in both directions, however. At the same time as the cities of the Indian *raj* sprouted Gothic churches and Palladian government houses, the cities of Britain expanded with suburbs full of one-storey "bungalows"—the style and the name of which derived from the Indian subcontinent; indeed, the word shares its root with "Bengal."

Analogously, Solomon's Jerusalem and Omri's Samaria, even as textual cities, let alone on the evidence of archaeology, are avowedly built by foreign craftsmen from foreign materials. They are not radically distinctive Judaean and Israelite alternatives to the great cities of other nations; they are emulations of them. They are not even the product of indigenous designers and builders, just as in biblical terms, the great Pharaonic store cities of Raamses and Pithon were the product of Israelite labour. The metropolis shows the extent of its power and influence by its command of the resources and riches of other nations.

The point is that the metropolis is both the object and the product of emulation. A prime example of this in the books of Kings is King Ahaz's replacement of the altar in the temple with one modelled exactly on the altar that he came across in Damascus when he met with Tiglath-Pileser (2 Kgs 16). Emulation and envy, as well as enmity, are part of a complex mixture of reactions to the metropolis. Isaiah 14:2 makes this potential reversal clear when it says of the people of Israel, "They will take captive those who were their captors, and rule over those who oppressed them." The vision, in this passage at any rate, is not of a radical undoing of oppressive structures. The problem is not that people are conquered and subjugated, but who gets to do the conquering and the subjugating. Here the aspiration is precisely of Israel become Babylon.

These ambiguities are particularly clear when these foreign cities apparently become the subjects of laments within the Hebrew Bible. F. W. Dobbs-Allsopp makes the case that something similar to the ancient Sumerian city-lament genre is present in the Hebrew Bible.[19] He

---

19. F. W. Dobbs-Allsopp, *Weep, O Daughter of Zion: A Study of the City-Lament Genre in the Hebrew Bible* (BibOr 44; Rome: Editrice Pontificio Istituto Biblico, 1993). See also John B. Geyer, *Mythology and Lament: Studies in the Oracles About*

points out the considerable generic similarities between Lamentations and Mesopotamian city laments and concludes that Israelite literature had a distinctive but recognizable native tradition of this genre. Within the Hebrew Bible, Dobbs-Allsopp finds it most frequently in the oracles against the nations and wonders why this should be. He cites the work of Jahnow[20] and Janzen,[21] who both give Mesopotamian examples of the shift from lament from the dead to curse of the murderer. Dobbs-Allsopp's point is that although Lamentations shows this pattern[22] he finds that the oracles against the nations have a modified intensification where lament and curse have the same object. "It is as if the laments themselves are lifted up as curses," Dobbs-Allsopp observes, going on to describe these instances as mock laments.[23]

I want to suggest that the postcolonial literature bears witness that even in these satiric oracles the double edge of lament and curse can cut both ways. The curse may be a symptom of lament. Anger, often directed against the one who dies, is a recognized part of the process of mourning and that anger, so Freud would suggest, may be the very reaction that

*the Nations* (Aldershot: Ashgate, 2004). The "about" in Geyer's title is significant, as one of his points is to question the assumption in the traditional title of "oracles *against* the nations." Geyer roots these traditions in mythological liturgies of purity in the temple that have later been given more concrete historical settings. His point, however, is that the oracles "are not expressions of xenophobia, they are concerned with a necessary step in the process of recreation" (p. 182). The object of condemnation is that which threatens God's holiness and that applies to Israel as much as the nations.

20. Hedwig Jahnow, *Das hebräische Leichenlied im Rahmen der Völkerdichter* (BZAW 36; Giessen: Töpelmann, 1923), 88–90, cited by Dobbs-Allsopp, *Weep, O Daughter of Zion*, 160.

21. Waldemar Janzen, *Mourning Cry and War Oracle* (BZAW 125; Berlin: de Gruyter, 1972), 27–34, cited by Dobbs-Allsopp, *Weep, O Daughter of Zion*, 160.

22. But see my "Reading Lamentations," *JSOT* 95 (2001): 55–69, where it is pointed out that the problem for monotheistic Israel is that the only possible suspect as murderer of the city is its patron and protector, Yahweh. The peculiar features of Lamentations arise because this logic is refused and the curse is displaced onto the victims, Jerusalem and her dead. Lament and curse become fused but for different reasons in this case.

23. Dobbs-Allsopp, *Weep, O Daughter of Zion*, 161. A development of this line of argument is offered by, among others, Reed Lessing ("Satire in Isaiah's Tyre Oracle," *JSOT* 28 [2003]: 89–112), who describes Isaiah's Tyre oracle (Isa 23:1–14) as a satire and Brian C. Jones's work on the satiric lament over Moab in Isa 15–16 (*Howling Over Moab: Irony and Rhetoric in Isaiah 15–16* (SBLDS 157; Atlanta: Scholars Press, 1996]). In both these cases, the argument goes that the wider context shows such hostility to the object of the lament that the turn to mourning can only be understood as ironic.

turns normal mourning into a pathological melancholia which has no end because the dead cannot ask forgiveness. There is something enviable, something worth lamenting, in the victim that is being mocked and the double edge can be turned against the mockers as well. The ironic lamenter, in his effort to belittle the enemy, may actually bear witness to the fact that the destroyed enemy represented his aspirations as well as a threat and indeed was a threat because it embodied aspirations that properly should belong to Judah. The ambiguity of the lament reflects a deep, but different, ambiguity in his reaction to the imperial power.

Such ambiguity comes to the fore specifically in regard to Babylon in a monograph by John Hill: *Friend or Foe? The Figure of Babylon in the Book of Jeremiah MT*.[24] What strikes him, as it does me, is that there are passages in Jeremiah, for instance in ch. 27, where the names "Judah" and "Babylon" could well be substituted for each other, passages which rail against Judah and ones which mourn over the fate of Babylon. These are set against passages such as chs. 50–51 where Babylon is unequivocally the enemy of God. For Hill, the tension in metaphor accounts for this and he sees the overall message of the book as asserting a theology of indefinite exile predicated on the idea that Babylon and Judah are more alike than different. Hill goes so far as to claim, in relation to Jer 29:49, "The relationship between Babylon and Judah is one of identity. Babylon is Judah!"[25]

We can go further than Hill and make the observation that metaphors do not obey the rules of algebra—to say "A is/is not B" is not the same as saying "B is/is not A." A standard example may help here: to say "All surgeons are butchers" is not the same as saying "All butchers are surgeons." The first activates the crudity and goriness and carelessness of the butcher; the second, the finesse and indeed artistry of the surgeon. Both activate culturally determined associations that serve to differentiate the two professions. After all, in literal terms, few people combine the roles of both surgeon and butcher. To juxtapose the alternative phrasings of the metaphor, however, brings to the fore the question as to how accurate these default associations are. Perhaps surgeons and butchers are more alike than we thought.

Can we try the same experiment with the conclusion of Hill's study? Babylon is Judah; Judah is Babylon. Does that suggest that while Babylon is the Lord's chosen home, and city of peace, Judah is the home of overweening pride and cruelty, hostile to God? Perhaps the two combine

---

24. John Hill, *Friend or Foe? The Figure of Babylon in the Book of Jeremiah MT* (Leiden: Brill, 1999).
25. Ibid., 152.

these features in a more subtle way. We end up with something much closer to Scott and Simpson-Housley's "vertical" account of city, where Babylon, Jerusalem and Eden are superimposed, and represent varying ideological accounts of the metropolis. A line of William Blake's encapsulates the ambiguity: "Whether this is Jerusalem or Babylon we know not." And mention of Blake immediately takes us to an imaginative identification of Jerusalem and London, and back to Rossetti and Doré and the superposition of London on Babylon and Rome.

Furthermore, Blake's line, from his visionary poem *Vala: or the Four Zoas*,[26] provides the epigraph for a much acclaimed novel by David Malouf, tellingly entitled *Remembering Babylon*, in which he explores the communal tensions around the emergence of a distinctive Australian identity, with implications for the antipodean who contemplates ruined London in Macaulay and Rossetti. The line also appears at the head and in the conclusion of Hill's work, with acknowledgments to Malouf. Both, however, omit the following line: "All is confusion All is tumult and we alone escaped [*sic*]." The indistinguishability of Babylon and Jerusalem in Blake's verse is given voice by the survivors of a catastrophe. In concluding this discussion, I want to suggest that the ambiguities in these Hebrew quasi-laments have resonances with aspects of contemporary postcolonial literature as survivors' literature.

Here I want to draw on the work of Sam Durrant in his *Postcolonial Narrative and the Work of Mourning*,[27] in which he studies the work of three novelists: J. M. Coetzee in South Africa, Wilson Harris in the Caribbean and Toni Morrison on African American experience. Durrant claims that what relates their disparate work is that all are ultimately concerned with the kind of communal act of forgetting that Freud points to in his *Moses and Monotheism*. In their different contexts, they deal with the ways in which oppressed peoples try to reconstruct a coherent

---

26. Intriguingly, this line and the one following it have an ambiguous textual status themselves. Although printed in some editions as lines 97 and 98 of "Night the Third" of *The Four Zoas* (e.g. as cited by Hill [p. 1] from *William Blake: A Selection of Poems and Letters* [ed. J. Bronowski; London: Penguin, 1958], 155), the notes to the poem in William Blake, *The Complete Poems* (ed. W. H. Stevenson; 2d ed.; London: Longman, 1989), relegate the lines to marginalia which are pencilled corrections by Blake to his manuscript of *The Four Zoas* applied to a block of material which he subsequently reused in his poem *Jerusalem*. These particular lines are part of the adaptations for the new context, but do not appear in exactly this form in that place. Tumult and confusion of place are enacted as well as encoded by these lines.

27. Sam Durrant, *Postcolonial Narrative and the Work of Mourning* (Albany: State University of New York Press, 2004).

narrative of the group's identity out of the disruption and loss that oppression and slavery have brought. That very history of oppression, however, means both that the narrative threads of history are brutally disrupted and that their history is complicit with that of those who are cast as the oppressors. There is no history without the other. For different reasons, both oppressed and oppressor come to share an amnesia about the events and consequences of that trauma, constructing stories and histories that elide the savage co-implication and mutual shame that the scrutiny of these events would provoke. This is both an objective and subjective amnesia. There is an actual loss of records, data and memories, but this is compounded by a willed amnesia manifested as a communal denial of the past and a refusal to acknowledge and learn from those records that do survive. The attempt to recapture a pure point of origin and a unique history for an oppressed, displaced and scattered people will end by emphasizing the fact that their history is inextricably implicated with the history of others, including those who appear in the story as the oppressors, to the extent that the point of origin becomes blurred. To quote Durrant again, "The inability to recover the prehistory of the tribe as an integrated and integrable narrative guarantees the endlessness of the process of collective mourning."[28]

Consequently, the effort to reconstruct a lost history of a nation, people or tribe after a traumatic experience or disruption is an act of impossible mourning. Precisely as the authors of these laments in the Hebrew Bible strive to recreate a past disrupted by the exile, they discover, repress and betray the fact that that past and their identity is inescapably shaped by the very nations from which they are desperate to distinguish themselves. The Hebrew Bible is a supreme example of the attempt to recreate a past when that past has been disrupted, to see pure origins where all is obscure, where Eden as the primeval point of origin is conceived of in terms that presuppose the great city that is the point of aspiration. As endless collective mourning and lament, the ambiguities it attempts to deal with are the ambiguities characteristic of the empire and its metropolis: hated, envied and mourned by those who suffer its cruelties, who are also those who hope to inherit and surpass its power. Postcolonial criticism has much light to shed on these ambiguous texts. Indeed, it suggests that just such ambiguity, rather than being a problem in these texts, is exactly what we should expect.

In 2009, the British Museum was home to a fascinating exhibition on Babylon and its cultural heritage, made more poignant by the damage sustained to the ancient city in recent years in the various Gulf Wars.

---

28. Ibid., 117.

Once again, London was home to Babylon, in all its splendour, decadence and decay. If catastrophe had then struck the city, Rosetti's future Australian, picking through the ruins, might well have been confused. The exhibition contained a striking picture by Julee Holcomber entitled "Babylon Revisited" of the modern city redesigned on the model of Breughel's famous image of the half-completed tower of Babel that makes the point of the continuity of the imagined city of the Bible with the imagined city which is London. In both, towering aspiration turned hubris portends collapse.

And what of the Bible in such a city, which is where we came in? After all we have said, what book is better situated to unpack the ambivalences of a great city falling on hard times and a population made up of more or less willing migrants from all corners of its political and economic empire? Perhaps that question can be answered best by looking at what seem to be the beginnings of a reversal of the gift of the Bible that was depicted in the painting by Baker we began by discussing. As an example of this, we could cite the publication of the volume edited by Hugh R. Page Jr. entitled *The Africana Bible: Reading Israel's Scripture from Africa and the African Diaspora*.[29] Page brings together biblical readings by scholars from Africa and from the African diaspora in the United States and Caribbean; the term "Africana" is inclusive in this sense. It offers reflections by these scholars on the books of the Bible, in this case all from what the book terms "Israel's Scriptures" and some general essays, reflecting the difficulties and concerns of African and Africana readers. I wonder if there is mileage these days in attempting the same kind of exercise in London itself. Who is reading the Bible here, and how do they relate the Bible to their various experiences of displacement and exile, either as immigrants to the city, from abroad, or from within the UK, or as displaced people, as many longstanding inhabitants of the city feel themselves to be, physically or emotionally removed from the communities and places that had meaning for them in the past? Like any metropolis, London is, at the risk of oxymoron, a home for exiles.

Towards the beginning of this chapter I referred to the series of lectures on what were then called "Colonial Problems" that took place nearly a century ago. Intriguingly, in the light of the present situation of universities, the preface makes no bones about the fact that that series was a deliberate publicity exercise designed to raise support and endowments for the setting up of a Professorship in Imperial Studies. King's

29. Hugh R. Page, Jr., ed., *The Africana Bible: Reading Israel's Scripture from Africa and the African Diaspora* (Minneapolis: Fortress, 2010).

College, at the heart of what was termed "the Colonial Quarter" of London, was particularly well placed, it was thought, to carry that forward, and indeed such a chair was established and still flourishes.

Is there a similar argument to be made that at this juncture, of all junctures, Sir Charles Lucas's plea for a book that does justice to religion as a force in empire should be remembered and revised? Is this not a time when the biblical imaginary that underlies London as the city of cities needs to be explored and rethought as a core part of the re-imagination of a city in a rapidly changing world? Is it not part of the role of scholars of Biblical Studies to help London, and the other great cites of the world, mourn and celebrate themselves? What the biblical scholars of the third world know well is how to read through structures of oppression in the Bible and in their lives, through anger and indeed hatred, to find the possibilities of continued life and renewed community. Maybe that is what the people of the metropolis always need to hear: the biblical message that it is within the city that is built to fall that the models and materials for rebuilding are to be found.

Part III

THE BIBLE AS GUIDEBOOK

Chapter 7

BIBLICAL TOURISM:
EÇA DE QUEIRÓS AND MARK TWAIN IN PALESTINE

Novels are a vital resource for understanding the development of the popular understanding of the Bible and particularly that sub-genre that explicitly uses novelistic techniques to engage with the problems of how the Bible has been and should be received. It was while researching the surprisingly extensive range of these works that I came across a novel by the great nineteenth-century Portuguese novelist Eça de Queirós entitled *A Relíquia* (*The Relic*),[1] a work which, besides being very entertaining, has a distinctively Portuguese but more generally applicable contribution to make to the wider understanding of biblical reception.

When it comes to analyzing those distinctives, however, I confess to being a mere tourist in the realm of Portuguese history and culture, probably the equivalent of someone to booking a cheap Easyjet flight and spending the weekend in Faro. The same could be said of my engagement with contemporary New Testament scholarship, making me rather a day-tripper into areas where others are at home. Yet I console myself that even the tourist's perspective may have value as long as the tourist never forgets his or her limitations. When it comes to visiting the strange world of the birth of Christianity, are we not all tourists, picking among ruins, and seeing, for the most part, what the guidebooks tell us to expect?

As mass tourism to Palestine took off in the nineteenth century, so Hilton Obenzinger has observed in his *American Palestine: Melville, Twain and the Holy Land Mania*, the Bible itself became not just a metaphorical guidebook to life but also a real one to the sites of the great events of the Old and New Testament.[2] Because they are journeying to the unfamiliar, tourists must depend for the guarantee of authenticity on

---

1. Editions consulted: José Maria Eça de Queirós, *A Relíquia* (Porto: Livraria Lello, 1935 [1887]); English translation *The Relic* (trans. Margaret Jull Costa; Sawtry: Dedalus, 1994). Page numbers in the text refer to this English translation.
2. Hilton Obenzinger, *American Palestine: Melville, Twain and the Holy Land Mania* (Princeton: Princeton University Press, 1999).

some guide or other: the label by the picture, the guided tour, the endless brochures, the tradition of the church and, in the Holy Land, the witness of the Bible.

For Edward Said, this phenomenon of the guide book marks an intrinsic relationship between text and tourism. It epitomizes for him what he calls the "textual attitude," which consists in assuming that the way to deal with unfamiliar or threatening circumstances is to fall back on texts, an attitude that could be said to typify much traditional biblical reading. As Said writes,

> Many travelers find themselves saying of an experience in a new country that it wasn't what they expected, meaning that it wasn't what a book said it would be. And of course many writers of travel books or guidebooks compose them in order to say that a country *is* like this, or better, that it *is* colorful, expensive, interesting and so forth… [T]he book (or text) acquires a greater authority, and use, even than the actuality it describes.[3]

Yet the very presence of the tourist can complicate the picture. Authenticity becomes hard to pin down as the inhabitants of the tourist centre quickly learn what is expected of them, leading to the burgeoning phenomenon of "staged authenticity," where the authentic is consciously "performed."[4] This leads in turn to the development of what is termed "anti-tourism": travellers who distance themselves from their fellow-tourists and who seek the "authentically authentic" experience off the beaten track, yet, who are, of course, never able totally to dissociate themselves from the role as tourist which they despise.

Such questions are brought to the fore in Eça's novel *A Relíquia*. Indeed, we could read the novel as a kind of parable of the inauthentic. Teodorico, the hero, or anti-hero, of the novel, embodies the ambiguities of pilgrim, tourist and anti-tourist. The novel is in the form of his memoir of a journey to the Holy Land. Sent by his insufferably pious but wealthy aunt to fetch her a relic from the Holy Land, he obeys, knowing that this is the surest way to inherit her wealth. He embodies the new phenomenon of the tourist to the Promised Land, as opposed to the pilgrim, although he adopts the role of pilgrim to satisfy his aunt. In brief, the pilgrim travels in search of an authentic spiritual experience, whereas the tourist travels to see where other people have authentic spiritual experiences.

Teodorico's desires are fulfilled when he takes up with a young lady in Cairo. She is Mary, a Yorkshire lass; for the young Portuguese traveller, she is thus a creature with her own exoticism. As a remembrance of their

---

3. Edward W. Said, *Orientalism* (London: Penguin, 2003), 93.
4. For a discussion of the importance of authenticity in the tourist sensibility, see John Urry, *The Tourist Gaze* (2d ed.; London: Sage, 2002).

passion, she gives him her nightdress, neatly tied in a brown paper parcel. Anxious to find the relic, however, he has a weird encounter with a thorn tree which he concludes could well be the source of the crown of thorns, an opinion which his learned travelling companion, who is a German biblical scholar called Dr Topsius, is prepared to confirm with all the authority of science, even although he does not believe a word of it. Their clever local guide fashions a crown of thorns from the tree and this too is wrapped in a brown paper parcel all ready to be presented to Aunty.

Mary's nightgown, however, is proving to be an annoying piece of unnecessary baggage and he gives the parcel containing it away. After many adventures, including an extraordinary trip through time that allows the two travellers to be present at the events of the crucifixion, they return to Lisbon.[5] Aunty opens the parcel containing the precious relic, only to find to her horror a nightdress with a loving inscription to "my gallant little Portuguese," signed "M. M." So end Teodorico's hopes of a fortune, although he ends the book quite respectably off, having managed to make a living from selling other fake relics he has brought back.

At the end of the book, Teodorico concludes that his biggest mistake was not his deception, but the one lie he was not bold enough to utter. If only he had said that the initials on the note, M. M., stood for Mary Magdalene, then Aunty would have revered the nightdress as a relic and left him her fortune. Not only that, he is sure that learned New Testament scholars would have revered him for providing such rich material for reconstructing the nightwear and the textile industries of the early Christian world.

Teodorico is very aware of the power of narrative and of writing. After all, a relic is just an object, when all is said and done. What gives it power is the story that is attached to it and the signature of whatever authority is prepared to vouch that it is what the story says it is. In the mysterious sequence where the two travellers are transported back to the Jerusalem of Jesus' trial, Teodorico has a characteristically mixed response to the thought that he might actually see Jesus. At first, he is suddenly aware of his own shortcomings and terrified of what would happen when the Lord saw him, and then becomes caught up in the possibility of hearing a cry or a word from his lips. This sentimental

---

5. In a characteristically sly aside, Eça has Teodorico remark, as he watches Jesus in front of Pilate, that he is not wearing any crown of thorns. Not only is the relic that he would have given his aunt a fake made by his guide and falsely authenticated by Topsius, there never was an original, at least in this story world.

identification almost immediately, however, is followed by his typical self-regarding reflection:

> I would be privy then to a new word uttered by Christ, one that had not been written down in the Gospels and I alone would have the pontifical right to repeat it to the prostrate crowds. My authority in the Church would shine like the newest of New Testaments. I would be a previously unknown witness to the Passion. I would become St Teodorico the Evangelist![6]

Here Teodorico reveals himself as the anti-tourist of the Bible. He eagerly seeks the authority of having his own particular authentic word, rather than following the crowd in their silly devotion to the evangelists. He wants both to single himself out from the mass of biblical readers and at the same time earn their praise. By giving him this speech, however, Eça slyly satirizes the motivations of the original evangelists. Were they the Teodoricos of their own day?

Eça, of course, is not the only writer of his time to give voice to such scepticism, although he is a particularly intelligent and witty exemplar who brings an intriguing Portuguese and Catholic dimension to the discussion. I suspect, however, though cannot prove, that he is aware of and influenced by one of the nineteenth century's best-selling works, Mark Twain's *The Innocents Abroad*. Given his knowledge of and interest in English literature, his fascination with this particular subject matter and the rapid popular success of Twain's book, it is certainly not unlikely that he knew it. Indeed, it is suggestive that *The Innocents Abroad* was first published in 1869, around the time that Eça was working on his account of Jesus' death in a series of articles entitled "A Morte" which are precursors to *A Relíquia*, although the latter was not published until 1887.[7]

Whatever the case, there is a palpable similarity of tone between the two books, different as they are in structure. Both are, in Franklin Walker's phrase, told in the voice of an "irreverent pilgrim."[8] *The*

---

6. Eça de Queirós, *The Relic*, 154.
7. In this connection, it is intriguing that in *The Innocents Abroad* Twain hints at other books that could be written, especially in the chapter on Nazareth: "Whoever shall write the Boyhood of Jesus ingeniously, will make a book which will possess a vivid interest for young and old alike" (p. 537). He then goes on to supply a brief digest of some of the apocryphal infancy gospels, and remarks on their usefulness as a guidebook to the traveller visiting the cathedrals of France and Italy, "with their treasures of tabooed and forgotten tradition" (p. 539).
8. See Franklin Walker, *Irreverent Pilgrims: Melville, Brown and Mark Twain in the Holy Land* (Seattle: University of Washington Press, 1974).

## 7. Biblical Tourism 83

*Innocents Abroad* originated when Twain was paid by the *New Yorker* to accompany a group of American travellers on a cruise to Europe and the Near East. In return for his fare, he supplied a series of weekly satirical essays, later revised and edited into the book. Although not strictly a novel, *The Innocents Abroad* does bring centre stage a narrator with the irreverence and wit of Teodorico, with the difference that he is an American Protestant rather than Portuguese Catholic, with therefore a more straightforward ability to scoff at what he finds to be Catholic superstition in the reverence for holy objects and sites in Palestine. Twain's character "Mark Twain"—for the narrator is a character—brings a self-confident Yankee sense of superiority to his encounter with the Holy Land and uses the same technique of bathos as he uses the disjunction between the shabby reality of present-day Palestine as viewed through a brash American eye with the sentimental vision of the tourist guides and the glories of the past.

In his *Orientalism*, Edward Said describes the sense of betrayal that underlies the Western traveller's discovery that the reality of the East does not live up to the fantasy. For Twain and Eça, the encounter with Palestine is a juxtaposition of two betrayals: by the country which disappoints expectations and by the Bible as the book which fostered these expectations. This issues, somewhat irrationally, in hostility and mockery towards Palestine, in both writers' works. It is only too human to turn in anger against the innocent disappointing object, against those who misled us, and against ourselves for being so easily fooled.

In the light of this, there is a certain irony that Twain's book itself was used as a guidebook by American travellers. His mocking account of how he wept at Adam's tomb made the site all the more attractive to tourists who wanted to follow in Twain's footsteps, not Christ's, and see the spot where Twain had wept. A measure of the book's influence emerges from an interesting note from a correspondent for the Hartford *Courant* in 1872: "Here at this hotel, Byzanci of Constantinople, I am not sooner housed than on my room table I espy a copy of the *Innocents*, whose well-worn condition contrasts oddly with the well-conditioned Scriptures furnished in hotels at home."[9] Twain replaces the Bible as the bedside reading of the tourist to the east.

More troublingly, Twain's avowedly satirical dismissal of all of the East of the Mediterranean, in particular anywhere under Turkish influence, as a corrupt and decadent desert finds its way into the speeches of David Ben-Gurion as he argues for the establishment of the state of Israel. It is Twain whom he quotes in justification of the claim that

---

9. This passage is quoted in Obenzinger, *American Palestine*, 164.

Palestine was an empty land. Whatever the strengths and weaknesses of that case, to offer Twain's version of Palestine as a historical account of the condition of the country in the nineteenth century is a gross misprision of Twain's purpose. This does, however, make the point that Twain's book, the first widely distributed satire on the craze for biblical tourism, is one that needs to be taken seriously in tracing the origins and development of the complex modern assumptions about Palestine and about the world of the New Testament and biblical scholarship.

For Twain, and for Eça, the Bible often seems like that most aggravating of texts, an out-of-date guidebook that was not very carefully edited in the first place. Anyone who has tried to navigate a city with a guidebook produced a decade ago will know how frustrating that can be. *A Relíquia* is a parable of the betrayal and disappointment that is always possible when textual expectation and experience fail to match. As a biblical reader, Eça has been given what the Portuguese Church and the society around him purport to regard as a parcel containing a relic, the authentic account of the way the world is and should be. He has opened it, in the company of Renan, Voltaire and, as I suspect, Mark Twain, to discover that the parcel only contains a common nightdress, a tissue of deceit.

The well-known epigraph to *A Relíquia* could be appealed to here: "Over the sturdy nakedness of the truth, the diaphanous veil of phantasy." Eça's take on the gospel is actually the reverse of this, however. It turns out that is the deceitfulness and allure of the diaphanous nightgown of writing that is the truth; the claim to truth made by the crown of thorns and the religious and political story for which it is a metonym is the fantasy.

Yet while last year's guidebook is a potential source of frustration, the guidebooks of a century ago recover a new kind of interest as evidence not just of sites now lost or changed out of recognition, but of an earlier gaze and an earlier interpretative framework shared between a lost traveller and his lost audience. Both Eça and Twain's works now have an interest for us as evidence of older attitudes and insights as well as, of course, information and insights about the geography and social customs of the countries they visited and of the societies they represented and satirized, though this needs careful sifting. At times the tourist, sometimes by not understanding what he or she sees, can put a finger on matters that the natives have forgotten or concealed or take for granted. Biblical scholars have much to learn from the growing literature on tourism and travel writing in their continuing attempt to come to grips with the problems of biblical authenticity.

Chapter 8

*THE BOOK OF DAVE* VERSUS THE BIBLE

*The Book of Dave*, Will Self's fifth novel, published in 2006, is a complex work set within the even more complex self-referential *roman-fleuve* that constitutes his *oeuvre*. Central to the novel is the book referred to in the title, a book that becomes a new scripture. At some point in the future, on the series of islands that are all that are left of a drowned Britain, the misogynistic rants of a London cabbie, the Dave of the title, become the sacred texts and social blueprint of a post-apocalyptic society. Dave, who, the reader realizes, is becoming increasingly deranged as his own story unfolds, is obsessed by the unfairness of the divorce settlement with his estranged wife and particularly over the issue of the custody of their son. His obsession finds expression in the book that he arranges to have inscribed on silver plates and then buries in his ex-wife's garden, hoping that his son will some day discover it and then understand his father's point of view. In the society of the future, the book has been discovered but has attained the status of scripture. The people of the future are living with the consequences of a repressive religious society that enforces Dave's misogyny and ritually calls over the cab routes of the now drowned city that the rulers are obsessively trying to restore.

The novel draws both explicitly and covertly on a wide range of sources and weaves them into an unusual structure. Its story-telling is not linear, but oscillates, in alternate chapters, between the story of Dave and his increasing psychosis as his marriage disintegrates, which is set in the 1990s and the early 2000s, and the story, set more than five hundred years in the future, of a young man, Carl, as he seeks to find love in the authoritarian and divisive society that is based on Dave's text. Even within the each of these two story lines, the chronology is not linear. This chronological instability adds to the often subtle way that the two stories and the two worlds intertwine. The subtitle to the book is significant in this regard. Self calls it "A Revelation of the Recent Past and the Distant

Future." Past and future are held together as mutually illuminating—the revelation of one is the revelation of the other. The past, even the recent past, however, needs revelation just as much as the future does. We understand more of the peculiarities of the Bible and language of the future society as we see their roots in Dave's life and we see the unintended consequences of Dave's actions as they play out in the life of the new community.

In an interview, Will Self divulged the two sources for the inspiration of this work. One was a series of raisings of the Thames barrier, which prompted him to wonder what would happen if London were flooded and then to ask himself who would be left as the best source of information of what the city used to be like. He concluded that it would be the London cabbie, with his "knowledge" of every street and corner within a six-mile radius of Charing Cross. The city could be recreated from the routes that a cabbie has memorized.

The other stimulus was his reading of *The Bible Unearthed* by the Israeli archaeologists Israel Finkelstein and Neil Asher Silberman.[1] As Self put it in another interview:

> They said something that chimed with me: that even though the whole thrust of biblical scholarship since the early 19$^{th}$ century has been to disprove the Bible as the literal word of God, nevertheless there's a strong residual feeling we have that there's some truth in the Old Testament, that there were kind of sheep herders in the bronze era up to these sorts of things. What these two did was to systematically go through the Bible to show there is no historical evidence for any of it whatsoever.[2]

Self rather exaggerates the claims of the two archaeologists, but by his account these two inspirations come together to inform a novel that is, among other things, a satire on the notion of an authoritative revealed text. As Self goes on to say in the same interview, "The book is arguing that what you need for a revealed religion is any old bollocks, it just has to there in the right place at the right time" (that is a verbatim quotation, I hasten to add). More moderately, writing in *The Guardian*, he says that what he learned from Finkelstein and Silberman is that "revealed religion is a necessary function of state formation, and that the content of this or that 'holy book' is more or less irrelevant to what people make of

---

1. I. Finkelstein and N. A. Silberman *The Bible Unearthed: Archaeology's New Vision of Ancient Israel and the Origin of Its Sacred Texts* (New York: Simon & Schuster, 2001).

2. These words are attributed to Self in an interview by Helen Brown for the Telegraph published on May 28, 2006 and available online at http://www.telegraph.co.uk/culture/books/3652752/A-writers.

## 8. The Book of Dave *Versus the Bible* 87

it."³ Self's substitution of *The Book of Dave* for the Bible is thus designed to debunk the claims made on the Bible's behalf. It is not only its authority which is undermined, but any claim it has to relevance.

I want to question that assertion. To pick up Self's colourful phrase, while the right place and the right time are unquestionably essential components of the success of any scripture, I do not think "any old bollocks" will do. The Bible is a particular kind of bollocks, and that matters. Within Self's novel, there is in fact a much more nuanced approach to the question of what constitutes a scripture than this quote and some others by Self would suggest. In the end, what Self is reacting against is not so much the Bible as a particular way of reading that is applied to the Bible.

The origins of this approach, however, are themselves biblical. I want to set the scene for the development of the kind of novelistic treatment Self represents by a very rapid account of the rise of the historical approach, which came to the fore in nineteenth-century Europe, and then reflect on how and why that gives rise to novelistic literature. I want to argue that the seeds of this are in the Gospels themselves.

I will be drawing here on two main sources. The first will be Albert Schweitzer's classic work *The Quest of the Historical Jesus*, which contains a magisterial, if at times tendentious, survey of novelistic treatments up to the turn of the twentieth century; this is now itself a remarkable witness to the culture embeddedness of so-called objective scholarship, a point Schweitzer is well aware of.⁴ The second is Stephen Prickett's *Origins of Narrative: The Romantic Appropriation of the Bible*, which offers an intriguing reading of the rise of realistic fiction, with the Bible as a key element in its development.⁵

To begin at the beginning, then, with the Gospels themselves. The first point to note is their plurality. The canonical Scriptures know four, but there are at least 30 other texts that have been known or rediscovered that bear that designation: the *Gospel of Thomas* may be the best known, but the *Gospel of the Hebrews*, the *Gospel of the Nazarenes* and many others are known, sometimes partially and in fragments. This means that at the

---

3. "In the beginning: Will Self on the genesis of *The Book of Dave*." Online: http://www.guardian.co.uk/books/2007/Jun/16/willself.

4. The edition referred to here is Albert Schweitzer, *The Quest of the Historical Jesus: A Critical Study of Its Progress from Reimarus to Wrede* (trans. F. C. Burkitt; Baltimore: The Johns Hopkins University Press, 1998). Burkitt's translation was first published in 1910, and Schweitzer's work first appeared in German under the title *Von Reimarus zum Wrede* in 1906.

5. Stephen Prickett, *Origins of Narrative: The Romantic Appropriation of the Bible* (Cambridge: Cambridge University Press, 1996).

heart of the Christian Church, and of the cultures which are influenced by Christianity, is a text characterized by plurality, and self-conscious authorship. We have one story told in many different ways—or is it more than one story? They certainly all centre on one character, Jesus of Nazareth, but is the Jesus of each gospel the "same" character? Is each of these ways valid, or are some to preferred to others? If so, on what grounds?

The fact that the Church settles for not just one version of this story, but for four, and only four, means that the Christian tradition is always aware that these stories can be constantly reworded and retold. At the same time, the juxtaposition of these different stories leads to centuries of argument over their validity, or, dare we say it, truth. Two thousand years later, the success of books like Dan Brown's *The Da Vinci Code* and the remarkable growth of interest in the Gnostic gospels and Dead Sea Scrolls bears witness to the perception of what I have elsewhere called "canon as betrayal." The act of canonization, seen by orthodoxy as a preservation of truth from its enemies, is interpreted as an act of suppression, an attempt by a powerful elite to suppress the truth. The rumours of conspiracy and lost documents have never been quietened, and as the Church loses power, these voices become ever louder.

We should not forget that these questions are nothing new, but are argued over vehemently in the earliest centuries. Many of the questions that later critics have with the partiality, the fragmentariness, the miraculous claims, the internal inconsistencies and the contradictions between gospels are rehearsed in the early Christian centuries. The *locus classicus* for this is in Origen's *Contra Celsum*, where the great third-century Church Father is driven to refute the sceptical and contemptuous dismissal of the biblical texts by the pagan philosopher Celsus. In the process, however, Origen makes great strides in the development of the Church's counter to this in his brilliant application of allegorical reading as a strategy. Origen makes a virtue of the surface inconsistencies of the texts to argue that this is the Holy Spirit's hint to us that we need to be reading at a deeper level to discover the spiritual rather than the literal meaning of the text. Through the good offices of Augustine and many others, this strategy develops as we know into the highly complex and refined allegorical readings of the Middle Ages. What this means, though, is that the meaning of the text is determined by something not on its surface, and the infinite possibilities of allegorization have to be controlled, ultimately by the magisterium of the Church. The art of reading becomes the skill of finding the meaning that one already knows must be in the text, as the Church's teaching says. There is only one story, the story reflected in the Church's dogma.

The Reformation, of course, disrupts this process fundamentally, although ultimately to the reformers' own discomfiture. Partly brought about by the rise of humanist scholarship and the critical reading of texts, and the discovery of new texts from Constantinople, it marks a new way of reading. In dismantling the old unifying principle of the magisterium, however, it revives the old problems of inconsistency and plurality. Where now is the one story? Where the one story was in medieval thought located this side of the text, so to speak, in the accumulated wisdom of the church's teaching, the obvious move was to move the unity of the story *behind* the text, into history. There may be many tellings, but only one thing can have happened.

The trouble is, of course, that this leads to putting the writers of the accounts, the disciples, into the role of witnesses in a forensic sense. If we want to discover what happened, we have to cross-examine them, and under cross-examination it may prove that they are not only fallible but actively deceptive. It may turn out that none of them is speaking the truth in terms of events that can be forensically pieced together. As Henning Graf Reventlow has shown, this cross-examination really begins with the English deists, for instance Herbert of Cherbury, who then influence the European Enlightenment, but it is synthesized and reaches into wider biblical scholarship with the work of Samuel Reimarus (1694–1768).[6] His *Fragments*, published posthumously by Lessing in 1778, are uncompromising in their view of the Gospels. *Prima facie*, the miraculous is ruled out of court. In Reimarus' view, the disciples are an illiterate bunch who have seen that they are on to a good thing with Jesus, who is a ready source of income. When he is executed, they hide the body and then proclaim the resurrection so that they can carry on with their livelihood, distributing other people's alms among themselves, and writing up their garbled, self-serving and barely literate accounts to maintain the illusion. This venal account of the disciples is presented as historically plausible by Reimarus, and indeed he hits on many of the key problems that historical Jesus studies still face. How is history to deal with the miraculous and the divine?

The publication of Reimarus's *Fragments* is usually taken as the beginning of the critical investigation of the historical Jesus, and the attempt to write a coherent life of Jesus on historical principles. His own work had relatively little impact outside scholarly circles.

---

6. See on this Henning Graf Reventlow, *The Authority of the Bible and the Rise of the Modern World* (trans. John Bowden; London: SCM, 1980).

The book which really took a wider readership by storm was David Friedrich Strauss's *Das Leben Jesu*, which appeared in 1836. While drawing on and developing Reimarus' critique with impressive textual skill, he also drew its sting somewhat by seeing the Gospels not as deliberate falsification, but as the inevitable result of the human propensity for myth. He assimilates Jesus' story to a Hegelian notion of the universality of Spirit. This did not stop him being both celebrated and vilified for his views, and translations of his work were rapidly produced and read.

In the context of the impact of Strauss's work on the novel, it should not be forgotten that the 24-year-old Mary Ann Evans, later known as George Eliot, devoted a year of her life to completing its English translation—which is still in print, incidentally. Strauss's work remains a benchmark in Gospel criticism, yet characteristically, at no point does Strauss read any one Gospel for its narrative sweep. Hans Frei, in his influential work *The Eclipse of Biblical Narrative*,[7] charts the loss of interest in the narrative shape of individual books in eighteenth- and nineteenth-century scholarship, and sets this against the rise of the narrative novelistic tradition. Frei sees this as a stark, and unfortunate, disjunction, though, as we will see, even this story can be told differently.

What Frei does do is to bring us back to the Gospels themselves. They are not Hegelian treatises, nor even lives of Jesus, nor historical reports in that sense. Nor are they, *pace* Frei, narratives in a simple sense. They are something rather odd, which is reflected in the oddness of their poetics. In his *Mimesis*, Eric Auerbach reinforces this point.[8] As an example, he reads the account of Peter's denial. He points out that the Gospels are filled with random characters with no narrative depth, brought into contact with Jesus and transformed: peasants, fishers, women, madmen, insignificant figures that would only be admissible in comedy in classical tradition. In terms of classical genres, this story of Peter is "too serious for comedy, too contemporary and everyday for tragedy, politically too insignificant for history."[9] What is also striking is that the narrative is conducted through dialogue, not set speeches.

Auerbach sees this literary revolution as a sign that the text arises from a great social revolution. He writes "The deep sub-surface layers, which were static for the observers of classical antiquity, began to move."[10] For

---

7. *The Eclipse of Biblical Narrative: A Study in Eighteenth and Nineteenth Century Hermeneutics* (New Haven: Yale University Press, 1974).

8. Erich Auerbach, *Mimesis: The Representation of Reality in Western Literature* (trans. Willard R. Trask; Princeton: Princeton University Press, 1968).

9. Ibid., 45.

10. Ibid.

Auerbach, what the Gospels offer, and what Reimarus and Strauss are uninterested in, is a stylistic revolution, one which the allegorical mode of reading tended to obscure with its fragmentation of the text and its seizing on detail and on resonance. Historical criticism equally tends to fragment the texts, as Frei points out. Instead of itself providing the grand narrative, to use a modern term, the Bible is reduced to evidence, and has to be fitted to another story, the rising story of scientific rationalism and liberalism.

But the very rise of historicism leads to another way of reading which has roots in pietism and the spiritualizing of history, another sort of allegorical reading in a way. Herder is cited as a key figure in bringing this approach to the intellectual world. The locus of stability for the text becomes its effect on the sensibility of the reader. The literature this gives rise to has an important root in the journal-keeping characteristic of the radical and pietist. Conceiving oneself in narrative terms, and the idea of a self-authenticating inner drama, is another way to stabilize the text's meaning, although it runs quickly up against the problem of the unity of the self. For nineteenth-century thinkers, the problem is the discovery that it is as hard to ground one's self in the self's history as it is to find the bedrock of the objectively historical. We still live in the aftermath of the various attempts to reconcile these two approaches, and it is in the debatable lands between the two that the modern novel has its rise.

Stephen Prickett, for instance, looks at the sermons of the novelist Laurence Sterne and concludes that Sterne reads his Bible as he might a novel. He traces a strand in English thought that sees the new style of biblical reading not so much as historical as a way of seeing biblical protagonists as characters, possessed of a new kind consciousness reflected in the genre of the novel.

These strands come together with particular force in novelizations of Jesus' life. The Gospels are not novels, as we said, but they may give rise to some of the problems, and provide elusive stylistic clues to the solutions, that novelists deal with. Schweitzer deals with some of the earliest novels, under the head of "the earliest fictitious lives of Jesus." In this field, it becomes rather hard at times to know where the boundary of fiction lies, because the Gospels themselves do not supply the kind of coherent narrative either of the outer events of Jesus' life, or of his inner psychological development, that the authors are seeking. As Auerbach points out, the Gospels are records of encounters. What in them is imaginative historical reconstruction, and what is fiction? Any coherent narrative has to be pieced together from hints and silences in the texts.

Be that as it may, it was in 1806 that Karl Heinrich Venturini published what Schweitzer takes to be the ancestor of all Jesus novels, and he makes the point that the bulk of its successors are to all intents and purposes more or less conscious or unconscious plagiarisms. It was somewhat provocatively and dauntingly entitled *A natural history* [i.e. as opposed to supernatural] *of the great prophet of Nazareth*. All the miracles are given natural explanations. For instance, Jesus had brought along some wine as a present to the wedding at Cana and handed it out at the end of the feast without saying were it came from. John, "perhaps the least thing merry himself," so Schweitzer quotes Venturini, got the story rather muddled.[11] Throughout this account, Jesus is the somewhat unwitting tool of the Essene brotherhood who smuggle his body away and bring him round from the crucifixion. Venturini anticipates a whole plethora of novels and sensational books based on such conspiracy theories.

Of all its descendants, however, also very indebted to Strauss, perhaps the most important for our purposes is Ernst Renan's *La vie de Christ* of 1863. Although not quite a novel, neither is this quite a work of historical scholarship. Renan's importance for the Catholic and Latin world was disproportionate, as most of the critical literature on the Bible had remained a German preserve. Rather amusingly, Schweitzer, who regarded German theology as the greatest product of the human mind in his time, and something that only the German temperament had the perfection of attributes to produce, regards Renan as allowing the French to discover under the cover of Gallic charm and finesse ideas that come from a foreign world, that is, German scholarship, which he can never quite assimilate, not being blessed with a German temperament.[12]

What Renan attempts is precisely a psychological history of Jesus, an account that gives a coherent shape to his mental development, although one which now strikes us as peculiarly a product of a time and sensibility not our own. His Jesus is an Orpheus figure, who by his charm and beauty draws everyone to him, nurtured as he is by the idyllic beauty of Galilean hill and wildflowers. His journey to the bleak and ugly city of Jerusalem, with its corrupt, narrow-minded and oppressive religious establishment, sours his sensitive soul, however, and he becomes aware that to him has fallen the mission of abolishing the Law. To Renan, this is some kind of violence to his Dionysian spirit. To modern eyes, there is a dangerous skirting of anti-Semitism and an out-and-out contempt for Islam in Renan's account, although, in his defence, his view of Judaism

---

11. Schweitzer, *Quest*, 45.
12. Ibid., 191.

## 8. *The* Book of Dave *Versus the Bible*

is a cipher for his view of the oppressive hand of the Catholic Church in his own day. The whole issue of the treatment of Judaism in this literature is an important one, and one that is still relevant in the criticism of contemporary novelizations.

The book is at times deeply sentimental; Schweitzer cannot resist his own jibes at Renan's rather ludicrous insistence on the "long-lashed beautiful gentle eyes" of the mule that was Jesus' preferred mode of transport. Renan's Jesus is not resurrected, but becomes divine by his self-sacrifice and his effect on the human heart thereafter. What is intriguing is that the notion of resurrection is given an explanation that will have a long afterlife in novelizations of Christ, and in a way which I suspect Schweitzer thought was just a bit too French. Renan asks,

> Did enthusiasm, always credulous in certain circumstances, create afterwards the group of narratives by which it was sought to establish faith in the resurrection? In the absence of opposing documents this can never be ascertained. Let us say, however, that the strong imagination of Mary Magdalene played in this circumstance an important part. Divine power of love! Sacred moments in which the passion of one possessed gave to the world a resuscitated God![13]

This moment is also redolent of the "feminization" of Christianity characteristic of the nineteenth century which has its own part to play in bringing the Bible into the parlour world of the female novel-reader. It is also fiercely parodied in Self's account of a gospel that is the product of a man's embittered struggle with his ex-wife.

This rather decorous hint of sexuality in Renan relates interestingly to Stephen Prickett's view that the plethora of novels on Christ in mid-Victorian England reflects a profound agon on the relationship between earthly and heavenly love. It is no secret that the love between man and woman is a constant theme of the novel from its earliest Greek and Roman roots, and also that the Gospels are not novels precisely in this sense too. Jesus is depicted as having no erotic relationships. Part of the tension but fascination of the synergy between the novel and the gospel is what happens to this key element.

For pious English Victorians, erotic love becomes the precursor to divine love, awakening a capacity which can only find full satisfaction beyond the human. For less pious writers, the hints and silences around Jesus' relationships are filled out in erotic ways. We see here too a change in sensibility in which Jesus' celibacy, instead of marking him out as a figure of heroic purity and self-control or as the epitome of manhood,

---

13. E. Renan, *The Life of Jesus* (Amherst, N.Y.: Prometheus, 1991 [1862]), 249.

makes him less than human. Renan may not be far along the line that leads to Kazantzakis' *The Last Temptation*, for instance, but he is a symptom of that beginning.

In Prickett's view, the nineteenth-century novel tradition, at least in England, was profoundly steeped in the biblical tradition and religious tendencies. In a way that relates interestingly to Auerbach's account of the stylistics of the gospel, Prickett sees a shift in the "sub-surface layers," to use Auerbach's phrase. As the Bible is dissected and shown to be itself the product of continual editing, rewriting and reappropriations, it becomes a paradigm not of text as stability, but of text in movement. There is a complex interaction here of cultural and religious shifts. The world of the late nineteenth- and twentieth-century writer is one where an unparalleled intellectual and social reordering is in train; or perhaps unparalleled is quite the wrong word. Is it not in fact paralleled in the social and intellectual reordering which the early Christians experienced with the destruction of Jerusalem, and the aftermath of their encounter with the life of Jesus, however they encountered him? Does the growth of the novel, which in some ways provides a counter to the gospel and yet adopts from it some of its concern with encounter and dialogue, and the dislocation between narration and history which the fourfold form of the gospel enshrines, reflect some parallel literary process, caught in the inherent narrative instability that affects both our account of external and internal history?

In view of this, how does Self's work fit into such a tradition? How does he himself regard his relationship to the Bible and its literary history? Considerable light is shed on Self's approach to the Bible in this work by his contribution to the series of prefaces and responses to biblical books that were provided by literary and other celebrities as a feature of the Canongate Pocket Bible series.[14] Self wrote on Revelation. He tells the story of a brilliant but troubled young friend of his who, as his sanity disintegrated, became obsessed with the book. "Like many people who are teetering on the edge of psychosis—one foot rammed hard in the door of perception lest it slam shut forever—Ben found in *Revelation* an awful immanent level of identification: an apparently fixed point around which his own frail psyche could orbit and then fission."[15]

This seems to relate to the way in which Self approaches the whole canon: *Revelation* is his interpretative lens. Already a rewriting of the

---

14. Self's contribution is included in a selection of the introductions and responses originally published in the separate books of the Bible that was released as *Revelations: Personal Responses to the Books of the Bible* (Edinburgh: Canongate, 2005).

15. Ibid., 378.

biblical tradition in its own terms, *Revelation* becomes the evidence of pathological reading practices. Those who wrote it read pathologically and are complicit in the development of later pathological readings. It is, Self states, a "sick text... In its vile obscurantism is its baneful effect."[16] He is disturbed by its persistence and its ramifications through the rantings of innumerable apocalyptic sites on the internet. Summing up his feelings, he is left with a sense of despairing awe: "To think that this ancient text has survived to be the very stuff of modern psychotic nightmare," he marvels.[17] As such, it is the instigator of a brand of exegesis which, as Self puts it, is "being squeezed out from the minds of the insane like variegated toothpaste ejected from a tube."[18]

The Dave who writes *The Book of Dave* is reminiscent of Self's friend Ben. Indeed, Dave himself later in his story repudiates his own book as the product of insanity and writes a sequel disavowing the demands he makes as the consequence of his obsessions. Revelation is itself a very particular re-writing of the biblical tradition, controversial from the start. Read through that lens, Self's Bible is already a rewritten Bible, reduced in some ways and expanded in others. In this he is no different from any other biblical reader, except that he then uses his reading to produce another sort of rewriting, setting "his" Bible Dave very deliberately and thoughtfully into a new nexus of intertexts and with new lenses. Quite apart from the ongoing self-referentiality of his own work, his debt to Russell Hoban's post-apocalyptic novel *Riddley Walker*, both in theme and in its experimental use of language, is palpable and acknowledged.[19] Self wrote a preface to a new edition of Hoban's book.

A second element which displaces the role of the Bible in the book is the conscious reference Self makes to the Book of Mormon. Dave comes across Mormons in the course of his friendship and his insistence of having his book inscribed on metal plates and then buried is in direct imitation of the official provenance of the Book of Mormon, copied from the golden plates concealed by the last Nephite prophet, Moroni and discovered by Joseph Smith. This is a powerful myth in its own right, but is very different from gradual story of selection and accretion that underlies the Bible's rise to its authoritative position.

In this light, one major lacuna in the plot of Self's novel is the lack of any account of how Dave's book was rediscovered and how it then came

---

16. Ibid., 381.
17. Ibid., 383.
18. Ibid., 380.
19. Self contributed the introduction to the twentieth anniversary edition of the novel: Russell Hoban, *Riddley Walker* (expanded ed.: London: Bloomsbury, 2002).

to be adopted as scripture and by whom. Probably wisely, Self evades the description of the process that would actually justify his view that any text could becomes scripture. His clear model, the Book of Mormon, whatever one may think of it as a text and whatever one makes of the story of its discovery and translation, is precisely not "any" text. Clearly it claims authority from the uncanny story of its origins, but it is crucial that it relates itself directly to the Bible, both in contents and in style. In addition, it arrives into a religious and political atmosphere of unrest and revival with a charismatic prophetic figure to build the institution that would preserve and reproduce it. How Dave's book achieves this status is never explained.

A third element of intertextuality that Self introduces is the work of Finkelstein and Silberman. This created something of a stir when it was published in that it attempted to give archaeological and extra-biblical evidence priority over the biblical text as a source of information on the history of ancient Israel, and indeed attempted to reveal the assumptions behind the framing of the question in that form. To set out to explore the history of Israel is already to assume that some entity called Israel can be identified that shows continuity between different time periods, and therefore *has* a history.

Is their book itself "Re-written Bible"? Sections of it avowedly are. They introduce the second section of the book as follows:

> So far we have examined the biblical version of Israel's formative history written in the seventh century BCE, and we have provided glimpses at the archaeological reality that underlies it [note the implications of that word "reality"]. Now it is time to tell a new story. In the chapters that follow, we will present the main outlines of the rise, fall, and rebirth of a very different Israel.[20]

What these chapters contain is a rewritten Bible, where a different set of events is presented and the origin, purpose, genre and authority of the biblical texts themselves are redescribed. As Finkelstein and Silberman's summary has it: "In specific historical terms, we now know that the Bible's epic saga first emerged as a response to the pressures, difficulties, challenges and hopes faced by the people of the tiny kingdom of Judah in the decades before its destruction and by the even tinier Temple community in Jerusalem in the post-exilic period."[21]

The interaction between past, present and future in these texts is something they emphasize. The biblical writers retell the past in order to

---

20. Finkelstein and Silberman, *The Bible Unearthed*, 145.
21. Ibid., 348.

offer a hope for the future to their present readers. They are not interested in history for dispassionate, academic reasons; they are interested in the ideological capital that it provides, enabling them to shape their readers' response to their present situation. *The Book of Dave*, in its dialogic structure, lays bare this process in an intriguing way, but belies Self's claim that any text would do. The biblical writers did not just write any book in Finkelstein and Silberman's view; they consciously and programmatically used what was familiar and already revered in sections of Judahite society in order to explain the past in a way that would shape the future. They emphatically did not produce a new text. The writers of the New Testament in turn consciously echo this process, and so to does the Book of Mormon, not to mention the Quran.

The point I want to take from all this is that part of the cultural legacy of the Bible and part of the secret of its longevity is that it is always already a re-written book at all levels. Editors rewrite within books, books rewrite other books, the New Testament writers rewrite Israel's story, and each other's accounts of that story. Rewriting never ceases: the Rabbis and the Church Fathers do little else, in the name of presenting the truth of the Bible. Biblical scholarship, including the work of Finkelstein and Silberman, is dedicated to rewriting the Bible, with the excuse that it is merely writing that has what the biblical writers lacked, namely, the knowledge or the honesty to write truthfully in the first place.

What *The Book of Dave* does, then, is to illuminate in a thought-provoking way some of the mechanisms and consequences of the misreading of such a text. Where it fails, however, is that its target is not, as Self seems to claim, the Bible, but already a rewritten and in some ways idiosyncratic Bible. Yet it is a book that can teach us a good deal about the importance of engaging with the Bible.

Speaking of the all-pervasiveness of London in his novels, Self uses the following typically dark, distasteful and London-centred metaphor, likening London to a smelly old drunk woman who sits beside him on the tube. "Like everyone else, I wanted to get up and move to the next carriage," he writes, "…But now we are inseparable, going round and around the Circle Line, arm in arm, perhaps for eternity."[22] There are those who might have a similar feeling about the biblical tradition, given its propensity for shoring up xenophobia, misogyny, and anti-intellectualism. Yet in our culture, there is no other carriage to move to, and the

---

22. The passage is from "Big Dome," an article originally published in *Granta* and reprinted (untitled) in *Feeding Frenzy* (London: Viking, 2001), 43; it is quoted in M. Hunter Hayes, *Understanding Will Self* (Columbia: University of South Carolina Press, 2007), 187.

old tramp is not all that she seems. There is not much she does not know, and the old girl can still sing some haunting songs.

To conclude, some words from Self indicate why it is worth wrestling with his complex text, and with the Bible itself. In the introduction he wrote to Alasdair Gray's *1982 Janine*, he asks why we should bother with difficult books. His answer: "For the simple reason that if literature doesn't have a capacity for awkwardness, then it cannot convey anything of the unreality of what it is like to be in this world."[23] Both *The Book of Dave* and the Bible can certainly do that.

---

23. Self's introduction appears in the Canongate Classics edition of Alasdair Gray's *1982 Janine* (Edinburgh: Canongate, 2003), xi. The book was originally published in 1984.

Part IV

THE BIBLE, MUSIC AND NATIONALISM

Chapter 9

WHEN JESUS WAS (NEARLY) A SCOT

The title of this chapter is admittedly a provocation, designed to explore the consequences of the prevalent desire to assimilate Jesus to a particular nationality. No one has ever seriously suggested that Jesus was a Scot. Granted that he came from a Northern region of mountains and lakes, granted that he and his followers spoke with a rough Northern accent, granted that there is no evidence that he ever wore a pair of trousers, even to posit such a question is an absurd anachronism. There is an apocryphal tradition that on his trip to Glastonbury with Joseph of Arimathea he went on to the Hebrides, but that is the extent of any support for anything like such a claim.

Nevertheless, I want to suggest that there was a small window in history when the claim might have been made until it was supplanted by the equally questionable, but, in its effects, far more dangerous, claim that Jesus was an Aryan. How this came about sheds light on the fraught debate about the status of the Old Testament, of Judaism, and of the European Jewish community in the late eighteenth and nineteenth centuries which itself set the frame for the catastrophic history of European Jews in the twentieth century. It also sheds light on aspects of Scottish history and on the potential anachronism of ascribing any nationality to Jesus, even in speaking of Jesus the Jew.

The two key figures in this story are Johann Gottfried von Herder (1744–1803) and the Scottish writer James MacPherson (1736–1796). In his prolific writings and translations, Herder, with great originality, rethought the basis of national identity.[1] In the German-speaking lands of Europe, there was a growing sense throughout the latter part of the eighteenth century that somehow their proper place in the emerging

---

1. A helpful discussion of this aspect of Herder's thought is to be found in F. M. Barnard, *Herder on Nationality, Humanity, and History* (Montreal: McGill-Queen's University Press, 2003), especially the first chapter, entitled "The Hebraic Roots of Herder's Nationalism," 17–37.

modern world was being denied them. This fuelled a general urge to establish a common German identity in order to counter the advantages in terms of trade and culture that a strong sense of national unity in France and Britain seemed to be fostering. In previous centuries, politics and ethnic identity had been separate spheres. The German-speaking peoples had been governed by a series of local potentates and were accustomed to constant wars and changes of borders and governance.

It was Herder's distinctive contribution to argue for the possibility of a new kind of national identity, based not on loyalty to local rulers but on the idea of the *Volk*, a population bound together by a shared language and traditions which pointed back to a common origin and a common homeland. Crucially, it was the Old Testament that provided his model. The biblical Israel, where one kin ruled a people united by its unique language and its unique traditions, its compelling myth of a common ancestry and its claim to its land, was the ideal. Of course, that ideal was shattered by history, if it ever was realized, but the continuity of Jewish identity for eighteen centuries was for Herder a clue to how the German-speaking peoples could reassert their own identity. In the absence of a unified government and in exile, the Jews were held together, by their traditions, their language and their literature.

As might be expected from a good Lutheran, Herder did not emphasize the role of the Law in this. The soul of any people, and Israel was again his prime example, was to be found in their poetry and the oral tradition. For Herder, poetry, and the older the better, was the articulation of the spirit of the *Volk* and gave a direct expression to its most atavistic impulses. His remarkable two-volume work *On the Spirit of Hebrew Poetry*, published in 1782, explores this literature with characteristic subtlety and insight, but with an equally typically improvisatory quality.[2] His interest in this is not simply theological and literary. It is in Hebrew poetry that the secret of the identity of the Jewish *Volk*, the archetypal *Volk*, is to be found.

This high view of the biblical Israel had two consequences in his reflections on the political situation of his day. One was that in his view the European Jewish community was no longer a *Volk*. It was no longer in its ancestral land, had no ruler, and, crucially, had effectively abandoned Hebrew as its common language. This Jewish community was not, and could not be, at home in Europe. Herder's conclusion from this can

---

2. Remarkably, Herder's *Vom Geist der Ebräische Poesie* has not been published in English translation since the pioneering work of James Marsh in 1883: J. G. Herder, *The Spirit of Hebrew Poetry* (vols. 1 and 2; Burlington: Edward Smith, 1833).

on the one hand be seen as a precursor of the characterization of the Jew as a rootless cosmopolitan and the programmatic anti-Semitism of the nineteenth and twentieth centuries, with its culmination in the attempt to eradicate this foreign intrusion into European culture. On the other hand, he can also be seen as a proto-Zionist, as his vision was that the Jews should return to set up anew a Hebrew-speaking nation in Palestine based on Jerusalem in order to recover the true sense of the Jewish *Volk*. Herder's writings contain no hint of any violent expulsion of the Jews or of any animus against them.

The other corollary was that the German-speaking peoples needed to recover their indigenous traditions and the ancient poetry of their own language if they were to take their place as a fully fledged *Volk* in European affairs. The biblical tradition, which had provided Herder with this model, could not perform this function in the German context. The Bible and its poetry was an import into the German lands and, precisely because it underpinned the identity of the Jews as a *Volk*, it could not perform that function for the German peoples. What was needed was access to an ancestral tradition that was of the land and the people. All this was affected by the renewed sense of the alienness of the Hebrew Bible that develops in late mediaeval Christian humanism and is exacerbated by the Reformation's sense of historicity and its repudiation of allegorical reading as a way of domesticating the text.

Suffice it to say that Herder, with many of his contemporaries, though in his case much more self-consciously and programmatically, seeks a replacement for the Bible as a basis for the recovery of the identity and self-consciousness of the German lands.[3] His solution was to collect and research German and North European folk-poetry as offering the best way to recover the spirit of the *Volk*, making him the father of modern folklore research. For him, the traditional songs and poetry of the peasants were the repository of the ancient, half-forgotten traditions that bound the peoples of the North together. These had been suppressed, often deliberately, in favour of the Judaeo-Roman traditions of the Church or by the importation of ideas from the Classical tradition.

For Herder, in contrast to the Humanists and many Enlightenment thinkers, the Classical traditions of Rome and Greece were just as irrelevant as the biblical traditions to the spirit of the Northern peoples. In any case, these classical traditions had been seized on by French thinkers as a way of rooting a distinctive French identity in something other than

---

3. For an interesting discussion of the wider debate at that time, see George S. Williamson, *The Longing for Myth in Germany: Religion and Aesthetic Culture from Romanticism to Nietzsche* (Chicago: University of Chicago Press, 2004).

Christianity. Indeed, from the point of view of the Classical tradition, the Germans and other peoples beyond the Rhine are outside the community of the empire, only appearing as occasionally heroic captives. From a German perspective, what binds the people together is their courageous resistance to Roman occupation.

Into this situation, enter James MacPherson. Born in 1736 in Badenoch in the Scottish Highlands to a Gaelic-speaking family, he was exposed both to a rich oral Gaelic tradition and to the problematic influence of England and the English language on his Scottish and Gaelic identity. During his childhood, the Highlands were still occupied by English troops in the wake of the Jacobite rebellion of 1715, and with the defeat of the second Jacobite rising in 1745–46 a programmatic suppression of Gaelic language and culture began, breaking up the old social system. Tartans and the bagpipes were banned on pain of death, for instance.

MacPherson was gifted enough to enter Aberdeen University, where he encountered a tradition of reading of the Classics which admired the tales of ancient German resistance to Rome and which identified proudly with this stance. After all, for Scots, Hadrian's Wall was and is physical testimony to the independence, courage and cultural independence of the Scots as they too defied Rome. It was in this climate that MacPherson made it his business to collect and preserve the fast-vanishing Gaelic traditions of story telling and song. In 1765 he published the cumulative results of his researches as *The Works of Ossian*.[4]

This book took Europe by storm. Not only was what was reputed to be some of the oldest poetry in Europe from the ancient Celtic tradition now made available in English translation, but MacPherson claimed that from the fragmentary material that he had collected he had uncovered evidence of an ancient bardic epic of which they had once formed a part; furthermore, he claimed he had indeed been able to reconstruct it. This epic, he stated, was composed by Ossian, a blind Scottish bard of the third century. The remoteness and isolation of the Highlands, which in earlier ages had meant that their inhabitants were marginalized and despised as barbarians, had meant, so he claimed, that these traditions were preserved in something like their ancient purity without other cultural overlays. The work of this "Celtic Homer" (MacPherson's own phrase), apart from its intrinsic antiquarian interest, now provided a counter-epic from the North that could stand on its own, in terms of antiquity and poetic merit, with either the Classical or biblical traditions.

---

4. There is a modern edition of James MacPherson's works published as *The Poems of Ossian and Related Works* (ed. Howard Gaskill; Edinburgh: Edinburgh University Press, 1996).

## 9. When Jesus Was (Nearly) a Scot

It is rather astonishing to chart the speed with which MacPherson's work crossed Europe and the effects it had at the time on literature, art, politics, and even fashion. Early nineteenth-century obsessions with moonlight, mountains, weeping maidens, doomed warriors and harps everywhere stem directly from *Ossian*. Napoleon carried a copy of *Ossian* with him everywhere he went and commissioned a series of Ossianic paintings to adorn the walls of Malmaison, and the Russian court went wild for the Ossianic craze.

For Herder, this was a revelation and he fell on the German translation of *Ossian* as providing evidence for an ancient epic grounded in the Celtic heritage of the North, even older than the folksongs he had gathered or the Scandinavian heritage of the Sagas and the Eddas. Here was the way to recover a sense of the *Volk* for the peoples of the North.

However, and here is the rub, although the Hebrew tradition has run its course and had to be replaced, Herder was still a member of the Lutheran Clergy. The Old Testament might be dispensable, and the Jewish underpinning and Roman overlay of Christianity might have to go, but Jesus had to remain. How could Jesus retain his significance as part of an indigenous Nordic *Volk* tradition?

This is the moment when Jesus might have been Scottish, or at least assimilated to a Celtic tradition. As it happens, that move never explicitly occurred, for interesting reasons. First, MacPherson's *Ossian* was exposed as a forgery. The controversy still continues in scholarly circles as to how well-founded a charge this was, but it had immediate effects. The most influential whistleblower was Dr Johnson (of dictionary fame), who rejected the poems as the concoctions of a charlatan. Asked if he really believed any modern author could write such poems, he replied, "Yes. Many men; many women; and many children." Johnson was, of course, notoriously anti-Scottish and did not know a word of Gaelic. MacPherson defended his sources and indeed threatened physical violence. The arguments raged long after his death. They are still not settled, although there is a modern consensus that MacPherson did use genuine collected material but subjected it to extensive editing and rewriting, including insertions of his own invention. His fatal mistake was to produce as evidence Gaelic manuscripts which proved to be back-translations of his own English version of *Ossian*, thus casting doubt over all his sources.

In actual fact, *Ossian* may be almost as genuine a reconstruction of an ancient epic as the later compilation of Finnish poetry into the national epic *Kalevala* by Elias Lönnrot, very much under the influence of Herder and MacPherson. The Estonian counterpart, the *Kalevipoeg*, which Friedrich Kreutzwald composed on the basis of Estonian folk traditions, is avowedly largely a creative invention of its compiler. These works, however, especially in the Finnish case, had a profound influence on the development of their respective nations. Ossian had no such impact on Scotland. This is not simply because of the cloud that the allegations of forgery cast over it. Even without that, it had an essential difference from these other epics. For the majority of Scots, even in their homeland, it was only accessible as a translation. It could not provide the foundation of a Scottish *Volk* sensibility because it represented only part of the tradition of Scottish culture.

The debunking of *Ossian*, however, also undermined any claim it might have to represent an alternative Nordic tradition to set against the Hebrew Bible. The upshot was that those seeking to anchor the Germanic tradition had to resume their search. This was just at the time when European scholarship was encountering the textual traditions of the East, in particular India. In a groundbreaking study, Sir William Jones, a gifted linguist dispatched to serve as a judge in Calcutta, recorded his theories about Sanskrit:

> The Sanscrit language, whatever be its antiquity, is of a wonderful structure; more perfect than the Greek, more copious than the Latin, and more exquisitely refined than either, yet bearing to both of them a stronger affinity, both in the roots of verbs and the forms of grammar, than could possibly have been produced by accident; so strong, indeed, that no philologer could examine them all three, without believing them to have sprung from some common source, which, perhaps, no longer exists; there is a similar reason, though not quite so forcible, for supposing that both the Gothic and the Celtic, though blended with a very different idiom, had the same origin with the Sanscrit; and the old Persian might be added to the same family.[5]

Jones is thus the pioneer of the idea that India and Europe had a shared linguistic and cultural heritage, an idea enshrined in the now widely accepted term "Indo-European" for the language family that he has outlined. What is not always remembered, however, is that behind his reasoning are specifically biblical assumptions, in which he follows the work of earlier Jesuit linguists, such as Coeurdoux. The proto-language which lies behind the modern diversity is, in Jones's view, the language of the sons of Japhet, the third of Noah's sons. As such, it is entirely distinct from the linguistic and cultural heritage of Shem, his first son,

---

5. Sir William Jones, "The Third Anniversary Discourse, on the Hindus," delivered to the Asiatic Society, 2 February 1786. Cited from *Sir William Jones: Selected Poetical and Prose Works* (ed. Michael J. Franklin; Cardiff: University of Wales Press, 1995), 355–70.

which gives rise to the Semitic languages and literature. So, in embryo here is a discovery and a theory which relates what he calls the Gothic languages, the earliest traditions of the Germanic peoples, to what was to prove to be an extensive and ancient literary tradition. Moreover, this tradition is not only distinct from the Semitic tradition but by all accounts turns out to be both older and more comprehensive. The literary heritage of the Vedas and other Sanskrit epics quite puts Ossian in the shade.

The further discovery that it was the so-called primitive Baltic languages, Latvian and Lithuanian, which resembled Sanskrit most closely in grammar and vocabulary, a discovery usually attributed to the linguist Franz Bopp, simply went to demonstrate the persistence and scope of this *ur*-tradition shared by this great sweep of the peoples of the North. Herder, living as he did in Riga for many years, was one of the few scholars who took the oral tradition of the much-despised Baltic peasantry seriously, and here was a vindication of his views. It was these illiterate people who had preserved the ancient forms that resonated with the astonishing cultural achievements of ancient Sanskrit literature and its derivatives.

Out of this discovery, in ways too complex and multifarious to detail here, but with a crucial impulse from Friedrich Schlegel, there developed an increasing sense of a common Indo-German heritage, given the name Aryan, which could confidently counter both the Classical and biblical traditions and which enshrined the mythical and poetic heritage of the Nordic *Volk*. Insofar as Jesus represented, in many people's opinion at the time, a drastic break with the narrowness and legalism of the Jewish tradition, Jesus showed himself to have his true affinities with that great Aryan tradition. Hence the interest in the later nineteenth century in positing Jesus' links with this Aryan world, and in particular with Persia and India. To take one example, the libretto that Richard Wagner drafted for his never-completed opera on Jesus of Nazareth makes Jesus' links with Buddhism absolutely explicit, although by this he means the particular German Romantic version of Buddhism that was articulated by Schopenhauer.[6]

With hindsight, we can see the unhappy consequences of this Aryanization of Jesus which had many influential advocates in the later nineteenth century, a story that has been traced by a number of scholars,

---

6. Stefan Arvidsson offers a searching overview of these developments in his *Aryan Idols: Indo-European Mythology as Ideology and Science* (Chicago: University of Chicago Press, 2006). The disastrous later developments of this tendency are well traced in Susannah Heschel's *The Aryan Jesus: Christian Theologians and the Bible in Nazi Germany* (Princeton: Princeton University Press, 2008).

but which has a long legacy. My aim here is not to follow that through, but to point out that the roots of this development were, as so often is the case, both biblical and counter-biblical. From the Bible comes the type case of the *Volk*, the ancient kingdom of Israel, but the identification of this case with the Jews leads to a search for a replacement to bolster the idea of a specifically German *Volk*. From the Bible comes the idea of a fundamental differentiation of human cultures, insofar as they can be traced back to the rupture between the sons of Noah. The division of the world into the realms of Shem, Ham and Japhet, quite explicitly represented in mediaeval maps, for instance, has enormous consequences for the development of imperialism and colonialism, but also profoundly affects the way in which the relationships between the Jews and Europe culture are conceived. The Jews are the sons of Shem in the territory of Japhet.

The biblical influence goes further, too. Western scholars read the Vedas as a counterpart of the Old Testament, importing an alien mode of interpretation into Indian culture. The same impulses that draw on this tradition to develop ideas of German nationality also underlie the development of an explicit Hindu and Vedic nationalism in India as a response to European imperialism.

In the middle of this story, with its lasting consequences for the power relationships of the modern world, is the lost moment of a Scottish Jesus, the Jesus who might have been, who can stand as a poignant comment on the complexity of Scottish identity as the nation which is not quite a nation. At the same time, an ambiguous light is thrown on modern debates about Jesus as a Jew, a term which is almost inevitably coloured by two thousand years of Christian and Western definitions and redefinition of the term "Jew." The idea of the Jews as themselves a *Volk* stems from Herder, and the idea of the Jew as defined against the Aryan is not something that can be retrojected into our reading of the ancient World, although it all too often subtly informs even the most responsible scholarship. Clearly, to call Jesus a Scot is nonsense; to call him a Jew also needs questioning, however, as the implications of that term in the ancient world are all too often distorted by modern preconceptions. There is sense to the claim that Paul was the first Jew in history because he was the first Christian; or, put another way, the first to view (his own) Jewish identity through Christian eyes.

## Chapter 10

## JONAH IN ESTONIA, JOSEPH IN LATVIA

The rather odd title of this chapter results from the conjunction of an interest in the Bible and postcolonialism on the one hand and, on the other, an interest in the history and the artistic achievements of the three small but intriguingly different countries that are lumped together as the Baltic States: Estonia, Latvia and Lithuania. In this presentation, I want to home in on the way in which particular biblical stories have been taken up in two works produced in Estonia and Latvia respectively by artists who used these stories as vehicles to express their nationalist convictions. The works to be discussed are the Estonian Rudolph Tobias's oratorio *Das Jonas Sendung*, and the play *Joseph and his Brothers* by the Latvian playwright Rainis.

What prompted these artists to turn to the Bible as a resource for this purpose, and how did they do this? I think we will find that there are intriguing differences between them, differences which relate to the real contrasts between the Latvian and Estonian experience as they assert their independence from the imperial power of Russia and the cultural influences of Germany and Poland. In turn, this may help us to reflect on the whole vexed topic of nationalism and the role of the Bible in the development of nation states, which may lead to further reflection on the development of the Hebrew Bible itself as a body of text produced by Hebrew writers in conditions of cultural and political suppression or oppression.

Until recently, most of the rest of the world, I suspect, knew little of these countries, partly because they are small, but also because their geographical obscurity, tucked away on a corner of the Baltic, was added to by the way that their cultures were programmatically suppressed under Soviet rule. Even getting to them was rendered extremely difficult. Sadly, one of the things they share is a history of being fought over by the dominant powers of the Baltic; although in the early medieval period the Grand Duchy of Lithuania was the largest country in Europe, stretching as far as the Crimea days, it and present-day Latvia and Estonia were subject to the attacks and the periodic rule of the Danes and the Swedes, with a powerful interest from the Germanic states, especially Prussia. The rise of the Russian Empire and its aspirations to the West through St. Petersburg then made these territories of strategic interest to the Tsars. It is only after the World War I, when both Germany and Russia were weakened, that they achieved a brief independence that was brutally brought to an end in the World War II. Left with an unenviable choice between Hitler and Stalin, the governments of all three countries opted against Communism, and therefore for Fascism. This led to a horrendous extermination of their considerable Jewish populations, but also to their becoming the targets of a ferocious reckoning by the Soviet powers after Hitler's defeat. The collapse of the Soviet Empire, which they fomented in their own way, brought about a new opportunity in the 1990s to reassert their dormant nationalism.

With a similar, though by no means identical, political history, Estonia and Latvia are often lumped together as Baltic states in a way that masks profound differences between them. Both contain ancient populations who have lived on the shores of the Baltic for millennia and which are quite different from the Slavic or Germanic/Scandinavian peoples around them; yet they are also quite different from each other. This is best demonstrated through their languages. Estonian is a Finno-Ugrian language, related to Finnish and, more distantly, to Hungarian. It also vies with Basque as being one of the hardest languages to learn. Latvian has only one immediate relative, Lithuanian, but both, much to the amazement of the early students of linguistics, were found to share a good deal of common vocabulary and grammar with what on the face of it may seem an unlikely partner: Sanskrit, the language of the ancient Vedic Scriptures in north India.

Thus, although both share the condition of having ancient languages with a rich oral tradition that have suffered centuries of being suppressed by educated classes that spoke German or Russian, the affinities of these languages are quite different, with important consequences. Both also preserve through their oral traditions a strong pre-Christian tradition with their own mythologies and pantheons which were developed into epic poems in the nineteenth century, rather on the model of the Homeric epics, or, if one is a little less charitable, of James MacPherson's *Ossian*, his more than semi-fictional blind bard of the ancient Celtic peoples. Estonia has its *Kalevipoeg*, compiled by Friedrich Kreutzwald, while Latvia's epic is *Lāčplēsis* (*The Bearslayer*), compiled by Andrejs Pumpurs. Enough background: to our tale. In what follows I propose to look at the two works I mentioned and their authors in turn, which will lead me to a few thoughts on their similarities and contrasts.

## Jonah in Estonia

On May 25, 1989, a remarkable event occurred in the Estonia Concert Hall in Tallinn: the first performance since its disastrous premiere in 1909 of Rudolf Tobias's monumental oratorio *Des Jona Sendung* (*Jonah's Mission*) in the restored edition sedulously prepared by the noted Estonian musicologist and pianist Vardo Rumessen. The critical reaction was more than enthusiastic. Other performances rapidly followed in Estonia and around the world and in 1995 the work was recorded by the Swedish label BIS in a performance under the world-renowned Estonian conductor Neeme Järvi. The respected British critic Martin Anderson, reviewing the recording in the leading American classic music magazine *Fanfare*, wrote:

> Rudolf Tobias's monumental oratorio *Des Jona Sendung* is one of the greatest choral-orchestral works ever composed, a score of towering strength and unflagging imagination. I know of no piece of music conceived on as constantly massive a scale—there are longer works and works that are more intense and works that aspire more explicitly toward the spiritual, but nothing that comes close to this gigantic score in its elemental sweep. I can state with complete conviction that *Des Jona Sendung* is a great piece of music. I have no doubt that it is worthy of the company of the greatest of its peers: the Bach Passions, Brahms' German Requiem, Berlioz' Requiem—I exempt only Beethoven's *Missa Solemnis*, which is *sui generis* and *sans pareil*.[1]

It would be hard to think of higher praise from such a source, and that alone would justify a further look at this astonishing work. Later in his review, Anderson makes the following telling remark: "If anything puts musical Estonia on the map, this will." The historical context makes this remark more significant than perhaps he realized. The date of the restored work's first performance is highly significant: just two years before Estonia became independent from the Soviet Union in 1991, and thus right at the time of the so-called Singing Revolution in Estonia where upwards of 300,000 people—a third of the Estonian-speaking population of the country—would gather in Tallinn to sing traditional songs in defiance of the Soviet authorities. Putting Estonia on the map—literally—was the dream of the participants in such festivals. In addition, an astonishing international awakening of interest of Estonian classical music, centering on such names as Arvo Pärt, Veljo Tormis and Eduard

---

1. Martin Anderson, "Tobias; Des Jona Sendung," *Fanfare* 19/3 (1996), n.p. Online:http://www.fanfarearchive.com/articles/atop/19_3/1932680.az_TOBIAS_Des_Jona_Sendung.html.

Tubin, was under way. The performance of Tobias' oratorio—a native Estonian work, long suppressed and based on an unambiguously religious text, in defiance of official atheism—thus crystallized a particular synthesis between music and nationalism, but this was only possible 80 years after its first performance and 71 years since the composer's death in 1918.

What makes this relevant to our concerns is the fact that this work is based on the book of Jonah. In essence, the suggestion I want to put forward is that there is an analogy between what Tobias has done with Jonah and what the writer of Jonah did with his own source material, in particular 1 Kings. Both drew on existing historical and artistic traditions but transformed them in such a way as to give their own works recognizable authority and approachability but also to lay those traditions open to scrutiny. Both transform their traditions to speak to their time and yet are heard after their time in new contexts, contexts in which they may be appreciated for reasons rather different from those originally envisaged. Tobias's oratorio thus becomes not just an intriguing part of Jonah's reception history, but may give some insights into the processes by which the book of Jonah came to be the way it is. I also want to consider, albeit briefly, the way that the music rather than just the libretto of the oratorio is itself a creative and revealing reaction to Jonah.

I shall first give some brief background on Tobias and how he came to write *Des Jona Sendung* and then focus on a particular topic that exercised him as he wrote it: the motivation of the Ninevites' repentance. I then want to compare his reworking of Jonah with the writer of Jonah's creative rereading of 2 Kgs 14 in the hope of establishing the point that this kind of study can genuinely contribute to our understanding of the Bible itself.

So, to Tobias. He is a remarkable if somewhat tragic figure. Born in 1873 on the small Estonia island of Hiiumaa, then part of the Empire of All the Russias, the son of a Lutheran parish clerk, he had a sound biblical and musical education. His mother tongue was German, as the cultural influence of the so-called Baltic German middle classes, to which his family belonged, was still strong, Estonian being largely regarded as the language of peasants. His initial claim to fame is that he was the first Estonian ever to be enrolled at the St Petersburg Conservatory, where he studied organ and composition, the latter under Rimsky-Korsakov. He specialized thereafter in church music, particularly in choral works. Ultimately he found Estonia too confining for his musical ambitions and eventually moved to Leipzig, partly in the hopes of finding a way of performing the great oratorio that he had been writing over several years. In the event, he succeeded, but the performance was a debacle. Tobias himself conducted, having failed to find a conductor willing to take the work on, while the huge orchestra the score requires was reduced to 24 scratch players. By all accounts the less said about the results the better. Thereafter, Tobias was able to arrange performances of a few numbers from the score, but it was never performed in its entirety again before his early death in 1918.

What was it, then, that led Tobias to the book of Jonah and to the composition of such a monumental score in these unpromising circumstances? In much of what follows, I am indebted to the writings and the gracious personal communications of Professor Vardo Rumessen, whose painstaking restoration work in the 1980s brought the score back to life, and would like publicly to acknowledge my gratitude to him. Tobias's avowed interest is in Jonah as the symbol of the moral resistance of a small people against an oppressive ruler. Rumessen suggests this may relate to the views of Rudolf Kallas, an Estonian pastor whom Tobias encountered in St Petersburg, who drew parallels in his own writings between the Estonians under Russian rule and Israel in Babylonian captivity.

Jonah the character is not really the hero of the oratorio, however. Tobias speaks of the "solid boulder" of Jonah's character as the "resistant material" (his words) from which the artist ought to work, and it is clear that Jonah's fanatical intolerance is something of which he has to be cured. The theme of the oratorio is Jonah as *sign*. Its deepest root is in Matthew's account of the sign of Jonah, rather than in the book of Jonah itself, which does, however, provide a narrative shape.

The oratorio is divided into three parts and five sections. These have rather idiosyncratic titles and are introduced by equally idiosyncratic explanations by Tobias himself which give interesting insights into his creative decisions. It begins with a prologue where Jonah seeks to flee from God's call. The first scene then depicts the storm and his being cast into the sea. The second scene is then entitled "The Night of Being Forsaken by God," and recounts Jonah's acceptance of his fate in the belly of the fish, which, however, only makes the briefest of appearances itself. The second part, and third scene, begins with a psalm of vengeance sung by the members of what Tobias calls the Ecclesia, the 7000 who did not bow the knee to Baal, the faithful but fanatical members of the community. This is countered by a mystical chorus, and gradually what Tobias calls "the fanatically piercing voice of Elijah" is replaced by a vision of the Christian saviour. In the fourth scene ("Judgment") the Ninevites are condemned but repent and the third and final part, which consists of one final scene, "The Sign of the Son of Man," holds out the prospect of reconciliation for those who do not resist divine mercy.

The libretto, in German, is a catena of biblical verses. Nearly every word sung is from a cited biblical verse and Tobias ranges across the Old and New Testaments to find appropriate sentiments. So, for instance, the Ninevites declare their philosophy in an irresistibly catchy way in words drawn from Isa 22 and Pss 14 and 12: "Let us eat and drink: for tomorrow we shall die. There is no God. Who is Lord over us?"

A detailed review of every aspect of this work is beyond the scope of this chapter. I propose to focus on what Tobias himself identifies as a key theme, the repentance of the Ninevites and their forgiveness. In the course of this we can also encounter some of the musical features of the score. We will begin with the Ecclesia's call for vengeance, which Tobias heads *Rachepsalm*. Intriguingly, Tobias gives this call for vengeance solely to female voices, remarking, "The hyena-like rage in the female voices…must be presented with declamatory emphasis (cf. the mothers in the second part of 'Faust', the curse of Eve from Byron's 'Cain')." This is then countered by children's voices singing God's praises. A mystical chorus proclaims God's judgment, culminating in a heaven-storming Sanctus.

On the one side, then, is God's judgment; on the other side, the only too seductive insouciance of the Ninevites which we have already heard, countered by Jonah's denunciations. The juxtaposition of the awesomely righteous God of the Sanctus and the godless Ninevites should, one would think, lead to the annihilation of the Ninevites; yet they repent. Here Tobias consciously departs in a significant way from the book of Jonah. He explains this as follows:

> Hence Nineveh's repentance begins which is quite difficult to motivate dramaturgically. In the original text, the crucial and dominant figure is the king of Nineveh (see Jonah 3:6–9). The composer has deviated from the original text, attributing the proclamation of repentance to children, to their pure souls. Their innocence is their privilege to be reconciliators and agents. For theirs is the kingdom of heaven.[2]

This departure seems to take its cue from the longstanding interpretative tradition that the "more than a hundred and twenty thousand persons who do not know their right hand from their left" in Jon 4:11 are the children of the city, linking this to the gospel vision of children as the models of the kingdom. Tobias' vision is of children, the innocent bearers of the future, as the agents of reconciliation between the penitent superpower and an Ecclesia, or Estonia, purged of the desire for vengeance. The

---

2. As we have seen, Tobias has already used the children to counter the psalm of vengeance.

politically unlikely repentance of the king in Jonah, which could be read as leaving power in the hands of the oppressive establishment, is not something Tobias wishes to endorse.

So Tobias draws on, and then subverts, this familiar biblical text. Musically as well as textually, this reliance on and yet displacement of tradition is evident throughout the work. Martin Anderson's fulsome review placed the work in the most distinguished company. This response testifies to the success of Tobias's strategy. He wanted to write the grand Estonian oratorio, giving voice to the spiritual suffering of an oppressed people in an international language. Bach and Handel are conscious models—the children's chorus, for instance, links to the use of this device in the St. Matthew Passion. In further conscious imitation of Bach, Tobias uses Lutheran chorales throughout the work, sometimes in almost literal quotation, although with his own twist, while in other places they are simply briefly quoted in complex textures.

Yet his musical language and some structural features of the work draw on the operatic and symphonic traditions as well. Wagnerian *leitmotifs*, harmonic devices and melodic shapes drawn from Brahms and Bruckner and Mahlerian grandiloquence blend with hints of Berlioz and Verdi. This might seem to suggest that Tobias's score is another sort of catena, but Tobias frequently, in my judgment, manages to achieve a unique synthesis.

One striking way the work is unified is by a characteristic three-chord progression which pivots on a lowered dominant ninth. This explicitly structures two orchestral interludes which are entitled "The Sign of Jonah" and "The Sign of the Son of Man," but pervades the whole score. For the listener, the odd effect of this progression is that it seems to wrench the music from key to key, rather than producing a subtle shift. The effect is, to my ears, startling and unsettling, but in each case the starting and finishing keys are in one sense as close as they could be to each other, only a semitone away, although in terms of harmony, the so-called cycle of fifths, they are poles apart. It is a simple device which is both eccentric and yet memorably effective, rooted in traditional tonality, but playing in the oddest way with it. This progression is not just a musical metaphor for the startling transformation which repentance and forgiveness can bring about; in musical terms, it enacts that transformation.

Nor is an accident that Tobias makes such use of it in two interludes which explicitly explore Jonah and Jesus as signs. A minor chord is followed by an unexpected dissonance, a kind of harmonic limbo, which abruptly lifts the tonality up a step and into the major. There is something here that enacts the transformations of both incarnation and resurrection.

So, in both libretto and music, we have a strange mixture of conventional and unconventional devices, drawing on the power of tradition to subvert it as it takes the voice of a small nation and rewrites it on the largest international scale.

Yet how does this all relate to the composition of the book of Jonah? Here I am drawing on an argument I have developed elsewhere that Jonah is itself an odd re-presentation of tradition.[3] Quite eccentrically, I propose that the Jonah psalm may well predate the prose of Jonah, which has been composed as a quaint double midrash on this psalm and on the only other mention of Jonah the son of Amittai in the Hebrew Bible, in 2 Kgs 14:25.

In the space available I cannot rehearse the entire argument I have set out elsewhere, but will concentrate on that mention of Jonah. 2 Kings 14:25 is part of a summary account of the reign of King Jeroboam II of Israel which seems to have given the Deuteronomistic compilers of the book a particular theological headache. In typical Deuteronomistic fashion, the verdict on the king is harsh and simple. He did what was evil in the eyes of the Lord by continuing the practices of Jeroboam I. The verdict may be clear, but there is a problem. Jeroboam II managed to hold the throne for forty-one years, one of the longest reigns recorded in Kings. A simple theology of retribution would lead us to expect that this wicked king would quickly meet his deserts. Not only did he survive, but he also expanded the boundaries of Israel, in itself a rather questionable virtue in the eyes of the Deuteronomistic writers. More than that, he did this in response to the Lord's word as spoken by one "Jonah son of Amittai, the prophet, from Gath-hepher" (the Hebrew is ambiguous as to whether Jonah or his father is designated as "the prophet"). Jonah, then, prophet or simply the son of a prophet, conveys a favourable word from the Lord to an evil king of the heretical northern kingdom which strengthens that kingdom.

Let us suppose, for the sake of argument, that a reader of the book of Kings, troubled by the shrill nationalism and complacent reliance on Israel's special status that he hears around him, happens on this story. Here he finds a prophet, or at any rate a messenger of God, whose word encourages the northern king. If that has pricked our reader's interest, the next verse will certainly deepen it. In it, there is an explicit

---

3. See my "Swallowed by a Song: Jonah and the Jonah Psalm Through the Looking-glass," in *Reflection and Refraction: Studies in Biblical History in Honour of A. Graeme Auld* (ed. R. Rezetko, T. H. Lim and W. B. Aucker; VTSup 113; Leiden: Brill, 2006), 337–58.

theological apology for this turn of events. The fact that such an account has to be given emphasizes the fact that this is not what one would expect. The apology turns on a divine word that, according to the writer of Kings, was *not* spoken. There was no decree that Israel would be utterly blotted out. The Lord thus used the unsavoury hands of Jeroboam to save Israel. Jonah here is the bearer of an unlikely word of succour to someone that the Deuteronomists at any rate see as an opponent to true belief.

Immediately, narrative gaps open up. What did Jonah feel about this role? Why do we hear nothing else of him? The Jonah of 2 Kgs 14 is a prophetic figure whose brief appearance crystallizes a theological conflict between the Lord's purposes and those of the Deuteronomists. He is a reminder to those in Zion that God's writ runs much wider than their parochial interests. This is a message that the book of Jonah conveys through its gap-filling satire on Jonah and his narrow sense of what it is appropriate for God to be concerned with. The writer of Jonah turns the Deuteronomistic tradition against itself in his plea for an Israel that grounds its identity in humility before God rather than enlisting him as an avenger.

This aim seems to me to parallel Tobias's as he seeks to use the great German musical tradition to voice the national suffering of Estonia and yet to advocate a peaceful and hopeful solution in the perhaps naïve idea of the redemptive office of children. He uses and rewrites Jonah as an allegory of national defiance that can turn to fanaticism and which needs its own experience of judgment and repentance while rightly exposing the corruption and oppression of the ruling powers. Tobias's plea fell on deaf, or perhaps deafened, ears in his own day, and for complex reasons, partly to do with his early death, partly to do with his choice of German as the language of his libretto and a religious theme—neither of which would commend his work in Soviet Estonia, or among Estonian nationalists, for that matter—had no effect on Estonia's political fate for over 70 years. The work's very obscurity, however, lends weight to the idea of a religious Estonian masterpiece rediscovered and to its power as a representative work for an Estonia emerging from Soviet domination.

The book of Jonah, too, has had to bide its time, its message of reconciliation having little noticeable effect in the history of Persian and Hellenistic Israel. Jonah's mission, however, turns out to include an extraordinary journey to Tallinn via Nineveh, where its message of reconciliation, transposed and elaborated in a very different key, reaches new ears and performs an extraordinary modulation of national and musical history in the modern renaissance of Estonia.

## Joseph in Latvian

The second work I want to examine in some detail is rather different. It is the play *Joseph and His Brothers* by Rainis, the pseudonym of the prolific Latvian poet, playwright and politician Janis Pliekšāns, who lived from 1865 to 1929. I cannot forebear from recalling how this came to my attention. For several years I taught a class in "The Bible and the Literary Tradition" at Leeds University. One of my challenges to the students was always that they should bring works I had not heard of that meant something to them into the class seminar and explain to the class how the particular author had made use of the Bible. In the class one year was a mature occasional student who gave a fascinating talk on a play by Rainis, as she herself was a Latvian by birth. What I have never forgotten, though, was her remark to me at the end of the class: "You know, that's the first time in all my years in Britain that anyone has ever asked me about my Latvian culture." That was both poignant and pleasing, and this section of this chapter is indebted to her input.

It is a mark of our cultural insularity that I had not heard of Rainis before. Unlike Tobias, he has not languished in obscurity in his own country. He has recently been named Latvian "Man of the Twentieth Century" and during his lifetime narrowly missed being proposed for the Nobel Prize. His lyric poetry is highly regarded and his plays were performed throughout the Soviet era and continue to be performed regularly. Together with his wife, herself a poet of note who wrote under the name Aspazija, he undertook a monumental series of translations of European classics into Latvian, including Dostoevsky, Shakespeare and Goethe. He was also active in Latvian politics. As an avowedly socialist young journalist, he was exiled to Russia by the Tsarist regime for several years. Back in Riga in time to participate in the abortive revolution of 1905, he was forced to flee to Switzerland, where he lived until 1920. In the remaining years of his life he returned to the land of his birth to become a member of parliament, director of the National Theatre and, briefly, Minister of Education in the newly independent Latvia. To this day, a national poetry festival is held on his birthday when people congregate at his statue in Riga.

This is a far cry from the obscurity of Tobias' life, but it is also an example of one of the paradoxes that postcolonial studies thrives on. Rainis's love for and, by all accounts, mastery of Latvian means that his remarkable works are unavailable to the vast majority of readers outside Latvia. Translations do exist, but they were hardly encouraged or promoted by the Soviet regime. This means that his fame remains local. Tobias, on the other hand, made a programmatic decision to write his libretto in German, and to exploit of the so-called international language of music in order to stake a claim on the international stage. At the time when he did this, the experiment failed both at home and abroad until his work found its moment in 1990 and then could be appreciated worldwide.

Out of Rainis' large body of work, I want to mention two plays, one very briefly. Rainis' great early success was a play called *Fire and Night* (1905), which was based on Pumpurs' epic *Lāčplēsis*. His work ends with the hero plummeting to his death in the river Daugava together with his enemy the Black Knight, who represents the forces of oppression. In the immediate context, these are the Teutonic Knights forcibly converting the Latvians to Christianity, but they could be easily be understood by Latvian audiences at the turn of the twentieth century as representing the Tsarist forces. As the hero plunges to his doom, his semi-divine ladyfriend Spidola cries out, "The battle is not over!" Here Latvia's stubborn preservation of its language and its pre-Christian traditions is held up as a rallying call for modern resistance. For this reason, this play is often cited as the first stirring of modern Latvian nationalism.

The second play, which dates from 1919, and so is written towards the end of fifteen years of enforced exile, is "Joseph and His Brothers." This work is written on a grand scale, and is indeed something of a polyphonic *tour de force* as the twelve brothers interact on stage. It follows the biblical story quite closely in parts, but inevitably telescopes incidents and adds characters and dialogue. Joseph, the dreamer, is quite clearly presented as the artist in exile, the imaginative thinker whose visions merely enrage his envious brothers but which come to their own in a foreign land. Yet the exiled Joseph is left both with a burning sense of betrayal and injustice and with a longing for the home to which he cannot return.

The first two acts play out the murderous plans of the brothers and end with Joseph cast into the pit. Act 3 opens by contrast in Pharaoh's palace, where Joseph is already the chief of the land, renamed Nofer, and the next three acts explore the psychological issues of his meeting with his brothers. In this Egyptian section, Rainis subtly insists on the parallels between Joseph's story and the myth of Osiris, the son of Isis who is slain and torn apart and yet miraculously made whole again by the waters of the Nile, but also, through the use of a recurrent motif of piercing by thorns, which parallels the death and resurrection of Christ.

The climactic moment of the judgment and recognition of Joseph contains a rather troubling element, however. The tension between Joseph as both Egyptian and Jew is brought to the fore in a way that paints Jewishness in a very dark light. Judah challenges Joseph's right to judge the brothers by saying "Only by a Jew can the Jews ever be judged," but Joseph counters by the claim, startling in its context, "Ha! I am a Jew!" He finally reveals he is Joseph and turns on the brothers with the following words:

> Aha! at last you fall and lie on the ground!
> What! has the arrow found you? is the rock shattered?
> The desert wind and sands have closed your mouths?
> Hunt away now from here, the ghosts of revenge
> About you, on your death journey! Hey! look out!
> Your fall is from the seat of heaven down to hell!

Benjamin, however, rallies his stricken brother Judah:

> Judah, stand up! For that wild furious man
> Is never Joseph! for he was kind and gentle.

Joseph's response is telling:

> Ha, ha! my laughter falls back on my heart.
> You stole from me the heart of Benjamin!
> Ha! that's not Joseph! He was kind and gentle!
> Look here and see what you have made of me!
> I was no Jew and now am I become one.

Joseph becomes a Jew when he resorts to the violence and revenge that characterized his brothers' dealing with him. This strand of the play grows stronger as it reaches its odd climax, where Joseph renounces life and departs to become one with the Sun-God, urging his brothers to love one another, and saying cryptically

> For I sank deeper down than a man should:
> Now must I higher rise than a man can,
> Alone I go and for the whole world's sake.

The unhappy implication is that the way in which Joseph has fallen below mankind is by becoming the avenging Jew.

This is troubling in itself, but all the more troubling in the light of the awful fate that was to befall the Jews in Latvia in the 1940s. Of the 93,479 Jews living in the country in 1935 it is estimated that over 70,000 perished, most before December 1941. Yet Rainis himself came under fire in the 1920s from the emergent Latvian fascist movement as a "Jew-lover," and in 1929, just before his death, Rainis visited a kibbutz in what is now Israel and praised it as a model of socialism which he would like to see introduced to Latvia. What it seems to me we have here is an almost unthinking approach to Judaism which is, I would argue, not unrelated to the odd status of Latvian and the notion of the

Indo-European languages which was explored in more detail in the previous chapter of the present volume, "When Jesus Was (Nearly) a Scot."

What is interesting in Rainis' use of the Joseph story is that it is Joseph's Egyptianness and his relationship to the Egyptian myth of Osiris that is stressed, to the exclusion of his Jewishness. The ending of the play, where Joseph, quite unbiblically, goes off into the desert to undergo a lonely transfiguration, rather like Oedipus in Colonnus, merely underlines the divergence between Rainis' Joseph and any Old Testament thoughtworld.

What I am suggesting here is that this is linked to the way that, for a range of intriguing cultural reasons, the Old Testament becomes the place where European culture in the nineteenth-century works out its anxieties of identity. This is because it represents otherness, an alien intrusion, which has to be expelled to maintain or regain a lost purity in Aryan culture. One of the many harsh ironies in this, however, is that the Old Testament itself provides the stories and the rhetorics that can be used to justify the use of extreme violence to purge a corrupt society and which advocate or indeed command in God's name the total eradication of foreign elements that could contaminate a society morally, politically and ethnically. Again, I stress that Rainis and his play are in no way covert Nazi propaganda and he would no doubt be horrified by the links I am tracing. The very fact, however, that people were unconscious of such deep cultural movements which swayed their opinion of Judaism made them peculiarly susceptible to the kind of anti-Semitic ideology later demagogues would spout.

In Tobias's case, however, quite apart from very different personal circumstances, the fact that he was working within Estonian culture is rather different. Estonia and Finland also found great strength in their national epics and their shared cultural heritage in their resistance to German or Russian imperialism, but there was no way to link this Finno-Ugrian heritage into the great classical cultures. As ancient and intriguing as Finno-Ugrian culture is, it had not impacted on Europe in the same way. Knowing that you are related to the speakers of Mordvin and Votic does not carry the same impact as being related to the Brahmanic tradition of India. Moreover, Estonia never had a substantial Jewish population and so was never prone to the same sort of cultural tension.

Different as they are, what these two intriguing works both show is that acknowledged and unacknowledged biblical influences have had lasting effects, for good and ill, on the Baltic States, but that the differences are as important as the similarities in understanding these cultures.

That the Bible has a profound significance is beyond dispute, but the exact nature of that influence, benign or malign, bears more detailed searching. In doing so we not only shed light on contemporary cultural situations, but can also be prompted to read the biblical stories in new ways and to understand more of the cultural and political pressures that may have contributed to their present form. In the process, too, we have to examine our own encounters with the alien and unfamiliar and decide what we are open to learning from texts and cultures that at first seem so foreign, and yet are so familiar.

Chapter 11

## BRUCKNERIAN TRANSPOSITIONS

There is a burgeoning interest in the relationship between the Bible and the western musical tradition. Understandably, much work in this field has fallen in line with the model J. W. Rogerson sets out in his characteristically lucid chapter on "Music" in John Sawyer's *The Blackwell Companion to the Bible and Culture*.[1] Rogerson there explicitly restricts himself to musical works that use biblical words or dramatize biblical stories while making the plea that these are recognized as serious exercises in biblical interpretation. While there is much to do in this regard, in this chapter I want to draw attention to the fact that there are lessons for biblical scholars that can be learnt from the classical music tradition and the history of musicology by taking seriously purely musical phenomena.

After all, musicologists are not above drawing analogies from biblical studies. Consider this quotation from an article by Derek B. Scott on "Bruckner's Symphonies—A Reinterpretation":

> Gregory Bateson's idea of a "plateau of intensity" which he finds, for example, in Balinese culture, has been taken up by Gilles Deleuze and Félix Guattari. They explain this plateau as "a continuous self-vibrating region of intensities whose development avoids any orientation toward a culmination point or external end." The idea leads them to envisage a book which, instead of chapters having culmination and termination points, is composed of "plateaus that communicate with one another across microfissures." The Bible might already be thought to approach this description, and so do Bruckner's non-culminative and fissured structures.[2]

---

1. In J. F. A. Sawyer, ed., *The Blackwell Companion to the Bible and Culture* (Oxford: Blackwell, 2006), 286–98.
2. Derek B. Scott, "Bruckner's Symphonies—A Reinterpretation," in *The Cambridge Companion to Bruckner* (ed. John Williamson; Cambridge: Cambridge University Press, 2004), 103–4.

Whatever the problems with this quotation in detail, and I think there are serious questions about how far the various people named understand each other, let alone the Bible, the fact remains that the Bible is being invoked to clarify a complex problem in the understanding of a purely musical form and indeed to account for its apparent failure to fit the expected norm of cumulative and seamless musical argument. The formal peculiarity of the Bible offers Scott an analogy that suggests that traditional formal analyses in musical criticisms may need revision and expansion. So, the comparison can go two ways, and classical music as it has developed in the Western world bears traces of biblical influence in unexpected ways.

This piques my interest in the possibility of reversing the process. For biblical scholars, are there useful musical analogies which might open our eyes to the fact that our expectations and understanding of form and structure in biblical books could be expanded? In the case in point, for instance, there is a common factor in that the length and complexity of both Bruckner's symphonies and the biblical histories or indeed prophetic books are culturally unprecedented. They pose similar problems to their composers in maintaining coherence and clarity across attention spans and therefore similar problems to critics and audiences in coming to grips with the formal solutions that they propose. One example of something like this approach is provided by Frances Young in her book *The Art of Performance: Towards a Theology of Holy Scripture*.[3] In it, she uses musical performance as metaphor to illuminate aspects of contemporary theological hermeneutics. In the prologue she explains, "as the writing got under way, the analogy with performance—particularly musical performance, though opera and drama sometimes takes over—took off and began to stimulate new insights in a remarkable way. If it begins to seem like 'compositional allegory' by the end, that will itself provide an example of the potential of seeing one thing under the image of another."[4] Young's work enacts what Gregory Bateson, alluded to above, called associative thinking, a way of thinking that, rather than developing an argument through linear logic, explores the heuristic possibilities which occur through a more or less unexpected metaphorical juxtaposition. Her principal concern, however, is with the use of the Bible within the Church and analogies around concert performance. I want to follow another line and suggest two distinct but linked areas

---

3. Frances Young, *The Art of Performance: Towards a Theology of Holy Scripture* (London: Darton, Longman & Todd, 1990).
4. Ibid., 3.

where music provides a source of analogies: the analysis of musical form and the social and cultural dimensions of the history of musical analysis.

To do this, I will turn to the works of Anton Bruckner, and particularly his symphonies, to illustrate what I mean and conclude by offering some brief general reflections on ways in which we could expand and extend our study of Bible and music.

Anton Bruckner's remarkable series of symphonies raises a whole series of questions that provide suggestive parallels to the art of biblical scholarship: questions of canon, of sources, of textual criticism, of the nature of authorship and originality and, importantly, of the influence of wider cultural and political forces on the seemingly dispassionate intellectual study of textual productions. On the issue of canon, for instance, the seemingly simple question "How many symphonies did Bruckner write?" is not so simple to answer. A look in a record catalogue shows the difficulty. There are nine numbered symphonies to be sure, although the last of these is unfinished. In addition, however, you will find in record catalogues Symphonies 0 and 00, the former written after the numbered series began. Apart from that, most of the numbered symphonies exist in several editions, often with quite radical differences. Contemporary conductors argue about which version to perform.

If biblical scholars had been allowed to get to work on these symphonies, however, I suspect there could have been many more. Bruckner's great opening movements, for instance, tend to proceed by setting out at least three contrasting blocks of material which are then developed, not in combination, but a block at a time, as if he were moving very heavy objects. He moves block A so far, then leaves it, and goes back to fetch block B, moves it up in line and goes back to fetch C. Any traditional source critic could easily postulate a whole series of Bruckners or a succession of Brucknerian schools who have broken up and redistributed originally separate and coherent narrative strands. Looking to Bruckner for analogies might suggest that there can be valid formal structures that depend on this sort of sequential stop and start.

The problem is compounded because Bruckner, as an obsessive devotee of Wagner's music, borrows extensive themes and patterns from Wagner's operas, especially in his earlier symphonies. Again, what would a source critic make of this? Imagine if in two thousand years a page of Wagner's *Die Walküre* and Bruckner's Third Symphony were found in the ruins of some great music library. "Who borrowed from whom?" might be the question.

We are in the happy position, of course, of having extensive documentation of Bruckner's work and manuscripts. These show, however, that the source critics might have a point. Bruckner was notoriously unselfconfident at times and was prevailed upon repeatedly by his pupils to revise many of his symphonies to be more in line with what they considered to be modern taste. Not only did he consent, but he often allowed his students to do the revisions themselves. This has led to a continuing point of debate in Bruckner studies as to what then constitutes the "authentic" version of any of the symphonies affected. If Bruckner assented to these revisions, are the revised versions his final thoughts? Or was the originality of his vision watered down by the interference of his pupils, so that we should turn to the earliest completed manuscript for the purest record of his intentions? Should we take a consistent view on this, or should we be more nuanced?

The great British Bruckner scholar and composer, Robert Simpson, whose own eleven symphonies build on and develop Brucknerian principles, argues, for instance, that the first version of the Third Symphony, while flawed, represents an original architectural achievement which Bruckner subsequently completely ruined in his revisions, while in the Fourth Symphony, the revisions rescue a deeply unsatisfactory work. In both cases, Simpson argues that Bruckner is himself learning through composition, groping towards a new form of structure but in moments of weakness trying to make his original vision conform to the conventions of sonata form. Simpson goes so far as to propose an eclectic version which might assist Bruckner in his struggles to express something he has not yet been able to articulate, but which we in hindsight can see better than he could.

Whatever the rights and wrongs of this, it puts a question mark over reading authorial intention and inspiration out of a work of art, or a text. The lessons for biblical scholars, who deal with postulated authors almost exclusively, should be clear. Yet the cultural and political complexities are more tangled yet. Simpson is a great champion of Bruckner but is responding to a view in the history of Anglo-Saxon criticism certainly in the early part of the twentieth century that sees Bruckner as rather an oddity, not quite part of the great canonical stream of symphonism. German-speaking criticism, on the other hand, has seen him as "canonical" from the outset, and has seen less difficulty with his structural originality. The difference in reception, so it is posited, can be accounted for in one word: Hegel. For critics who worked in the German cultural ambit, where Hegelianism was part of the air one breathed, Bruckner's structures embodied thesis, antithesis and synthesis, and his movement represented the epitome of sheerly musical *Aufhebung*. Anglo-Saxon critics were on the whole resistant to such interpretations; again, the analogies to biblical scholarship are not far to seek.

Besides these cultural differences, and indeed hardly separable from them, were political differences. Here a great deal of work has been done in Bruckner scholarship which has uncomfortable but important questions to put to biblical scholars. What are presented as the methods and findings of disinterested scholarship may not be so innocent, or, if they are, may be taken up and used in politically charged ways. In the 1920s for instance, there was a notable division in German-speaking scholarship between those critics who traced Bruckner through Wagner to Bach as a great German composer whose work was rooted in folksong and those who asserted that his roots were in Schubert and the Viennese classics and saw him as the great Austrian composer, inspired by his fervent Catholic faith.

In this somewhat fraught climate, and given the textual confusion of Bruckner's scores, what could be more obvious than that an authoritative edition should be commissioned, the so-called *Bruckner-Gesamtausgabe* completed in 1932. Its editor, Robert Haas, however, wrote in 1934 that Bruckner's world-view was "entirely founded on the German character, [that] its musical setting allowed the German soul to pour forth untroubled, that every cosmopolitan refinement and foreign admixture of blood was missing from objective necessity, and [that] even the formative experience of Catholicism left no trace."[5] In the light of this, it is unsurprising to learn that Haas had strong sympathy for the National Socialist cause. Why this matters for our purposes is in the implications of the third phrase for Haas's editorial practice. Haas opted to favour the pre-publication final manuscripts of Bruckner's scores in most cases. This in itself is a defensible critical position, but it takes on another aspect when we realize that part of his explicit motivation was to remove any trace of editorial revision by Bruckner's predominantly Jewish pupils— hence the allusion to "cosmopolitan refinement and foreign admixture of blood" above.

As the critic Julian Horton puts it:

> To an extent, Haas's critical methods reflected contemporary politics: he was not simply concerned with reproducing the autograph sources, but also with saving Bruckner posthumously from what were considered to

---

5. Robert Haas, *Anton Bruckner* (Potsdam: Akademische verlagsgesellschaft Athenaion, 1934), 6, as quoted in Christa Brüstle, "The Musical Image of Bruckner," in Williamson, ed., *The Cambridge Companion to Bruckner*, 244–60 (256).

be the pernicious interventions of Jewish elements. Haas's philological method was therefore compromised; he frequently sacrificed textual accuracy in favour of spurious ideological justifications.[6]

Bruckner, characterized as the naïve religious peasant genius, was seen as giving unsullied expression to the German soul. The fact that he was Austrian was also important. It is no coincidence that in a a speech given by Joseph Goebbels at the dedication of Bruckner's bust in the Walhalla on June 6 1937 he proclaimed that "Anton Bruckner, as a son of the Austrian land, is particularly destined to symbolize in our time too the inextinguishable intellectual and spiritual community of fate that embraces our entire German folk."[7] In the same speech, he pledged the Führer's support of the *Gesamtausgabe* project, all, of course, in the political climate that would soon lead to the *Anschluss* of June 1938. After the war, the edition was revised on rather different principles by Leopold Nowak, who took a much more eclectic view and was prepared to incorporate elements of the later revisions in his versions as representing positive afterthoughts by Bruckner.

The point of rehearsing this story here is that even in the abstract and seemingly isolated world of musicology and dry business of the preparation of an authoritative edition, major political and social factors can be at work. If this is true of music, how much more should we be aware of it when claims of disinterested scholarship are made in relation to a text with the political and cultural significance of the Bible?

As for Bruckner himself, there is also considerable evidence of the rise of a Bruckner myth which at times explicitly drew analogies between what was represented as his lonely and unrecognized commitment to an unwavering faith in the cynical and uncaring world of Viennese music and the fate of Christ. Examination of the sources shows that Bruckner was far from unrecognized in his lifetime, but this fitted with an idea that Schopenhauer among others made popular of the artist as a melancholy suffering genius. A popular idea of him as a wildly impractical and naïve man who was simply touched by an almost supernatural genius as he improvised in the organ loft and composed also grew up. He embodied one aspect of the idea of the artist as inspired almost in the form of an

---

6. Julian Horton, *Bruckner's Symphonies: Analysis, Reception and Cultural Politics* (Cambridge: Cambridge University Press, 2004), 14. To be fair, it should be noted that Horton sets out this evidence as part of an argument against the tendency to dismiss a critical method or conclusion simply because of the unwelcome political affiliations of the critic or the ideas. While this is a valid and important point, in Biblical Studies the discussion of such issues may not be so far advanced.

7. Quoted in Brüstle, "The Musical Image of Bruckner," 257.

idiot savant. Granted that Bruckner was a socially awkward and obsessive man, the evidence shows that he was could be witty and convivial. His self-imposed renunciation of original composition for seven years in his thirties as he completed the exacting apprenticeship in counterpoint under his teacher Sechter and the opinion of his examiners for the Vienna Conservatory—"he should have examined us"—make clear the formidable intellectual and technical armoury with which he approached his compositions.

Again, the point of this is that here is a creative artist who died a little over a century ago whose motivations and character have been mythologized and turned to a variety of political uses. What does this say about the influence of such models on our attempts to reconstruct and understand the motivations and political position of any biblical author? What might it have to teach us in looking at the history of biblical scholarship itself?

In conclusion, then, I offer the thought that for biblical scholars music and musicology are the seedbed for a range of analogies. There are analogies at the level of the study of form, of the construction of large-scale heard works that must cohere over time. I also suggest that these fields offer the opportunity of *kal wehomer* arguments of the form: if x is true for music with its non-verbal character and apparent remoteness from direct theological, social and political rhetoric, how much more must it be true of the Bible, a transparently theological, social and political verbal construct. The influence of wider cultural and political currents on what proclaims itself as objective scholarship must be taken into account. More particularly, the development and critique of the romantic notion which depicts the composer of music as the epitome of the creative artist as a solitary, inspired and inarticulate genius has direct analogies in the history of debates about the nature of intention, inspiration, authorship and creativity in biblical texts.

Such associative thinking has both heuristic and pedagogical advantages.[8] It may open new possibilities for the researcher, suggesting

---

8. Consider, for instance, the fact that musical scores are a way in to understanding what it is to be partially literate. What proportion of even the educated population in Europe could sit down with the score of a Beethoven symphony and read it in solitary silence? Not many. Did Beethoven write the score with this purpose in mind? Well, perhaps, but not as his primary purpose surely. Music thus gives a way of conveying the otherwise mysterious phenomenon for most students of restricted literacy. Pointing out that anyone could learn to read music, but that most people are quite content to let the professionals do it for us, and that even among those who do read music, not so many can read a full orchestral core, let alone write one, makes clearer the status of writing and literature in an ancient society.

unfamiliar questions but also giving analogies that can be used in teaching, either moving from a familiar or at least accessible realm to the less familiar phenomena of ancient Israel or placing ancient phenomena in the defamiliarizing aura of classical music.

Let us then close with a brief quotation from one of Bruckner's pupils, Max von Oberleithner, which serves to underline why Bruckner at least might be worth our time as biblical scholars. Von Oberleithner describes how Bruckner combined an almost religious veneration for the strict rules of counterpoint he had learned from his teacher Sechter with complete imaginative freedom in his compositions: "In this, he [Bruckner] was like a bold interpreter of the Holy Scriptures who never completely disregards the basic idea."[9] That at least is good advice for all biblical scholars, even if working out its implications could take the rest of our careers.

---

9. Max von Oberleithner, *Meine Erinnerungen an Anton Bruckner* (Regensburg: G. Bosse, 1933), 14–15, quoted in Stephen Johnson, ed., *Bruckner Remembered* (London: Faber & Faber, 1998), 100.

Part V

ANIMAL BIBLE

Chapter 12

## THE LION KING

Some time in 2007, a political campaign advertisement appeared on Youtube, claiming to be endorsed by the White Witch of Narnia. Entitled "The Truth about Aslan," the text runs as follows:

> What do we really know about Aslan? Aslan wants to bring an end to Narnia's winter wonderland, plunging our country into a state of global warming. Aslan is also a carnivore, putting every citizen of Narnia on *his* diet. Even his biggest supporters agree he is not safe. Aslan is on the move, but if he loved Narnia so much, why did he move away in the first place? Aslan: bad for us, bad for Narnia.[1]

Now I take it that I can assume that most readers will get the reference, and the joke. Not everyone thinks this is funny. The comment pages are full of outraged protests that anyone could even dare to criticize Aslan. As one not untypical comment puts it, "This is stupid video and I didn't like neither don't respect who was talking bout Aslan, so please remove this stupid thing." Other comments along the lines of "Jeez, it's just a story-book lion, dude; it's not like it's Jesus" or "Jeez it's just a parody, dumbass," reveal the different reading strategies correspondents adopt. Now, making fun of respondents to Youtube videos is cheap, but the point is that this shows the power that this metaphorical representation has over certain readers, and the difficulty that human beings have in learning to negotiate what is metaphor and what is not, how what is said depends on who speaks and who hears and how metaphors have implications which may lurk unnoticed until activated.

What I hope this example does is open up the tensions in the use of animal metaphors in delimiting the bounds of the human, metaphors that are almost taken for granted. Aslan, the epitome of the Lion King, shows that that juxtaposition plays out differently depending on where you

---

1. Video accessible at http://www.youtube.com/watch?v=PaQD-nizpbo. With acknowledgments to the original poster "johnritc."

stand. In particular, I want to look at the lion as metaphor and metonym as it serves to configure the human in the Hebrew Bible and in those traditions that build on the Bible. I will then turn to Derrida's reflections on animals in his seminars collected as *The Beast and the Sovereign* and the presentations collected in *The Animal that Therefore I Am* to see how these interact. I will not claim that this leads to some new revolutionary manifesto, but in the course of researching this material I have found that I have had to correct some assumptions and have realized some implications that I had overlooked.

C. S. Lewis's use of Aslan the lion, rather than any human character, to represent the sovereign figure in Narnia is generally assumed to depend on his familiarity with the biblical tradition. For a remarkably comprehensive and thorough exploration of the role of the lion within the Hebrew Bible and its ancient context, I would point you towards Brent Strawn's *What Is Stronger than a Lion? Leonine Image and Metaphor in the Hebrew Bible and the Ancient Near East*.[2] Out of the wealth of material, textual and visual, that he assembles, there is one particular point that I want to home in on. He finds what he describes as a "glaring omission" in the Hebrew Bible when set against its ancient Near Eastern context. This is the *lack* in the Hebrew Bible of an association between the lion and the figure of the king.[3] In its contrast to the wider cultural norms from Egypt to Assyria, this is surprising. The iconography that associates king and the lion is so typical of Assyrian and other cultures that it is a cultural commonplace even in popular depictions. However, the Hebrew Bible contains no celebration of the king as displaying the power of the lion against his enemies, nor of the king as the great protector of his people against lions, real or metaphorical. Nor is the common trope of the identification of the king and the lion to be found. Even the few verses that might be cited in contradiction to this claim, Strawn argues, are markedly different in tone.

Instead, leonine imagery is reserved for Yahweh. In Strawn's view, the balance of probability is that this is a product of the process of accretion that gives rise to the biblical character of Yahweh, whereby attributes and characteristics of a series of deities are assimilated. Intriguingly, given the fact that leonine imagery is, if anything, more associated with feminine rather than masculine deities, such as Ishtar and Astarte, Yahweh's leonine qualities may reflect an aspect of his

---

2. Brent A. Strawn *What Is Stronger Than a Lion? Leonine Image and Metaphor in the Hebrew Bible and the Ancient Near East* (Orbis Biblicus et Orientalis 212; Fribourg: Academic Publishing/Göttingen: Vandenhoeck & Ruprecht, 2005).

3. Ibid., 236.

femininity. Be that as it may, the biblical tradition stands out as the one where the human king is not equated with the lion. The lion is Yahweh. The Lion King as sovereign beast is set against and differentiated from the human.

As Strawn rightly points out, this is commonly seen to be an ambivalent metaphor, where Yahweh can be represented either as the roaring lion who is opposing Israel's enemies, or as turning on Israel itself, regarding it as prey, graphically in Amos. However, Strawn reminds us, it is not that these are two different aspects of the lion. The lion is consistent; the difference depends on where we are standing. Lion statues are widespread in the ancient world, seemingly used as the guardians of thresholds, for the very good reason that there is a world of difference in being face to face with a lion, or standing behind it. Once allowed past the threat of the lion, one moves into its protection. The lion does not move, the spectator moves; but its symbolic force changes. Yahweh is represented as a lion, but so also are Israel's enemies, and the inimical forces of wild nature. What can protect me can also threaten and the image of the lion uncannily ties together protector and threat, ruler and unruly.

As I have indicated, Strawn's study is indispensable, but I want to supplement it by drawing on the work of Thomas Allsen who has undertaken a wide-ranging study of the institution of the royal hunt in Eurasia.[4] In the Mesopotamian context, the lion, he argues, embodies the paradox that the king draws spiritual power from the untamed powers of the wilderness and yet exercises that power to bring order and discipline to the world. Nature is at once nurturing and threatening. In the lion hunt, the king both shows his courage and his power to dominate nature, but also takes on the strength and power of his adversary.[5]

Iconically, the Mesopotamian king is never more kingly than when in single combat with a lion. Considerable resources were spent to maintain a captive population of lions that the king could hunt and kill in the carefully stage-managed context of the royal hunt in the royal parks, thus reinforcing the basis of his sovereignty and providing the court and population with evidence of the fitness of his rule. The pervasiveness of depictions of the royal hunt in a number of media shows the importance of the hunt as a way of demonstrating and communicating the king's status.

---

4. Thomas Allsen, *The Royal Hunt in Eurasian History* (Philadelphia: University of Pennsylvania Press, 2006).
5. Ibid., 216.

The use of hunting animals as partners in the hunt is also a significant and shared cultural feature. Dogs, raptorial birds and even the great cats, particularly cheetahs and caracals, have been co-opted to the human side of this conflict, often carrying out the killing on behalf of their masters. The evidence that lions were ever successfully used in this way is scant, though Allsen cites some rumours of such use, made more dubious by the confusion of terminology about the great cats.[6] Whatever the truth, the image of the king who not only confronts wild animals and subdues them but then turns them to his own use is a powerful one. By hyperbole, this power of the king can easily be extended to the lion. An extension of this power is the use of wild beasts as the instruments of punishment and the guardians of the king's reputation and authority. This was bound up with a wider view that saw the attacks of wild beasts as a sign of divine punishment.

Is it helpful to see the association between Yahweh and the lion in terms of the royal hunt, then, a hunt where lions are part of the pack but may also be the prize trophy? The ancient world then becomes Yahweh's royal hunting park, his *paradeisos*, where the nations become alternately the prey and the hunting partners and Israel itself can be spectator or victim. The sovereign shows his sovereignty by his ability not only to control or tame the beast, but to embody it, turning its ferocity to his own ends, with the drama of the royal hunt as the seal of that metaphorical fusion; not only does Yahweh himself act like a lion, but, as the prophets in 1 Kgs 13 or 1 Kgs 20 found out, or the people of Samaria in 2 Kgs 17, Yahweh uses lions as his executioners. His sovereignty is defended by the very beasts against whom he serves as protector.

It is here that we can turn to Derrida. In his seminars on *The Beast and the Sovereign* he offers extended meditations on the relationship between the animal and the political, meditations which go well beyond the scope of this chapter.[7] I want to focus on a particular paragraph where Derrida is discussing Hobbes' view in his *Leviathan* of the nature of the civil

---

6. See p. 75, where he cites the second-century writer Aelian as saying that India has many lions, the smaller of which can be trained to hunt deer. The possibility of confusion with cheetahs or even trained leopards is real and this is clearly far removed from the ancient Near East.

7. These seminars, which were the focus of Derrida's attention in the final years of his life, are now being published posthumously in several volumes. At present, the following are available in English: Jacques Derrida, *The Beast and the Sovereign*, vol. 1 (trans. G. Bennington; Chicago: University of Chicago Press, 2009), and *The Beast and the Sovereign*, vol. 2 (trans. G. Bennington: Chicago: University of Chicago Press, 2011).

contract as one that can only be made between human beings. Derrida interprets him as seeking to save the possibility of human sovereignty. This means that Hobbes excludes any covenant with God. Derrida writes,

> And what I would like to emphasize, is that this exclusion of any convention with God will be, as it were, symmetrical with another exclusion, that of a convention with the beast. This symmetry of the two living beings that are not man, i.e. the beast and the sovereign God, both excluded from the contract, convention or covenant—this symmetry is all the more thought-provoking for the fact that one of the two poles, God, is also the model of sovereignty...[8]

In a characteristic and untranslatable pun, Derrida writes that this equation means that "Dieu *e(s)t* la bête," His translator valiantly wrestles with the text as he explains, with brackets around the "s", "With or without the *s*, God is the beast/God and the beast," or as Derrida puts it, "God is/and the beast, with or without being." This association of God and the beast as the two excluded poles in Hobbes' attempted construction of an entirely human polity resonates with the discussion of the naming of the animals in Derrida's essay *L'animal que donc je suis*. This title is again an untranslatable pun: it can be translated as either "the animal which therefore I *am*" or "the animal which therefore I *follow*"; the significance of this for our discussion will become clear.[9]

Derrida undertakes quite an extensive exegesis of the naming of the animals in Gen 2. He points out that in this chapter the naming is undertaken by the solitary Ish before the creation of Ishah, not the man-woman pair of Gen 1:26. In doing so he draws heavily on Chouraqui's idiosyncratic translation of the Hebrew Bible. Ish alone names the animals which God makes and then brings before him. However, in the wider context of Gen 1 and 2, the one who names the animals comes *after* them; in ch. 1 they are created on the fifth and sixth days. Who follows whom? Derrida elides the detail of the creation of the animals in 2:19, but stresses the tension between God's desire to oversee the naming and to leave the man free to name as he chooses. "God lets Ish call the other living things all on his own, give them their names in his own name, these animals that are older and younger than him, these living things

---

8. Derrida, *The Beast and the Sovereign*, 1:49–50.
9. *L'animal que donc je suis* originated as a ten-hour address to a seminar that was dedicated to Derrida's work on animals. The text of this and other material derived from discussions on the same topic was edited together into a book by Marie-Louise Mallet which has been translated by David Wills as *The Animal That Therefore I Am* (New York: Fordham University Press, 2008).

that came into the world before him but were named after him, on his initiative, according to the second narrative."[10]

According to Derrida, this moment fills him with dizziness, a sense of vertigo, which he connects to the feeling of being naked before his cat. Derrida's discussion in *L'animal...* notoriously begins with his recounting of the shame that he feels before the gaze of his little cat. As Tom Tyler puts it,

> Despite appearances, Derrida's cat is wilder than the lion of Barthes or Aesop. She is not a cipher, nor an instance of "the animal," nor a stereotype. Derrida's cat is *fera*, following her own wishes, fancy free. She does not rage about with tooth and claw, but wanders from one room to the next, insistently roaming first this way, then that. She is, in short, an amiably unruly, indexical individual.[11]

Here, Derrida links the feeling he has under his cat's gaze to his reaction to what he calls "God's exposure to surprise," an emotion that is surely one of the paradoxical points of ignorance of any omniscient being. How can an all-knowing God be surprised? God leaves himself open to being surprised by the man's choice of what to call the animal. At this point, the question is raised by the text as to whether God's gaze and the animal's gaze can be equated: "I hear the cat or God ask itself, ask *me*, 'Is he going to call me, is he going to address me? What name is he going to call me by, this naked man...?'"[12]

The question this raises in the wider consideration of what marks the delimitation of the human is the coincidence of the gaze. The man, the Ish, is caught between two gazes, that of the beast and the sovereign, the animal and Yahweh, but these gazes are dizzyingly coincident, both intent on knowing what he will say next. Responsibility to one is responsibility to the other. This seems to me an insight that is also borne out in the use of the metaphor of the lion within the Hebrew texts, where Israel is caught between the gaze of its enemies and its protector, between the wilderness and the temple, but, disconcertingly, the two gazes turns out to be one and the same. Precisely because in the biblical world it is not directed at the singular person of the king, it puts the individual reader of the text in front of that gaze.

The cat's gaze asks "What will the man call me?" One name that man could give, a name that, as Derrida later explains, "is a word that men have given themselves the right to give," cannot be given at this point:

10. Ibid., 17.
11. Tom Tyler, "*Quia Ego Nominor Leo*: Barthes, Stereotypes and Aesop's Animals," *Mosaic* 40 (2007): 45–59 (56).
12. Ibid., 18.

the name "animal." Imagine God's expression if the man had pointed at each of his varied creations in turn and named them "animal…animal… animal." "Animal" is not something you call an animal. Indeed, much of Derrida's subsequent discussion is devoted to the unsatisfactoriness of the singular designation "animal," a problem of language that he encodes in the teasing term "animot," a portmanteau of "animal" and "mot," which is a homonym of the French plural "animaux" that therefore has unsettling effects on the French ear when used in conjunction with singular articles and verbs. Singularity and plurality are called into question by this coinage.

The biblical text never answers that question of the name directly. The man reviews and names the animals, but we do not learn what name he gives to any specific animal. What we do learn is that the man comes to shun the gaze of both animal and God. The realization of nakedness causes man and woman to hide from God's gaze and to shield their naked bodies from any gaze. A further implication, however, of Derrida's discussion is that the very use of the word and category "animal" is itself an attempt to evade the gaze of the specific animal, the individual of another species, in the effort to build a community based solely on the human, as the man cleaves to the partner that was already part of him, bone of his bone, rather than cross the divide between human and beast, human and God. We might argue that that dilemma, and that almost inevitable response, has shaped Western attitudes both to politics and to the natural world ever after.

By removing the screen or filter of the king as the one who represents the union of sovereign and beast, the biblical tradition locates each individual human before the inexorable gaze of Yahweh as the sovereign beast, characterizing the human as a point of answerability. In pursuit of this evasion of the dual gaze of beast and sovereign, humans design for themselves the coverings of clothing, language, law, politics and religion.

When, then, Derrida raises the question of "the animal that therefore I am," or "follow," once again playing on the ambiguity of the French "je suis," he destabilizes the category of the human and of the I at a profound level. But lest we become entangled in existential and metaphysical issues of "being," we must not forget the importance of "following."

In Lewis's Narnia, the great queen Jadis who becomes the White Witch has her own slogan, "Ours is a high and lonely destiny."[13] That is the slogan of the one who refuses to follow. As we have seen above, it

---

13. C. S. Lewis, *The Magician's Nephew*, in *The Complete Chronicles of Narnia* (London: Collins, 2000), 30.

makes all the difference where we are in relation to a lion. To follow a lion is rather different from facing one, or being followed by one. Jadis refuses to follow the lion, and seeks to become herself the sovereign beast and indeed to hunt down the lion. What Derrida reminds us, and what the biblical tradition scandalously reveals, is that hunter and hunted may turn out to be the same. In the effort to avoid being prey, we may seek to become the hunter, and find in the process that we have voted for the White Witch.

Chapter 13

CONVERSATIONS WITH DONKEYS

Twice in his works, Tertullian recounts the story of a freelance fighter with the wild beasts in the arena (in one version a Jew) who exhibited in Carthage a placard on which he had written: "The God of the Christians—*onokoites*." This was the caption to a picture of a man with the ears of an ass and one hoofed foot, carrying a book and wearing a toga. Tertullian writes, "Both the name and the figure made us laugh."[1] If nothing else, it is reassuring that he found something to laugh at— usually he comes across as distinctly humourless. Be that as it may, "*onokoites*" is a mysterious word. One interpretation, borne out by the picture, would translate it as "born of a donkey." The implication is that Jesus is a hybrid of a human and a donkey.

It is easy to dismiss this as a cheap and generic jibe at Christianity. As Ingvild Sælid Gilhus argues, this particular line of denigration is part of a trend in Roman culture during the period in which Christianity was developing from a sect to a state religion.[2] Animals are progressively devalued and human beings are accorded increasing status. The worship of animals as gods becomes seen as a mark of cultural inferiority. In the midst of this wider cultural development, she points out, Christian writers project Christians as a *tertium gens*, a third race. This initially serves to set the boundaries between Christians and Romans on the one hand and Christians and Jews on the other. However, in the eyes of the wider culture, this concept becomes mapped on to the symbolism of the differentiation between animal and the human, with Christians as the third race becoming symbolically human–animal hybrids. As she indicates, this was compounded by the Christian insistence on the reality of the incarnation. As she says, "the product of a union between the Jewish

---

1. Tertullian, *Apologeticus* 1.16.12; cf. *Ad Nationes* 1.11.
2. See Ingvild Sælid Gilhus, *Animals, Gods and Humans: Changing Attitudes to Animals in Greek, Roman and Early Christian Ideas* (Abingdon: Routledge, 2006).

god, who by outsiders was caricatured as an ass, and a human mother logically became a mixture between ass and man, an *asionocephalus*."[3] Christian writers reply to this calumny by stressing the full humanity of Christ and by deflecting the donkey slander back onto the Jews, using this as a way further to differentiate themselves from the Jewish tradition.

The question that intrigues me here, however, is: Why a donkey, of all animals? Tertullian himself explains the root of this slander as lying in Tacitus's tale that the Hebrews, having been driven out of Egypt and dying of thirst in the desert, were induced by Moses to pledge their loyalty to whatever saved them, at which point a herd of wild asses appeared. Following them, they found a spring, and thereafter worshipped the head of an ass, an image of which was installed in the temple in Jerusalem. This slander of the "donkey God" of the Jews seems to have been widespread and may go back to the Egyptian demonization of Seth, the donkey god, as the god of the Hyksos invaders and thus of the hostile Eastern tribes. Josephus indignantly counters several instances of similar slanders in his sources. Through Tacitus and then Plutarch it becomes widely distributed in the Roman world.

The well-known Alexamenos graffito discovered in Rome, and often taken as the first representation of the crucifix as an object of veneration, might confirm this, although some of the argument is circular. It shows a man on a cross with an equine head, apparently being worshipped by a second figure, with the crudely written caption "Alexamenos worshipping his god." Nothing explicitly labels this as an anti-Christian graffito, and there are other explanations possible, but the fact remains that this victim of crucifixion is out of the same stable as the drawing by Tertullian's villain.

The point is, of course, that the slander battens onto a lewd interpretation of the doctrine of incarnation and implies that Jesus himself is the product of inter-species sex, between the donkey God and his human mother, with, no doubt, as Richard Bulliett suggests, the lubricious tales of such writers as Apuleius and Lucian resonating in the background.

Try this for size from Apuleius' novel, *The Golden Ass*. The narrator, Lucius, who has been transformed into a donkey, is hired for the night by an amorous noblewoman. He tells us, though:

> I was distressed, however and not a little frightened as I wondered how I, with so many and such large legs, could mount such a delicate lady; or how I could embrace such a soft translucent body, all compact of milk and honey, with my hard hoofs; or how I could kiss those fine lips

3. Ibid., 235.

reddened by ambrosial dew with my great monstrous misshapen mouth with its stone-sized teeth. Finally, even though she was itching for it to the tips of her toes, how could the woman [and here I revert to Latin to spare the reader's sensibilities] *tam vastum genitale susciperet*?[4]

The lady proves more than up to the challenge, however, and the spectacle of their night of passion so excites Lucius' keeper that he decides to set up a public display in the amphitheatre where a woman who has poisoned five members of her family will be forced to couple with the donkey. Horrified at the thought of sleeping with this female monster, Lucius escapes and is transformed back in to his human form.

Apuleius contrives a pious ending out of this perversity, but not so Lucian of Samosata, who, in his even more scurrilous version of the story, has the restored Lucius in his human form seek out the amorous noblewoman:

> When the night was now advanced and it was time to go to bed, I got up and stripped as though conferring a great favour and stood naked before her, imagining I would please her still more by the contrast I formed with the ass. But when she saw that every part of me was human, she spat at me and said, "Get to blazes away from me and my house; don't sleep anywhere near me."
>
> When I asked what heinous offence I'd committed she replied, "By heavens, I didn't love *you* but the ass in you and *he* was the one I slept with, not you. I thought that, if nothing else, you would still have kept trailing around with you that mighty symbol of the ass. But you have come to me transformed from that handsome, useful creature into a monkey."[5]

Lest we think that this is merely a product of the depraved pagan imagination, we should not overlook the striking parallels with the fevered imagination of Ezek 16. In his no-holds-barred excoriation of the unfaithfulness of Israel in explicitly sexual metaphors, Ezekiel depicts Oholibah, the harlot who represents Israel, as precisely the counterpart of Lucian's lustful noblewoman dreaming of lovers with "members like asses."

---

4. Apuleius, *Metamorphoses*. Vol. 1, *Books VII–XI* (Loeb Classical Library 453; trans. J. Arthur Hanson; Cambridge, Mass.: Harvard University Press, 1989), 10:23, 256.
5. Lucian of Samosata [attrib], *Lucius, or the Ass*, in *Lucian of Samosata* (Loeb Classical Library 432; trans. M. D. MacLeod; 8 vols.; London: Heinemann, 1967), 8:27–145 (143).

But does the connection end there? The mockers of Christianity in the ancient world, as we have seen, did not think so. And do they not have a point? After all, what species *is* God? If he is anything other than human, and the biblical tradition, for all its anthropomorphisms, is very keen to stress that he is not a man, then any doctrine of incarnation must knock up against the taboo against relationships between species. The strange incident of the relations between the sons of God and the daughters of men in Gen 6 which leads to the shortening of human life, and which so disturbs the writers of *Jubilees* and 1 Enoch, shows the dangers of breaching this boundary which can only give rise to monsters. Reflecting on this may at least alert us to the scandal of the incarnation in an unfamiliar way.

But still, why a *donkey*? Tertullian and Tacitus are clearly finding explanations after the event for an existing association between the Jewish God and donkeys. Why this association, however? Pushed too far, that question may not ultimately be answerable. The power of symbols cannot be reduced to discursive explanation. It does, however, send us back to look at the role of donkeys in the Hebrew tradition with a renewed sense of interest. In particular, it made me prick up my ears, so to speak, at a reported remark of the noted French film director, Robert Bresson, who said in an interview, "The donkey is the entire Bible, both Old Testament and New Testament." We will return to Bresson later, but, to bear out his remark, once you begin to look, there are a surprising number of donkeys in the Bible, in surprising places, and even more whose existence is assumed but never mentioned.[6]

Donkeys not only carry the story of the narrative of the Hebrew Bible, literally providing explicitly mentioned or tacitly assumed transport for characters and goods, but they also occupy a peculiar position in the legal material. They are the only animals, apart from humans, of which the first born is *not* to be offered to Yahweh. This may be a deliberate repudiation of the otherwise common use of donkey sacrifice in the ancient Near East to seal treaties. There is a difference, however, between humans and donkeys: a donkey is either to be redeemed with a lamb, or have its neck broken; a human child, however, must be redeemed. Donkeys end up in a unique marginal space between humans and the

---

6. For a compendious and exhaustive account of the role of the donkey in the Hebrew Bible and in ancient Near Eastern cultures in general, see Kenneth C. Way, *Donkeys in the Bible World* (Winona Lake: Eisenbrauns, 2011). Way does not explore the particular metaphorical and symbolic use we are tracing in any detail, however.

other domestic animals, something that Howard Eilberg-Schwartz picks up in his *The Savage in Judaism*, where this ambivalent status of the donkey is read as standing for similarly ambivalent role of the resident alien in Hebrew society.

In a Bible full of donkeys, the donkey of donkeys, surely, is Balaam's ass, or more accurately, she-ass, in Num 22. The rabbinic tradition even manages to find sex in this story in its obsession to root out any excuse to vilify Balaam. Taking a cue from Num 22:27, where the ass "lay down under Balaam," the rabbis come up with a suitably raunchy and transgressive interpretation of the nightly rites Balaam undertook to work himself into a state of prophetic ecstasy.

Leaving such crudities aside, what singles this donkey out, of course, is her speech. Only she and the serpent of Gen. 3 break the boundary between human and animal that is marked by speech and there are some interesting links between the two chapters. In the Hebrew Bible, they are the only animals with which humans can hold intercourse, or conversation, across the species boundary. This allows scope for more nuanced reflection on the role the donkey has played as a symbol to negotiate the relationships between sexuality, language and the boundary between human and animal.

Elsewhere I have argued that deep in the structure of the biblical texts is what I call an "anxiety of utterance" that identifies the male dread at the powerless of having to entrust the production if a male heir to the hidden processes of female sexuality with the dread at the powerlessness of the fact that an uttered speech has to be entrusted to the hidden processes of another's understanding. After all, Num 22–24 is a story of unexpected utterance, the donkey's, but also Balaam's own unaccountable blessing to Israel. The donkey who utters embodies this anxiety that links speech and sex and also the anxious possibility of transformation. But again, why a donkey?

This brings us back to Robert Bresson whose cinematic masterpiece *Au Hasard Balthasar* places a donkey, Balthasar, at the centre of the film. At one point Bresson told a friend that Balthasar was a depiction of the biblical ass from Abraham to Jesus. The film is hard to summarize, especially as Bresson deliberately makes the narrative elliptical to the point of confusion. However, Balthasar becomes the still point around which the abusive relationship of the young thug Gerard and the painfully passive Marie plays itself out. Charles Barr says of Balthasar, "He doesn't only remind Marie of sex, he represents it. Standing there, eating grass, he movingly evokes natural sensual appetite." She fondles Balthasar as a rehearsal for her relations with Gerard, just as he torments the donkey as a rehearsal for his cruelty to her. Remember, it is Balaam's merciless beating of his ass that prompts her speech. Bresson himself explains, "The love of adolescents can be addressed to vague, hazy objects. Love needs to find an object. The donkey is already an intermediary."

Balthasar does not speak, but at crucial moments his braying breaks in on the soundtrack, often marking a moment of recognition, for good or ill. Bresson relates this use of the uttering donkey to his being struck by what he calls a "moment of genius": the passage in Dostoevsky's *The Idiot* where Prince Myshkin tells General Yepanchin and his family of the disorientation and dread his intensifying attacks of his epilepsy caused while he was abroad, crushing him with a sense of alienness. The prince explains:

> "I shook off this blankness completely, I recall, one evening in Basle, as we were entering Switzerland, and what roused me was the braying of an ass in the town market. That ass really astonished me; it greatly took my fancy for some reason, and at the same time my head seemed to clear suddenly."
>
> "An ass? That's odd," remarked Madame Yepanchina. "Though what's odd about it, one of us could well fall in love with a donkey," she remarked, glancing angrily at the giggling girls. "It happened in mythology. Continue, Prince."[7]

In both pieces, wordlessly, the startling bray, the utterance of the donkey has revelatory power tied to the anxieties of sexuality. In the same vein, but now given words, is a typically intriguing piece by Hélène Cixous in her *Messie*: "Conversations with Donkeys," from which the title of this chapter is derived:

> The Bible does not report the conversation which Abraham had with the donkey on Mount Moria. Thus it is enough to follow them and hear them speak. I want to give the donkey with Abraham his speech back. One does not say stupid things to a donkey, does one? Nor to a cat.
>
> Telephone conversation:
>
> —It's me, your donkey, he said.
> She is surprised because she thought *she* was the donkey.
> —*You* are my donkey? [Tu es mon âne, toi?]
> —I love it infinitely.
> —But I didn't say, "You love my donkey [tu aimes mon âne]." I said, "You *are* my donkey??"

---

7. Fyodor Dostoevsky, *The Idiot* (trans. Alan Myers; Oxford: Oxford University Press, 1992), 59.

—Ah! yes. But a very little one. But I have big ears.
—In the end, you are the whole of my menagerie.
My greatest difficulty is in moving from my menagerie to philosophy.[8]

A close variant of this passage recurs in her collection *L'amour du loup et autre remords*. There she does not repeat the telephone conversation, but sets it in the context of a meditation on blindness, on writing and on the nature of the book and the Bible. The difference between her Bible and God's, she claims, is that in her Bible one laughs, but not in God's Bible:

> It is only in dreams that we are strong and generous enough to look God in the face while he bursts out laughing. That creation, really! Those creatures! It takes some doing! And I also laugh to have caught God doing what he has never done elsewhere.[9]

Intriguingly, the misunderstanding between Abraham and the donkey turns on a mishearing of being and loving. Something around that transition is epitomized in humour, although I think Cixous is unfair in denying laughter to the Bible's God. After all, even Tertullian laughed at the donkey.

This note of laughter bring us to one final ass who utters. In the Fourth Part of Nietzsche's *Also Sprach Zarathustra*, Zarathustra encounters two kings who are driving a single laden ass. This catches his attention, and in conversation with the kings it transpires that they, like him, are seeking the Higher Man, and bringing him the ass as a gift. This ass, too, utters. "But here it happened that the ass, too, found speech; it said clearly and maliciously 'Ye-a,'" or in German "I-A" [ja], a self-parody of Nietzsche's own eternal Yea-saying.[10]

Sometime later, when the kings and various other strange visitors have gathered in Zarathustra's cave, he is startled when silence falls and he re-enters the cave to find them all worshipping the ass, using a liturgy in which the ass replies "I-A" to each petition. The petitions satirically assimilate the donkey to the patience and acceptance of Christ. Zarathustra counters this with a louder "I-A" of his own.

Writing of this passage in her "Nietzsche and the Mystery of the Ass," Kathleen Marie Higgins points out that although Zarathustra berates the Higher Men for this reversion to worship, he also praises their foolishness

---

8. Hélène Cixous, *Messie* (Paris: Des femmes, 1996), 101–2.
9. Hélène Cixous, "Writing Blind: Conversation with the Donkey," in *Stigmata: Escaping Texts* (trans. Eric Prenowitz: London: Routledge, 1998), 139–52 (143).
10. Friedrich Nietzsche, *Thus Spoke Zarathustra* (trans. R. J. Hollingdale; London: Penguin, 1969), 260.

in worshipping a donkey of all things. There is a transformative power in the donkey, which is the transformation of laughter. As Higgins puts it, "…the asinine stage itself has value, both for the insights gained through it and for the comedy it presents to observers."[11]

To bring us full circle, Higgins concludes that if Christians did worship Jesus in the form of an ass, they were not wrong: "The ass, as the symbol of a crucial stage in spiritual development, is ultimately our redeemer."[12] Somewhere in the absurdity of human sexuality, which is brought to shocking clarity in the clashing hooves, tombstone teeth and outsized genitals of Lucian's donkey coupling with the matron or by the ineffable God impregnating the Jewish virgin, the shocking confrontation with sex across boundaries, voiced by the donkey's impossible utterances, is a glimmer of redemption through holy laughter. Madame Yepanchina is (happily) right: one of us could well fall in love with a donkey.

---

11. Kathleen Marie Higgins, "Nietzsche and the Mystery of the Ass," in *A Nietschean Bestiary: Becoming Animal Beyond Docile and Brutal* (ed. C. D. Acampora and R. R. Acampora; Lanham: Rowman & Littlefield, 2004), 100–118 (115).

12. Ibid., 116.

Part VI

THE SPORTING BIBLE

Chapter 14

WRESTLING THE BIBLE

A lurid sunset sky; gaunt black-and-white pictures of ruined buildings and human skulls scattered on a battlefield. A portentous voice warns of coming judgment. Bible references flash across the screen (no words, simply the references): Jer 30:3; Joel 2:31; Zeph 1:8; Rev 16. We see images of the sun turn to darkness and the moon to blood. "No soul shall be saved" intones the voice. "The heavens will shake, the earth shall be laid bare… It's going to be a triple threat match for the world heavyweight title."

As some of you may have recognized, what I am describing is the promotional video for Armageddon 2003, one of the major events in the annual calendar of the WWE, World Wrestling Entertainment, Vincent McMahon's empire which is reputedly worth over 1 billion dollars and which claims over 50 million regular viewers world-wide. For those less familiar with the phenomenon, the interest of the WWE for its fans is not simply in watching large half-naked men beating each other into submission in a variety of ingenious ways (so ingenious that they can return the next week without so much as a bruise on them having been left apparently for dead the week before). Just as important are the lurid plotlines that take place behind the scenes where the cameras just happen to catch the athletes and their coaches in "candid" moments. It is not enough for the real star wrestlers to be able to hold their own physically. Skill in verbal taunts and in making devious alliances is just as important. The vendettas, love affairs and family betrayals make any soap opera seem tame and lead to such gripping billings as "the world's first step-daughter/step-mother grudge match" and "Scott Steiner versus Test; If Test wins, he gets Scott and Tracy's services; if Scott wins, he gets Tracy."

What has all this to do with biblical studies, you may ask? A surprising amount, is my answer. Not only do implicit and explicit biblical allusions abound in wrestling in a way that is culturally intriguing, but my contention is that the popularity of both the Bible and wrestling stems from their ability to engage similar basic human reactions to perceived justice and injustice.

Roland Barthes in his classic essay "The World of Wrestling"[1] makes the crucial point that the essence of wrestling is what he calls the "spectacle of excess." The basis of this spectacle, Barthes tells us, is "Suffering, Defeat and Justice." Of these, the key point is Justice. To quote Barthes again, "Justice is...the embodiment of a possible transgression; it is from the fact that there is a Law that the spectacle of the passions derives its value."

As Barthes makes clear, the Law in question is not to be equated with the official rules mediated by the referee. What really excites the public is the cheat who claims the support of the rules to save his own skin, diving for the ropes to break a hold that his skill will not let him break, but quite prepared to punch and gouge behind the referee's back. The referee's function is to be the embodiment of the blindness of official justice. It is the audience who become the outraged witnesses of a breach of the rules. The manifest disregard of the rules in any WWE match is actually the condition for Law to become visible. The audience is primed to condone any act of revenge on the part of the wrestler who has been the victim of such cheating. This may break the rules, but it restores the Law.

The vindication of Law through the condoned breach of rules as Barthes describes is something known to story-tellers from time immemorial, biblical ones included. I cannot now read the book of Judges, for instance, without casting the characters in a WWE extravaganza. Samson could readily be transplanted to the wrestling ring. Strong, popular, able to smart-talk his way out of situations and to set up provocations to his enemies (remember the riddle, and the way in which he sets fire to the fields), over-the-top yet justified in his vengeance (burning his impertinent father-in-law's house, showing off by carrying the gates of the city to the top of a hill), able to beat overwhelming odds—yet not invincible. Women and betrayal bring him down. Degraded and blinded, cheated by Delilah and taunted by his enemies, he can still bring the house down with one mighty effort.

Throughout Judges, and indeed in Genesis and in Samuel/Kings, narrative shapes and moral outcomes that offend a strict sense of fair play but which take delight in the cunning trick, and the effective

---

1. Roland Barthes, "Le monde où l'on catche," in *Mythologies* (Paris: Editions du Seuil, 1970 [1957]), 13–24; "The World of Wrestling," in *Barthes: Selected Writings* (ed. Susan Sontag; London: Fontana/Collins, 1983), 18–30.

revenge, are played out. David himself, in the book of Kings at least, often operates by rules that seem closer to the WWE than to the Beatitudes. He has the requisite charismatic charm, and indeed the way with words, that makes a star of the ring. These are popular narrative forms, popular heroes. After all, these are stories that had to live through retellings and they give good value.

In the great story of wrestling which shapes Israel's identity as a culture in Gen 32, a mysterious masked figure (the tradition of masked wrestlers carries on to this day) wrestles Jacob till the break of day. Against all the odds Jacob prevails, even though his opponent cheats by dislocating his hip. Jacob is the arch fast-talking subverter of the rules who has the tables turned on him time and again and, unwittingly, ends up by fulfilling the divine plan. By a remarkable, and I suppose accidental, coincidence, this story enacts the archetypal conflict of professional wrestling where a wrestler whom the crowd is meant to warm to, called a "face," is pitted against the bad guy, known a "heel." "Heel" and "face"; Jacob at Peniel: the man named the "Heel" claims he has seen the "face" of God.

Jacob is also involved in the other story that brings wrestling explicitly into the Bible. In Gen 30, the childless Rachel, jealous of her sister Leah's fertility, induces Jacob to sleep with her maid Bilhah who can then give birth on Rachel's knees. This happens twice. Rachel calls the second child Naphthali, which means "I wrestled," because, she explains, "With mighty wrestlings I have wrestled with my sister, and have prevailed." The sisters wrangling for their common husband's favours are not an edifying, but an understandable, couple, quite easily imaginable as the pretext for a bout in the world of the WWE.

Much the same could be said for episodes from a wide range of ancient and folk literature. The *Iliad* and the Icelandic *Sagas*, for instance, show the same delight in heroes who can combine cunning revenge, spectacular savagery and clever wordplay. I want to go on to claim a more particular link between the WWE and the Bible, however. In some intriguing respects, I suggest, Vince McMahon is God, or perhaps more accurately, Yahweh is Vince McMahon. There are aspects of the character of the God of the Hebrew Bible that come uncannily close to those displayed by Mr McMahon. Vince McMahon, just like the biblical God, is owner, creator and final arbiter of the spectacle—and at the same time a character who appears on stage in that spectacle. The twist is that the ultimate guarantor of justice is himself involved in the spectacle of excess, thus destabilizing the whole system of justice on which the spectacle depends to frame and limit its apparently unbounded transgression.

In McMahon's case, there is a key moment which inaugurates this duplication of roles: the great betrayal in Montreal. In brief, the champion wrestler of the day, Bret Hart, had fallen out with Vince and was leaving the franchise. By custom, the wrestler who is leaving leaves the title behind with him. Bret had been drawn to lose his title to another wrestler, Shawn Michaels, whom he despised. Vince had agreed that honour could be saved by an arranged disqualification. However, when Sean Michaels pinned Hart at the point when the disqualification was due to be enacted, McMahon, who was at ringside, instructed the timekeeper to ring the bell after only a count of two, thus ensuring Hart's defeat. Bret Hart can then be seen going to ringside on live television and spitting full in Vince's face. By all accounts, he then followed Vince back to the dressing room and assaulted him.

What this did was bring the boss into the action as the subverter of the Law. Commentators ever since have wondered whether this incident was staged or real. This question goes to the heart of wrestling, with its mysterious concept of "kayfabe," the unwritten code that prevents wrestlers revealing the choreography and fixing of results which is determined by the writers. Real or staged, commentators on WWE see this as the crucial moment when McMahon "broke the third wall." No longer could the fiction be maintained that the outcome of the contests depended only on the skill and ability of the wrestlers in the ring and the upholding of the rules of the sport after such a blatant piece of interference by the supreme manager. What could have been the end of the business was, however, turned to its benefit in a stroke of genius on McMahon's part. His inspired solution was thenceforth explicitly to bill the WWE as "Sports Entertainment," obliquely admitting that the heroes of the ring were actors who played out a drama that he, Vince, had shaped.

What grew out of the Montreal event was a double Vince: Vince, the actual power behind the scenes, and Vince the character, who was now to be seen in apparently candid shots arranging matches to do down the crowd's favourite wrestlers, and who would now appear in the ring himself to slap down any upstarts. Furthermore, not only Vince but also his entire family are involved in WWE. His wife, son and daughter are all on the payroll of the company and the family dramas become enacted in the ring. Even the commentators appeared to be shocked, however, when his daughter Stephanie, given the control of the Raw franchise, defied her father and was then called out by him in the ring for, I quote, "the first ever father–daughter 'I quit' match." The spectacle of the then nearly 60-year-old Vince, in remarkable physical shape, beating up his own daughter in front of her mother's eyes is seriously disturbing, especially as the rules of this particular match mean that victory is won when your opponent explicitly says "I quit."

Yet, shocking as this is, it is far from the "first ever" father–daughter "I quit" match. Wotan and Brunhilde come to mind, and the *Iliad* at one level is just such a contest between Zeus and his daughter. Yahweh in his solitary sovereignty might seem to be exempted here, but one only has to turn to the books of Lamentations or Ezekiel. Daughter Jerusalem takes a fair pounding from her father Yahweh and again the rules are "I quit." Indeed, these texts depend on the fact that the solitary Yahweh has to come into the ring with Israel. Precisely because there is no divine family for Yahweh, he has to appear on stage with his own creations to fight these things out. As Vince snarls to his wife in one of their many in-ring encounters, "This isn't business anymore, it's family." Israel is not business for Yahweh, it is family: that is the tragedy and glory of their intertwined tales.

After all, how different is Vince's entry into the story in Montreal from the fatal moment when Yahweh himself steps down to walk in Eden in the cool of the evening and becomes embroiled in a still-controversial argument with Eve over death, the settlement of which might be seen as the bedrock of the whole subsequent plot of the biblical narrative? Did Yahweh set Eve and Adam up? Who is in control, and who is the embodiment of Law, rather than of the official rules, in the biblical story? This step into the garden, or the ring, generates a double Yahweh, Yahweh as character and Yahweh as supreme guarantor of the narrative, with complex literary and theological consequences.

Now, you may think, as I began to suspect myself, that this comparison is getting rather far-fetched. Truth, or kayfabe, is stranger than fiction, however. A new storyline emerged in WWE where Vince announced that he was going to make the life of the same Shawn Michaels, a self-confessed Christian wrestler, "hell." As part of the vendetta, Vince challenged Shawn to a tag team match against himself and his son Shane. Shawn's partner, however, was to be God. On April 17, 2006, Vince announced the birth of a new religion, McMahonism, in which he is Lord, Master and God of all sport entertainment and challenged God to show up if he had a problem with that. Mysterious explosions foiled Vince's attempts to beat up Shawn Michaels, at which point Vince announced that he would send his "only begotten son Shane" to fight Michaels next week.

This culminated in a match on April 30, 2006, where God was formally announced as Michael's tag-team partner only to be denounced as a "quitter" by McMahon when he never turned up. Ultimately, Shawn

Michaels beat up both his boss and the boss's son, but only after he was defeated in a match by precisely the same tactic that defeated Bret Hart, a defeat Michaels, of course, played a part in. Once again, he was pinned only for a two count but the bell was rung and he was deemed to have lost the contest. This time, however, Mr McMahon makes explicit the fact that he is bending the rules to do to Michaels what was done to Hart.

Truth and fiction here meld, as they do when Yahweh in Ezek 20 finally reveals that the laws he gave were bad laws, designed to horrify Israel. At the end of that chapter, after a great rhetorical outburst by Yahweh culminating in the threat of unquenchable fire, we find a strange comment in Ezekiel's own voice: "Ah, Lord God! They are saying of me, 'Is he not a maker of allegories?'" At precisely the point where God reveals the fictive nature of his own laws and seems to assert his absolute power, the issue of fictionality, of make-believe, is explicitly articulated by the text, in a troubling breach, perhaps, of the divine kayfabe. Is that power, too, a fiction?

I contend that some of the most disturbing aspects of the God of the Hebrew Bible are structurally related to the mixed position of the author/character that is the strength, but also the weakness, of Vince McMahon's dominance of Sports Entertainment. What is intriguing is the line between fiction and fact that the author-as-character can set up, manipulate and even fall victim to himself. We need to be alert to the way in which the demands and constraints of storytelling and the constant need to reawaken an audience's interest will shape a character. When that character is presented as the structuring feature of the story-shaped world, the consequences for those involved in the story can be incalculable. Vince McMahon's tussle with God is precisely a struggle over who controls the story and who embodies the Law.

It is in the areas that liberal and rational biblical scholarship finds most offensive in the biblical texts—apocalyptic, the supernatural (especially the demonic) and the allure of violence—that the WWE draws on the Bible and illuminates it by recapitulating some of its most characteristic structural tensions. On such matters, it may be that the highly paid and highly skilled analysts and manipulators of American popular culture who have made WWE such an international success may have more to contribute to understanding the outrageous and enduring cultural power of the Bible than do the tweedy denizens of biblical academia.

Chapter 15

# The NASCAR Bible

Life sometimes outpaces imagination. One example of this occurred on my only visit to Mount Rushmore, sadly on a day so foggy that the Presidents' heads, and indeed the whole mountain, were invisible from the viewpoint. As I made do with a trip to the gift shop, I had what I thought was the satirical thought that a lot of money could be made from selling cuddly toy versions of the Presidents. I came out the proud owner of a stuffed plush Teddy Roosevelt.

Something similar occurred in my researches into the Bible and popular culture. Having become intrigued by the surprisingly explicit role of the Bible in WWE (World Wrestling Entertainment), I fell to wondering about its role in that other sporting and commercial phenomenon of contemporary America, NASCAR (National Association for Stock Car Auto Racing). This led to various forays into the internet. As a result, I am now the proud owner of one of the many releases from Zondervan Bibles: *The Holy Bible: Stock Car Racing Edition*, published in October 2009. It contains the complete New International Version translation in red-letter format, interleaved with parables and testimonies from the world of NASCAR in twelve four-page full-colour articles distributed throughout the text.

The existence of such an edition, which I will from now on refer to as the SCR version, is testimony to a synergy of marketing between one of America's major sporting and cultural institutions, on the one hand, and, on the other, evangelical Christianity, in particular Motor Racing Outreach (MRO), an organization devoted to bringing the gospel to the racing community.[1] The point is made succinctly in the explanation

---

1. Founded in 1988, this organization now has a wide ministry to fans and to drivers and their families, including religious services and bible studies at race meetings. Besides the Stock Car Racing Bible, its website, to be found at http://www.go2mro.com, lists a number of publications which offer devotional material tailored to race fans, with titles such as *When the Thunder Rolls; Whoever Gets to Heaven First Wins*; and *Going the Distance: Building Strong Relationships*.

of the role of MRO that is provided in the SCR version: "The thrill and excitement of the race and a sense of belonging draw people to NASCAR. MRO believes the same will draw men and women to Jesus Christ."

NASCAR has a vested interest in portraying itself as a family affair, rooted in core American values, with respect for the Bible a cultural given. Evangelical Christians and Bible salesmen see an opportunity for mission and outreach in the millions of loyal followers of NASCAR. What is interesting is that this image represents a more or less deliberate rewriting of the history of NASCAR, sometimes to the annoyance of its original supporters. It also reveals what aspects of the biblical message the sponsors of this Bible wish to get across and what analogies they find in the world of NASCAR to help in this. At the same time, the use of traditionally Christian language and concepts by NASCAR fans as they account for its importance to their lives and sense of communal identity is another element in this symbiosis between what might seem unlikely partners, seen from the outside.

For those who may not be clear what NASCAR is, I will offer a brief overview, before going on to look in more detail the complex interdependence of sport, Christianity and nationalism in the identity of the NASCAR fans. After a brief examination of the SCR Bible itself and how it reflects and reinforces this identity, I shall conclude with some final remarks on the significance of this for biblical scholars.

## *The NASCAR Nation*

NASCAR involves teams who race cars that are highly modified but still recognizable versions of those available on the general market from major manufacturers around a track, sometimes for three and a half hours at a time. This is no obscure hobby. Nearly five million people attended NASCAR race meetings in the USA in 2007, while around 250 million watched the NASCAR Sprint Cup Series on television. It also made more than two billion dollars in licensed sales and attracted billions more in corporate sponsorship, being known for the brand loyalty of its fans.

What is the reason for this phenomenal success? Mark Martin in *NASCAR for Dummies*[2] puts it down very simply to the fact that driving is a skill that the majority of Americans share. In a way that is not true

---

2. Mark Martin (with Beth Tuschak and Mike Ford), *NASCAR for Dummies* (3d ed.; Hoboken: Wiley, 2009). The fact that this guide has reached three editions is testimony in itself to the wide and growing interest in the sport.

for many sports that demand specialist training or unfamiliar equipment, in essence NASCAR remains something that almost anyone in the crowd could envisage themselves doing. The reality is of course rather different; training, team membership and very expensive equipment are essential for any good racer, but the identification is there. Unlike Formula One, for instance, the cars remain outwardly recognizable as the cars the spectators themselves drive, despite the far-reaching modifications they undergo.

We can unpack this further. For most Americans, a car is both a ubiquitous necessity and a site of fantasy. The young boy who dreams of his first car dreams of independence and mobility: in a word, freedom. Furthermore, although driving is a skill that most people have, it has had to be acquired and publicly acknowledged. This is one test the majority of the population have had to sit and have passed. Proverbially, no-one thinks he or she is a bad driver. Again, everyone knows the frustrations of sitting in a traffic jam and the minor triumph of stealing a march on other drivers by spotting a quick way through. Stock car racing buys into these common experiences and fantasies; it simply heightens them and allows the crowd to live them vicariously. The spectators feel that, with a bit of practice, they could do this too.

At the same time, driving is the most dangerous activity most people indulge in on a regular basis and few people have not either experienced or witnessed potentially life-threatening situations on the road. It is also while driving that the average citizen is most likely to run foul of the law, perhaps indulging in the risky thrill of edging over the speed limit or taking a chance on a changing traffic light. Although this is now downplayed by NASCAR's current promoters, the pioneers of stock car racing were bootleggers, using their skills as drivers and mechanics to outrun the excise men as they transported moonshine from the Appalachian foothills into Atlanta.[3] Their criminality was romanticized through association with the atavistic resentment among the thrawn Scots-Irish settlers of the Carolinas of the imposition after the Civil War of what many saw as "Yankee law" and the values of the Puritan north. They became symbols of the remnants of Southern resistance.

The stereotype of a NASCAR fan is that he—and the choice of pronoun is deliberate—is the epitome of the Southern white working-class. This is no longer the case. The engagement with corporate America

---

3. This half-forgotten story is retold in Neal Thompson's *Driving with the Devil: Southern Moonshine, Detroit Wheels, and the Birth of NASCAR* (New York: Three Rivers, 2006).

in sponsorship has driven and been driven by a widening fan base and the spread of NASCAR beyond its Southern home territory. Indeed, its spread has been taken as a key indicator of what some political commentators have diagnosed as the "Southernization" of the United States, especially during the Bush years.[4]

This is a contentious topic and beyond the scope of this discussion, but any such process is double-edged. As Southern values become more widespread, they inevitably lose their local distinctiveness. The rise of NASCAR in the North comes at the expense of the repression of its bootlegging past and the promotion of its American, rather than its Southern, appeal and relevance. "NASCAR *is* America," asserts Jim Wright, a professor of sociology who has analyzed his own obsession with the sport and applies his professional analytic skills to his fellow fans.[5]

In that process, the Bible is an important symbol in that it signifies both the South, as in the phrase "the Bible Belt," but also the whole nation, in the "biblical values" that underpin what it is to be American. Indeed, part of the unease that underlies analyses of the "Southernization" of the US is over the place of the Bible in American public life. On the one hand, there are those who are anxious over the encroachment of a particular interpretation of biblical values, stereotypically associated with the South, into the political decisions of the nation. On the other hand, there are those who are anxious over the encroachment of the Federal State into areas of decision-making where the Bible has traditionally been the benchmark for communal values.

Tense though this is, what it means is that the Bible can function to some extent as a marker of Southernness that has purchase beyond the South. As NASCAR's management seeks the commercial opportunities afforded by an expansion across the whole of the US and seeks to attract major national sponsorship, the Bible, carefully handled, is a useful ally. Theological or denominational disputes are kept out of the picture, so that it is presented as a unifying symbol of shared communal values and the shared aspirations of the American way of life.

---

4. See on this J. I. Newman and M. D. Giardina, "NASCAR and the 'Southernization' of America: Spectatorship, Subjectivity and the Confederation of Identity," *Cultural Studies<=>Critical Methodologies* 8 (2008): 479–506 (479), published online at http://csc.sagepub.com/cgi/content/abstract/8/4/479 on August 8, 2008.

5. Jim Wright, *Fixin' to Git: One Fan's Love Affair with NASCAR's Winston Cup* (Durham: Duke University Press, 2002). Those of an academic bent who find the devotion to NASCAR rather baffling may find some clues to its attraction in this book.

## 15. *The NASCAR Bible*

### *NASCAR Hermeneutics*

What we find in the presentation of the Bible in the SCR version is an emphasis on the connection between the life of the reader and, ostensibly, the text. Each of the four-page inserts starts with a slogan from NASCAR that is then linked to questions about the reader's self-understanding with references to relevant biblical passages. The fourth page is given over to a testimony by or about a leading figure in NASCAR.

The headings of the twelve inserts give a flavour of their tone

1. Why do we race?
2. Gentlemen, Start Your Engines
3. Staying on Track
4. Flags
5. Let's Get This Party Started
6. Spotters
7. War Wagon
8. Unseen Strength
9. Hand Signals
10. Let's Go
11. Position Players
12. Caution

Life, the message seems to be, is a risky but rewarding race where we all need help but where we can all be winners if we take courage and rely on friends and family. With a bit of guidance, we can keep on track and even come back from seemingly catastrophic crashes using the ordinary resources of the community. The social schema of the NASCAR race becomes the metaphorical frame within which the Bible can be read.

Space does not allow the analysis of all the inserts, but one particular trope that is distinctive to NASCAR is the metaphorical use of the "Spotter." In NASCAR terms, the spotter is a member of the driver's team who is perched high up in the stand and linked by radio to the driver. Because of the congestion of the race and the restrictions on the driver's vision because of the safety equipment required, the spotter is vital in alerting the driver to upcoming danger and also to opportunities to slip ahead of his rivals.

The metaphorical application is clear. The insert on the spotter asks, "Do you have a spotter, a friend who can provide Biblical counsel in a moment of crisis?" and "On the other side of the coin, do you have the Biblical perspective to help a friend who can't see beyond his or her circumstances to get the bigger picture?" In the wider NASCAR world, "Jesus is my spotter" is a slogan that adorns tee-shirts, mugs and baseball caps and is the title of a well-known NASCAR gospel song written by Tim Malchuk and Joe McCaffrey, available from the MRO website.

A selection from the lyrics reads:

> Twisted steel, fire and smoke
> On this track that ain't no joke
> 'Cause at every turn there's danger 'neath my wheels.
> I got bumped 'bout two laps back
> Almost made me leave the track
> But by the grace of God I'm still running with the field
>
> The voice that's in my radio
> Is guiding me on where to go
> To keep me safe this long hot afternoon
> But something's wrong ahead of me
> It's getting hard for me to see
> There's only one way I can make it through
>
> *Chorus*
>
> 'Cause I know what I believe
> And I know that God is watching over me
> When all is said and done
> In my heart I know
> Jesus is my spotter
> And I've already won.

That sense of individual guidance through a difficult race with the promise of an eternal victory party at the end underlies the hermeneutic and the peculiar mix of independence and dependence that is the ideal held out for the spiritual and social life of the NASCAR fan.

## *The Relevant Irrelevance*

In the end, however, what is most striking about the SCR version is how little interaction there is between the inserts and the text. The full-colour glossy inserts contrast with the plain printed texts and tend to be the points at which the Bible falls open. The distribution of the inserts appears to be random and mechanical, as they are spaced equally throughout the Old and New Testaments. Although the inserts include some, but surprisingly few, biblical references, they seldom urge the reader to refer to wider passages in the Bible and certainly give no advice on how to tackle the more difficult texts that surround them.

Of course, there are some intriguing, but apparently accidental, juxtapositions. Why should a section on "War Wagon" be inserted in the middle of Song of Songs 5:6? One could apply some ingenuity, but to no great purpose, in justifying such things; in this case, could we make anything of a link to Songs 6:12: "Before I realized it, my desire set me among the royal chariots of my people"? Mind you, biblical scholars might take pause at the thought of the ingenuity that may be expended on biblical texts to make sense of what may in the end be accidental or random juxtapositions in the assembly of biblical books themselves.

What this version represents, almost in spite of itself, then, is the relevance of the Bible as symbol in the continuing debate over the nature of American identity, and the irrelevance of much of the Bible as text in that debate. Just as the NASCAR driver can rely on his spotter and does not need to see the road or his rivals, so the biblical reader can rely on a few moral slogans to see him through and need not worry himself about his limited view of the intricacies of the race.

As biblical scholars, this may remind us of the potential significance of the text we study as a commercial and political entity, but it also shows the insignificance on the wider scale of much of the scholarship we are proud of. How biblical scholarship can best emulate NASCAR's success in attracting major sponsorship without losing its distinctiveness and independence is a question that is more and more pressing. It may be that NASCAR can provide both an example and a warning in this regard.

One intriguing instance of this is a novel published in 2006 by the best-selling author Sharon McCrumb.[6] It is entitled, significantly, *St Dale*, and follows a diverse group of NASCAR fans on a pilgrimage by bus to sites associated to the NASCAR driver who more than any other has taken on a quasi-religious aura as a role models: Dale Earnhardt. As evidence of his status, Earnhardt is the only dead driver to be featured in one of the SCR version inserts. This begins with a quotation from him: "The winner ain't the one with the fastest car, it's the one who refuses to lose." The message that determination can overcome seeming inequality of opportunity is a key one for the political hermeneutic of the edition.

Known as "The Intimidator" because of his relentless pursuit of rivals and his ruthlessness in pushing his way to the front of the pack, Earnhardt died in a spectacular crash at the Daytona 2001 race meeting. This is a key moment in NASCAR history and his death quickly saw him elevated him to an Elvis-like iconic status. To this day, the number "3," the number of the car he drove, has a quasi-religious significance for his fans, appearing on innumerable souvenirs and items of memorabilia. His home town, Kannapolis NC, not only hosts a more than life-size statue of Earnhardt and a museum of his life, but also advertises a pilgrimage route to places of significance in his life which is laid out round the city and this is much visited.

---

6. Sharon McCrumb, *St Dale* (New York: Kensington, 2006).

In her novel, Sharon McCrumb reuses the format of Chaucer's *Canterbury Tales* but puts Earnhardt in place of Thomas à Becket, complete with miraculous appearances. Asked about the reason for Earnhardt's appeal, she replied, "He is a twentieth-century Thomas à Becket: a poor boy who made good in a system stacked against him, and who retained his humility to the last."

As she explains further, however, part of her motivation in writing the novel is to reverse the cultural flow. Students who otherwise would never dream of reading Chaucer may be induced to do so once they have been hooked by the prospect of understanding more about their hero, Dale Earnhardt, and the novel has a useful appendix of suggested teaching material that could be used to supplement its reading in a school classroom.

What applies to Chaucer, of course, applies to the Bible. The development of biblical myths, so one could argue, follows the same kind of logic and the assimilation of the dead driver to an angelic or even Christlike figure in the internal mythology of the text would give considerable scope for investigating this parallel. Furthermore, no reader of Chaucer can get far without encountering language, images and narrative allusions that are biblically derived. Perhaps Sharon McCrumb may suggest an odd way in to reviving interest in Biblical Studies as well as Chaucer Studies in American schools. Perhaps every professor of Biblical Studies needs to know his or her NASCAR in order to trace the odd intersections between the Bible and popular culture at its most crass, at least in the eyes of the kind of people who set themselves up as the arbiters of high culture. Once unchained, the Bible finds itself among some unlikely companions. The more obvious attempts to insert the Bible into the discourse of the NASCAR fans may miss the fact that at less obvious but more potent levels, the Bible relates very well to the unconscious drives that fuel devotion to the sport.

Part VII

THE SURVIVAL OF THE BIBLE

Chapter 16

## Dispelling Delusions:
## Dawkins, Dennett and Biblical Studies

Religion, and by extension Biblical Studies, has taken quite a beating from the advocates of a strictly scientific approach to understanding human psychology and social structures. Two of the leading figures in this debate, Richard Dawkins and Daniel Dennett, both published best-selling books in 2006 that seek to show that religion can be adequately explained as a natural phenomenon in terms of evolutionary theory and cognitive science. Dawkins, then the Charles Simonyi Professor of the Public Understanding of Science at Oxford, published *The God Delusion*,[1] and Dennett, Professor of Philosophy and Director of the Center for Cognitive Science at Tufts University, came out with *Breaking the Spell: Religion as a Natural Phenomenon*.[2]

Although there are clear areas where the two agree, and indeed where they explicitly make use of the other's work, their approaches and agendas are far from identical. Dawkins goes on to denounce religion and its practitioners as destructive influences which should be got rid of. Dennett, more irenically, sees religion as inevitable, but untrue. Both books have been international bestsellers and a rash of more or less temperate statements of support by fellow-travellers have hit the book-shops, as have a smaller rash of more or less pertinent refutations.[3]

---

1. Richard Dawkins, *The God Delusion* (London: Bantam Press, 2006).
2. Daniel C. Dennett, *Breaking the Spell: Religion as a Natural Phenomenon* (New York: Viking, 2006).
3. As typical examples, Alastair McGrath, Professor of Historical Theology at Oxford University, has attempted to turn the tables on his colleague with *The Dawkins Delusion? Atheist Fundamentalism and the Denial of the Divine* (London: SPCK, 2007), while from the other camp, Christopher Hitchens's *God Is Not Great: How Religion Poisons Everything* (London: Atlantic, 2007), and Sam Harris's *Letter to a Christian Nation: A Challenge to Faith* (New York: Random House, 2006), have also made it to the best-seller lists.

As for the advocates of Biblical Studies, there is an implication from the supporters of Dawkins and Dennett that they should be dismayed by this onslaught and be reduced to a frantic gathering of fig-leaves to sew together in an attempt to cover the intellectual nakedness of the subject and the futility of their careers so that they can go on making money out of selling superstitious obscurantism to credulous fools, while battening parasitically on the intellectual reputation of the universities and other august institutions where they are employed.

Fortunately, some robust defences of the teaching of Biblical Studies have appeared at the same time. I quote:

> The King James Bible of 1611—the Authorized Version—includes passages of outstanding literary merit in its own right, for example the Song of Songs, and the sublime Ecclesiastes (which I am told is pretty good in the original Hebrew too). But the main reason the English Bible needs to be part of our education is that it is a major source book for literary culture... Ignorance of the Bible is bound to impoverish one's appreciation of English literature... An atheistic world-view provides no justification for cutting the Bible, and other sacred books, out of our education.[4]

Where do you suppose those sentiments came from? Well, it is Richard Dawkins himself, in *The God Delusion*, although more needs to be said. For someone who came up with the idea of the meme, the unit of cultural information that is replicated and transformed on analogy with the gene, it turns out that he has a rather narrow view of culture, for one thing,

As for Dennett, "I love the King James Bible," he unambiguously declares towards the end of his earlier book *Darwin's Dangerous Idea*.[5] One delusion that Dawkins and Dennett help us to dispel straightaway is that an interest in the Bible is to be equated with any theological commitment and that to defend it is to defend some dogmatic version of Judaeo-Christian theism. Biblical Studies cannot avoid interacting with religion and theology, but it is certainly not confined to such topics. We could draw an analogy from the study of the Greek and Roman Classics. Nobody asks professors of Classics whether they offer the appropriate sacrifices to Zeus or whether they are suspicious of their possible leanings towards the Eleusinian mysteries. It is good that Dawkins sees the wider possibilities of such studies.

---

4. Dawkins, *The God Delusion*, 341, 343, 344.
5. Daniel Dennett, *Darwin's Dangerous Idea: Evolution and the Meanings of Life* (London: Penguin, 1996), 515.

However, such politeness masks some more profound difficulties. After all, the titles of both the books in question are hardly irenic, given Dawkins' characteristically blunt reference to "delusion" and Dennett's milder but just as reproachful implication that adherents to religion are under a spell. As Dawkins particularly knows, polite exchanges do not make much of a lecture, or sell many books.

In a nutshell, what I want to do in this chapter is, cheekily, to play these two luminaries at their own game and suggest that it is just as possible to account for their writings in the terms of biblical studies as it is for them to account for religion in terms of their chosen discourses. I am explicitly not going to argue for or against the doctrine of evolution as against the theory of creation (and I have quite deliberately confused the terms here to represent the confusion of the debate). For what it is worth, I was trained as an evolutionary biologist and continue to find the explanatory power of the theory of evolution compelling to the extent that I would say that, given our present understanding of molecular biology, if biological evolution did not occur and is not occurring, then something must be actively preventing it. Still, that is not my topic here.

My concern is not with biology but with the Bible. In the epigraph to his first chapter, Dennett quotes a paper of mine in which I used Dawkins's and Dennett's concept of the meme to point out that much of the history of the Biblical tradition can be illuminated by thinking of it as "The Selfish Text."[6] Just as Dawkins turns the tables on human pretension in "The Selfish Gene" by describing us as merely the temporary vehicles through which genes ensure their replication, so I suggested the slogan "Western Culture is the Bible's way of making more Bibles." This time, rather than accounting for the Bible's success in terms of memetics, I want to suggest that Dawkins and Dennett's texts manifest epistemological and rhetorical strategies that have a clear filiation to the biblical tradition. There would be, and could be, no *The God Delusion* or *Breaking the Spell* if there were no Bible and if there had been no Biblical Studies. Such books could only be written in a biblically shaped society, one where, if you like, memes transmitted through the biblical tradition have been and are still at large.

So now let us move on to deal with these two writers in turn in an attempt to substantiate that claim.

---

6. Hugh S. Pyper, "The Selfish Text: Memetics and the Bible," in *Biblical Studies/Cultural Studies* (ed. J. C. Exum and S. D. Moore; Sheffield: Sheffield Academic, 1998), 71–90.

## The Prophetic Dawkins

In *The God Delusion*, Dawkins argues from the perspective of a convinced Darwinian. His first point is that the hypothesis of a creator is unnecessary to account for the existence and diversity of life; secondly, he argues that the idea of God itself can be accounted for within evolutionary psychology as a delusory response to the uncertainty of the world and, thirdly, that it is a dangerous delusion that leads to ignorance, repression and violence and one we would be well rid of. Fortunately, in Dawkins's view, a forthright application of enlightenment rationality will scotch it. For Dawkins, religion as he characterizes it is not simply an error, a product of confusion and ignorance, but a vice, a product of a wilful act of self-delusion. Religious believers are not just mistaken; they are wrong in the strong sense of morally, culpably wrong.

But as I read Dawkins, the voice I hear is a familiar one; it echoes that of Isa 44. This chapter contains a scathing denunciation of idolators which is rich in sarcasm. The writer scornfully points out that the idolator's god is fashioned by the strong arm of the blacksmith, who nevertheless gets weary and needs to stop for a drink, or else by a carpenter who cuts down a tree, uses part of it to fuel a fire to cook his dinner and the rest to make a god which he then worships, praying "Save me, for you are my god!"

Verses 18 to 20 round off the attack, in the NRSV translation:

> They do not know, or do they comprehend; for their eyes are shut, so that they cannot see, and their minds as well, so that they cannot understand. No one considers, nor is there discernment to say: "Half of it I burned in the fire; I also baked bread on its coals. Now shall I make the rest of it an abomination? Shall I fall down before a block of wood?" He feeds on ashes; a deluded mind [*note that phrasing*] has led him astray and he cannot save himself or say, "Is not this thing in my right hand a fraud?"

Here, I would submit, is the essence of Dawkins. There is the same tone of exasperation that we find in his work, not just at the folly of the idolator, but at the fact that he fail to make the minimal effort of thought that would reveal the logical inconsistency of what he is doing. The idolator's failure is a moral one. Neither the biblical writer nor Dawkins can otherwise explain such a lack of logical analysis except as culpable and willed self-delusion and an inability, surely a perverse refusal, to see what is obvious. Idolators suffer from a God-delusion, and dispelling such delusions is what these passages of Isaiah are about.

The anti-idolatrous polemic in Isaiah is scattered throughout the book. In ch. 2 of Isaiah, the people throw away their gold and silver idols to the moles and bats as they seek to find shelter in caves and crevices. Isaiah 46 makes a mockery of the statues of Bel and Nebo being loaded onto the backs of cattle as they make an ignominious retreat from the fallen city. These gods who were meant to "carry" the burden of the people are now burdens themselves that have to be carted off.

It would be beside the point to go to such biblical texts to get an accurate opinion of the religious beliefs and practices of the people of Babylon, of course. The writers of Isaiah are not social anthropologists concerned to approach the religious viewpoint of their target culture with critical empathy. Neither, then, need we expect a balanced critique of religion from Dawkins. That is not his purpose, however much he uses the rhetoric of reason in the debate, just as his creationist opponents seek to use the rhetoric of science.

Both Dawkins and his antagonists in the battle over the scientific basis of biblical account of creation, in my view, are guilty of a skewed portrayal of the biblical material on creation in their polemics. We all know the biblical creation story; God killed the sea monster Rahab and then set limits to the sea—sorry, no, that's in Ps 74 and Isa 51. We all know that really God first created a companion, Sophia, and in her company set bounds to the sea and built the mountains—no, sorry, that is Prov 8. We know that God built the earth on supporting pillars—sorry, no, that's Job. I know, it's Genesis we should be reading. There we read that God created the earth in six days, animals first and then man by his creative word, and made man and woman together on the seventh day. We also read in the next chapter that God first made man from earth, then woman from his side and finally created the animals as his companions.

The point is, of course, that the Bible offers us several creation stories, not one, and thus several creator Gods. It seems to me profoundly unbiblical to take these stories and turn them into one story which the Bible itself does not seem to know, or to have much concern with. Both creationists and Dawkins do this, even if Dawkins had a better claim to the age-old defence, "They started it!" If academic Biblical Studies over the last 250 years has taught us anything, it is that the bible is polyphonic, or, to use a biological metaphor, polyploid. It contains many voices, many Gods, some of which are contradictory and some of which are hidden or submerged, like recessive alleles. The Bible is a series of arguments over hypotheses over the idea of God. Some of the hypotheses proposed, the God of Joshua, for instance, the divine vindicator of tribalism, massacre and holy war, we might well hope are delusions. It is a perfectly respectable way of dealing with the biblical material to see it as recording a process whereby the crude denunciation of idolatry becomes more and more refined so that the danger that is addressed does not lurk in physical representations but ideological constructions. One of these ideological idols, I would submit, is the kind of creator God that some sorts of biblical readers come up with. The hypothesis of the creator and designer God beloved of the Intelligent Design school seems to me to be a highly problematic rationalization of something much more interesting at work in the Bible and in the natural world.

The corollary of this is that Dawkins and Dennett have reason to be grateful that the early Church, after a protracted struggle, decided to retain these texts. The idea that the God of Christianity was also the creator of the manifestly imperfect universe in which we live was scandalous to many of those whom we now identify as Gnostics. Some of them repudiated Genesis and indeed the whole Old Testament on such grounds. Had they won the day, however, what would have happened to any development of physical sciences? If, like the Manichaeans, you conceive of matter as itself evil, in the sense that it is a trap for the pure spirit which continually strives to escape it, you are not likely to spend much time on examining its laws or exclaiming at the wonder of natural phenomena.

The Bible contains a surprising amount of material that is precisely directed against the unintelligent multiplication of spurious religious explanations. If we turn to the creation story of Gen 1, which is so often the bone of contention in these debates, and lay aside for one moment the restricted reading strategy that can only ask the question "What really happened?," we find a text that systematically demystifies and depersonalizes the structure of the world. In other ancient Near Eastern creation myths, the cosmos is presented as a battleground between different gods, each responsible for different functions and, as often as not, providing from their own bodies, living or dead, the material stuff of the universe. In Gen 1, the universe is evacuated of any divine material or any community of Gods. One God alone speaks and order and matter appear. The sun and moon, supreme divinities in their own right in most myths of creation, are not even dignified with a name. They are merely the great and lesser lights. The stars, rather than controlling the times and seasons of the universe, are merely there to mark them. Of course, this is not a modern scientific account of the development of the universe and of life, but it provides an algorithm, in Dennett's terms, for this process of demystification. Creation has its own integrity, is separate from God and responsive to law rather than arbitrary whim.

Here again an implicit target is the creation myths of Babylon and other surrounding cultures. We might not be so surprised that the biblical writers have in it for the practices and beliefs of the Babylonians. After all, the Babylonians have lorded it over them and it is always good to get your own back. The more surprising thing is that this turns out not to be the principal target. After all, it is not likely that the people of Babylon will be reading or hearing the book.

The same kind of denunciation is turned against the cultic practices and beliefs of the religion of Yahweh. Genesis 1 is countering those other creation myths found vestigially elsewhere in the Bible. In Isaiah, in no uncertain terms, God is represented as rejecting not just idols but the feast days and sacrifices of Israel, because of their immorality: "What to me is the multitude of your sacrifices?" says the Lord. "I have had enough of burnt-offerings of rams and the fat of fed beasts" (Isa 1:11). I cannot endure solemn assemblies which are accompanied by iniquity," he continues. "Cease to do evil, learn to do good; seek justice, rescue the oppressed, defend the orphan, plead for the widow" (Isa 1:13, 16–17). In such passages, although not consistently through the Hebrew Bible, there is a strong polemic against the ritual practice of religion precisely because of its tendency to ignore and even to condone injustice. This is a biblical voice that we hear in Dawkins's work, too. In the same way, Gen 1 implicitly silences the ancient strand of polytheism and divine conflict has left its traces in the biblical tradition and pre-emptively counters Gnostic spiritualization through its assertion that the world is not to be explained in terms of conflicting wills but through the intrinsic categories of its own description.

Indeed, we might even describe such attitudes as biblical memes for autoimmunity. This self-limiting aspect of the biblical texts is an important element in their survival and the survival of the communities that incorporate them as a source of memes for their own survival. They help to provide a survival strategy for the community when the otherwise focal elements of the temple and of sacificial worship become impossible to maintain. Such texts offer a way of maintaining communal coherence through the effort to sustain the weak of the community in a time of disaster, precisely the strategy that is required. They also check any tendency to interpret disaster as a consequence of the unknowable whims of rival gods. Abandoning the temple and sacrifice in such circumstances is not an abandonment of the core of communal identity but paradoxically the very thing that reinforces it. The tradition carries within it memes that can be activated which seem to be antithetical to it, just as the development of advanced organisms requires that each cell carries genes which when activated would destroy them so that the strategic death of particular tissues can be used in the architecture of the final organism.

Dawkins, I submit, is a locus of expression of this biblical meme. Of course, such iconoclastic memes can run out of control and be fatal to the culture that sustained them, just as an individual organism can die through the inappropriate and self-destructive activation of its own immune system. That is not a reason to be ungrateful for the immune response, however, or for the force of Dawkins' critique.

## *Dennett the Sage*

Let us now turn to the somewhat different case of Dennett. He is less inclined than Dawkins to denounce religion, but explains it as an almost inevitable aspect of the evolution of the human mind, which may well have its dangers but which is not easily, or usefully, got rid of. Given the kind of biological system we are and the evolutionary mechanisms by which consciousness comes to be, on his account, religion is just the kind of thing such minds would generate. "At the root of human belief," he writes, "lies an instinct on a hair trigger: the disposition to attribute *agency*—beliefs and desires and other mental states—to anything complicated that moves."[7] This is an instinct that is highly adaptive for any animal that has to deal with potential predators and prey.

As we argued above, however, the biblical tradition contains at least one strand that precisely seeks to limit this attribution of agency. There is, however, another biblical voice in his work: the voice of the pioneering Director of the Centre for Cognitive Studies in Jerusalem—Qohelet, as the Hebrew tradition names him, the narrator of the book of Qoheleth or Ecclesiastes, and Dennett's lineal predecessor.

A pioneering cognitive scientist? The case could hardly be clearer. In Eccl 1:12, we read "I, Qoheleth, applied my mind to seek and to search out by wisdom all that is done under heaven," and five verses later, "I applied my mind to know wisdom and to know madness and folly" (Eccl 1:17). Qoheleth wants to understand understanding. Two phrases grab our attention here: "I applied my mind"—literally, "I gave my mind/ heart." Qoheleth does not turn to tradition or to external authorities to answer his problem, but *thinks* about it. Secondly, the phrase "under

---

7. Dennett, *Breaking the Spell*, 115.

heaven" or "under the sun." It becomes clear as the book develops that this phrase is a methodological declaration. In using it, Qoheleth sets aside any supernatural explanation. Qoheleth assumes a cosmos whereby the sun is set in the physical barrier of the firmament, but, in his scheme of things, that barrier also marks the boundary of the world "under the sun" which God has left to its own devices.

Furthermore, he not only thinks about his problem, but attempts to carry out a controlled experiment using empirical data. Indeed, we need to step back a bit and say that Qoheleth, the narrator of the book of that name, *is* a cognitive experiment by the authorial voice of the book, a tool for investigating the central claim of the wisdom tradition of the ancient Near East, represented in the Bible by the book of Proverbs for instance: the claim that we are faced with a stark choice between wisdom and folly and that wisdom is the choice that guarantees prosperity and survival.

The book of Job puts this formula to one sort of test. The writer of Qohelet takes a different, experimental approach. You want to know whether wisdom or folly is better? Well then, try both, and who better to take as your model than the wisest of kings, Solomon? In order to control the variables in the situation, we need also to be sure that we cannot argue that the subject is somehow constrained in his access to the resources needed for both wisdom and folly. The writer sets up Qoheleth as the richest and most able of men. He has, if you like, an unlimited research budget. His conclusion at the end of ch. 1? "In much wisdom is much vexation and those who increase wisdom increase sorrow."

Having exhausted wisdom, the logical step is to test folly. However, there is a contradiction here. Qoheleth writes, "I searched with my mind how to cheer my body with wine—my mind still guiding me with wisdom—until I might see what was good for mortals to do under heaven during the few days of their life." "My mind still guiding me with wisdom"—there's the problem. In order for Qoheleth to know whether wisdom or folly are better, he has to experience both, but he has to remain wise as he does it. He is trying soberly to watch himself being drunk to see if it is a better state than sobriety.

He hits upon an unresolvable problem intrinsic to wisdom. It can never "know" folly because the fool is characterized precisely by his lack of reflection on his experience. It is therefore impossible to use wisdom to assess the superiority of wisdom. Nor can we make an argument from external observation to decide whether the wise man or the fool has the better bargain. In the end, as Qoheleth constantly reminds himself: "What happens to the fool will happen to me also: why then have I been so very wise?" (2:15). Wise men and fools both die, and sooner or later both are forgotten. In a phrase that recurs throughout the book, there is no "profit," nothing left over, no tangible result, no benefit, from wisdom—except, perhaps, the dubious one that it comes to know its own profitlessness. Wisdom, which seeks to overcome delusion, is itself delusional if it thinks it can succeed.

There is a great deal more to be said about this amazing book, but the point I want to make is that for all the differences between the book of Qoheleth and Dennett's work, there is a fundamental similarity in the experimental approach to understanding consciousness and a similar conclusion that the sovereign "self" is illusory. In Dennett's view, a theory of consciousness is not an attempt to describe some kind of subject who observes and controls the processes of the brain, but must constantly resist and break down any such description. It seems to me that Qoheleth comes close to a similar insight, or more accurately, the complex history of interpretation of the book shows that its readers have great trouble in finding a coherent, master voice within it. In its own way, it enacts the polyphonic pandemonium that is Dennett's account of the mind.

Notoriously, Qoheleth also refuses any special quality of the human that distinguishes us from animals: "I said in my heart with regard to human beings that God is testing them to show that they are but animals. For the fate of humans and the fate of animals is the same" (3:19). Humans are a phenomenon within the natural world whose regular yet self-cancelling processes are so memorably described in the portrayal of natural cycles in the first chapter or in the indelible "meme" from ch. 3 which has entered our cultural store: "For everything there is a season and a time for every matter under the sun."

Once more, I stress that I not claiming that Qoheleth and Dennett are saying the same thing, any more than I would claim that Dawkins and the writers of Isaiah say the same thing. What I am suggesting is that there are biblical memes, if you like, being expressed in Dennett's text. In Dennett and Dawkins's own terms, though they might disagree with each other on how this should be stated, it is not to be wondered at that their own written works turn out to be modes of transmission of memes which have persisted in Western culture more successfully than most. As Qoheleth writes, "of the making of books there is no end"—not, I would submit, because there is so much knowledge to impart, but because culture and consciousness endlessly orbit the black hole generated by the opaqueness of consciousness to itself

## Conclusion

In conclusion, I want to move on to present a threefold reflection on what we have discussed here in terms of some implications for three different audiences: the professional biblical scholars, the academic community of a secular university, and the seekers for understanding, religious and non-religious, at whose service the first two must be.

*To colleagues in Biblical Studies:*
I hope that we are encouraged to engage with these debates and to respond positively to the genuine if sometimes uninformed interest in the Bible that exists in wider cultural debates. Both Dennett and Dawkins take the Bible seriously, and that is to be welcomed. Both also have a good deal to suggest to us about the cultural processes by which the Bible came to be and how it is presently used. They can remind us how various a tradition we deal with.

Even in his most trenchant criticisms of the religious world-view, Dawkins has a point. His moral indignation at religion is not simply negative. What he reacts to most strongly is the way that religion, in his understanding, evacuates the world of wonder. In a typically controversial image, he urges us at the end of *The God Delusion* to throw off the "burkah" of religion which enables us only to glimpse reality through a narrow slit. "Science flings open the narrow window through which we are accustomed to viewing the spectrum of possibilities." Surely Biblical Studies cannot be worse for that. I am reminded of the sharp observation of another non-biblical scholar who has recently devoted considerable effort to examining the field, the distinguished historian Donald Harman Akenson. In his book *Surpassing Wonder: The Invention of the Bible and the Talmuds*, he has this to say of his experience in researching the scholarly literature:

> When one immerses oneself in recent scholarship concerning the Bible... the effect is curiously anesthetic, even depressing. Hardly anyone seems to be having any fun, and if they are, they do a good job of keeping their pleasure well hidden behind stone faces and dirge-like prose. Instead it seems to me that biblical scholarship should be one great ode to joy.[8]

To which I say, Amen—oops, that's a give-away. Biblical Studies is great fun, and Dawkins and Dennett, if nothing else, do convey a sense of excitement in their respective intellectual enterprises, a bit of which could well rub off on the rest of us.

---

8. Donald Harman Akenson, *Surpassing Wonder: The Invention of the Bible and the Talmuds* (Chicago: University of Chicago Press, 1998), 5.

*To colleagues from the university:*
I hope that this chapter helps to dispel some of the delusions about the discipline of Biblical Studies. No-one need expect simply to have their prejudices reinforced and to have what they learned at Sunday School endorsed and supplied with footnotes. Biblical Studies is, I would claim, a unique resource for that much touted but less enacted aspiration, interdisciplinarity. It has the advantage of not being defined by a methodology, a language or a field of inquiry, but by a text, a text which just happens to be the most widely distributed in the world and one which has one of the longest, unbroken, best documented and most various traditions of reception.

We deal with one of the richest meme banks in our cultural sphere; indeed, I have sometimes described the Bible as "a jungle book," full of richness and diversity, seductive and highly dangerous, but an irreplaceable resource. If a university means anything, it should be the place where we explore, unravel and rethink precisely these resources. I have said before, and I will take this chance to repeat, that the big lie that we need to counter collectively is the idea that we have universities in order to serve the economy, training the new workforce. Nonsense: we have an economy so that we can sustain the leisure for people to have universities. In all this, Biblical Studies has much to offer; there at least, Dawkins, Dennett and I agree.

*To the seekers after truth:*
Towards the end of *The God Delusion*, Dawkins quotes approvingly the well-known statement by J. B. S. Haldane, "Now, my own suspicion is that the universe is not only queerer than we suppose, but queerer than we can suppose." Biblical Studies, if it is worth anything, ought to be demonstrating that the same statement can be made about the Bible itself: it is queerer than we can suppose. Of course, that says nothing either way about whether it is true, or helpful.

What it does say to me, however, is that, if you want to use the Bible as the basis of a theology (and that is certainly not the only thing you can do with it), queerness has to be taken into account. For the theologian, as for the biblical scholar, Dawkins and Dennett should be listened to as salutary critics, not opposed as a threat. Even Dawkins' uncompromising scientific atheism must be taken seriously. My own position is that if you want to do Christian theology from the Bible then you need to take seriously the great programmatic principle of St Gregory of Nazianzus "What is unassumed is not healed"—or, as we might translate it, "What is not taken fully on board cannot be made whole." In a universe where an honest assessment of the evidence leads many observers to conclude that God is absent or non-existent, any account of God that fails to take seriously the viability of a universe without God will be inadequate. Nothing less than a God who can paradoxically know what living without God is like can offer the healing that Gregory points to.

But that is if you want to do Christian theology with the Bible. I hope what I have outlined shows that there are many other reasons to read it. For those without theological interests, the Bible remains the primer in queerness, in Haldane's terms. Qoheleth has not yet been exhausted by 2500 years of reading. Just do not forget to apply the same critical criteria to the Bible as you would to other books, and by the same token, apply the criteria you would to the Bible to the likes of Dawkins and Dennett. Ideological criticism has to cut both ways.

So, at the end of this discussion, what delusions do I hope have been dispelled? Firstly, I hope to have dispelled the delusion that Biblical Studies is an uncritical adjunct of dogmatic theology; secondly, the that the debate between Dawkins, Dennett and religion is a simple matter of rationality against irrationality; thirdly, the delusion that there is only one "god delusion"; fourthly, the delusion that the Bible itself is unaware of the possibility of religious delusions; fifthly, the delusion that Biblical Studies is a marginal special interest in the study of humanities in a secular university; sixthly, the delusion that Biblical Studies has to be deadly dull; and seventhly, the delusion that universities exist to serve economic interests, rather than the other way round. There may well be others, but seven (a good biblical number) will do.

# Epilogue

In the same novel, *Pastors and Masters*, by Ivy Compton-Burnett from which I derived the epigraph to the introduction of this book, there is an instructive vignette where Mrs Merry, a headmaster's wife, is shown in the act of teaching the Bible to the boys at her husband's school:

> Mrs Merry taught the scripture of the school, and there was a general sense of her fitness for the task, based upon her temperament rather than her scholarship. Mr Merry often mentioned the fact of her teaching it to parents.
>
> The boys, who had a tendency to giggle this morning, took their seats about her table.
>
> "It is the scripture lesson," she said, with peaceful lips. "I think we are forgetting that."
>
> The boys read aloud a chapter verse by verse, and Mrs Merry added observations, in a gentle, rather peculiar voice used only on these occasions. At questions she turned to the commentary, and read it out; and it was felt that difficulties had been met as far as reverence permitted. An especial discrepancy caused an increase of mirth. Mrs Merry looked straight at the questioner.
>
> "I don't think we will cavil about it, Johnson. We will just think of it. That will be the best, and the most difficult thing. The book says nothing, you see."
>
> It was felt that a cheap effort had been made; but the laughter held its own.
>
> Mrs Merry looked very long at a boy.
>
> "It is only the Bible, Bentley; only the most sacred book in existence that you are laughing at."[1]

---

1. Ivy Compton-Burnett, *Pastors and Masters* (London: Gollancz, 1972 [1925]), 12.

"It is only the Bible." What in context makes that an ironic statement has been the basis for the previous chapters. It is easy, as the pupils find, to hit upon difficulties and absurdities in the Bible of a kind that would not usually be put before children. It is also only too true that temperament rather than scholarship is thought to be the prime qualification to teach the Bible, although we would do well to be wary of espousing the cause of a scholarship that takes no account of temperament. Also only too recognizable is the resort to one or other authoritative commentator who, in Compton-Burnett's sly phrase, resolves difficulties as far as reverence permits. Less common, and also easily parodied, is the irenic response Mrs Merry offers when these devices fail to answer the real questions that the discrepancies in the text do raise. Instead of cavilling about such a difficulty, she recommends that readers should "think of it." This will be the best and the most difficult thing, she counsels. At least she makes a virtue of taking the most difficult approach.

Thinking of a difficulty, however, is not the same as thinking about it, or thinking it through, we might argue. Mrs Merry's reading strategies are programmatically limited by her conviction that we need to show reverence to this most sacred of texts, and by her lack of critical knowledge of the text and its interpretation. Yet if this really is irresolvable for whatever reason, then contemplating the very fact of that difficulty may not just be the best, but also the only responsible thing that the reader can do.

# BIBLIOGRAPHY

Akenson, Donald Harman. *Surpassing Wonder: The Invention of the Bible and the Talmuds.* Chicago: University of Chicago Press, 1998.
Allsen, Thomas. *The Royal Hunt in Eurasian History.* Philadelphia: University of Pennsylvania Press, 2006.
Martin Anderson, "Tobias; Des Jona Sendung," *Fanfare* 19/3 (1996), n.p. Online: http://www.fanfarearchive.com/articles/atop/19_3/1932680.az_TOBIAS_Des_Jona_Sendung.html.
Apuleius. *Metamorphoses.* Vol. 1, *Books VII–XI.* Loeb Classical Library 453. Translated by J. Arthur Hanson; Cambridge, Mass.: Harvard University Press, 1989.
Arvidsson, Stefan. *Aryan Idols: Indo-European Mythology as Ideology and Science.* Chicago: University of Chicago Press, 2006.
Ashcroft, Bill, Gareth Griffiths and Helen Tiffin. *The Empire Writes Back.* 2d ed. London: Routledge, 2002.
Auerbach, Erich. *Mimesis: The Representation of Reality in Western Literature.* Translated by Willard R. Trask. Princeton: Princeton University Press, 1968.
Barnard, F. M. *Herder on Nationality, Humanity, and History.* Montreal and Kingston: McGill-Queen's University Press, 2003.
Barrow, John, and Frank Tipler. *The Anthropic Cosmological Principle.* Oxford: Oxford University Press, 1988.
Barthes, Roland. "Le monde où l'on catche." Pages 13–24 in *Mythologies.* Paris: Editions du Seuil, 1970 (1957). English Translation: "The World of Wrestling." Pages 18–30 in *Barthes: Selected Writings.* Edited by Susan Sontag. London: Fontana/Collins, 1983.
Bashō, *Haiku.* Translated by Lucien Stryk. London: Penguin, 1995.
Blaikie, James. *The English Bible and Its Story: Its Growth, Its Translators and Their Adventures.* London: Seeley, Service, 1928.
Blake, William. *The Complete Poems.* Edited by W. H. Stevenson. 2d ed. London: Longman, 1989.
Bloch, Ernst. *Atheism in Christianity.* Translated by J. T. Swann. London: Verso, 2009.
Bloch, Ernst, and Theodor Adorno. "Something's Missing: A Discussion between Ernst Bloch and Theodor W. Adorno on the Contradictions of Utopian Longing." Pages 1–17 in *The Utopian Function of Art and Literature: Selected Essays.* Edited by J. Zipes and F. Mecklenburg. Cambridge: MIT, 1988.
Boer, Roland. *Criticism of Heaven: On Marxism and Theology.* Leiden: Brill, 2007.
Bottigheimer, Ruth B. *The Bible for Children: From the Age of Gutenberg to the Present.* New Haven: Yale University Press, 1996.
Brenner Athalya, ed. *A Feminist Companion to the Latter Prophets.* Sheffield: Sheffield Academic, 1995,

Bronowski, J., ed. *William Blake: A Selection of Poems and Letters*. London: Penguin, 1958.
Brüstle, Christa. "The Musical Image of Bruckner." Pages 244–60 in Williamson, ed., *The Cambridge Companion to Bruckner*.
Carroll, Lewis. *The Annotated Alice*. Edited by Martin Gardner. London: Penguin, 2000.
Cave, Nick, et al. *Revelations: Personal Responses to the Books of the Bible*. Edinburgh: Canongate, 2005.
Cixous, Hélène. *Messie*. Paris: Des femmes, 1996.
———. *Three Steps on the Ladder of Writing*. Translated by S. Cornell and S. Sellers. New York: Columbia University Press, 1993.
———. "Writing Blind: Conversation with the Donkey." Pages 139–52 in *Stigmata: Escaping Texts*. Translated by Eric Prenowitz. London, Routledge, 1998.
Compton-Burnett, Ivy. *Pastors and Masters*. London: Gollancz, 1972 (1925).
Darwin, Charles. *The Expression of the Emotions in Man and Animals*. London: John Murray, 1872.
Dawkins, Richard. *The God Delusion*. London: Bantam Press, 2006.
Dennett, Daniel C. *Breaking the Spell: Religion as a Natural Phenomenon*. New York: Viking, 2006.
———. *Darwin's Dangerous Idea: Evolution and the Meanings of Life*. London: Penguin, 1996.
Derrida, Jacques. *The Animal That Therefore I Am*. Translated by David Wills. New York: Fordham University Press, 2008.
———. *The Beast and the Sovereign*, vol. 1. Translated by G. Bennington. Chicago: University of Chicago Press, 2009.
———. *The Beast and the Sovereign*, vol. 2. Translated by G. Bennington. Chicago: University of Chicago Press, 2011.
Dickinson, Asa. "Huckleberry Finn Is Fifty Years Old—But Is He Respectable?" *Wilson Bulletin for Librarians* 1 (1935): 80–85.
Dillard, Annie. *An American Childhood*. San Francisco: HarperPerennial, 1998.
Dobbs-Allsopp, F. W. *Weep, O Daughter of Zion: A Study of the City-Lament Genre in the Hebrew Bible*. Biblica et Orientalia 44. Rome: Editrice Pontificio Istituto Biblico, 1993.
Doré, Gustave. *London: A Pilgrimage*. London: Grant & Co., 1872.
Dostoevsky, Fyodor. *The Idiot*. Translated by Alan Myers; Oxford, Oxford University Press, 1992.
Durrant, Sam. *Postcolonial Narrative and the Work of Mourning*. Albany: State University of New York Press, 2004.
Eça de Queiroz, José Maria, *A Relíquia*. Porto: Livraria Lello, 1935. English translation: *The Relic*. Translated by Margaret Jull Costa. Sawtry: Dedalus, 1994.
Finkelstein, I., and N. A. Silberman. *The Bible Unearthed: Archaeology's New Vision of Ancient Israel and the Origin of Its Sacred Texts*. New York: Simon & Schuster, 2001.
Frei, Hans. *The Eclipse of Biblical Narrative: A Study in Eighteenth and Nineteenth Century Hermeneutics*. New Haven: Yale University Press, 1974.
Geyer, John B. *Mythology and Lament: Studies in the Oracles About the Nations*. Aldershot: Ashgate, 2004.

Gilhus, Ingvild Sælid. *Animals, Gods and Humans: Changing Attitudes to Animals in Greek, Roman and Early Christian Ideas*. Abingdon: Routledge, 2006.
Gray, Alasdair, *1982 Janine*. Canongate Classics. Edinburgh: Canongate Press, 2003.
Grayling, A. C. *The Good Book: A Secular Bible*. London: Bloomsbury, 2011.
Greene, Graham. *Collected Essays*. London: Vintage, 1999.
Haas, Robert, *Anton Bruckner*. Potsdam: Akademische verlagsgesellschaft Athenaion, 1934.
Harris, Sam. *Letter to a Christian Nation: A Challenge to Faith*. New York: Random House, 2006.
Hayes, M. Hunter, *Understanding Will Self*. Columbia: University of South Carolina Press, 2007.
Herder, Johan Gottlieb. *The Spirit of Hebrew Poetry*, vols. 1 and 2. Translated by J. Marsh. Burlington: Edward Smith, 1833.
Heschel, Susannah. *The Aryan Jesus: Christian Theologians and the Bible in Nazi Germany*. Princeton: Princeton University Press, 2008.
Higgins, Kathleen Marie. "Nietzsche and the Mystery of the Ass." Pages 100–118 in *A Nietzschean Bestiary: Becoming Animal beyond Docile and Brutal*. Edited by C. D. Acampora and R. R. Acampora. Lanham: Rowman & Littlefield, 2004.
Hill, John. *Friend or Foe? The Figure of Babylon in the Book of Jeremiah MT*. Leiden: E. J. Brill, 1999.
Hitchens, Christopher. *God Is Not Great: How Religion Poisons Everything*. London: Atlantic, 2007.
Hoban, Russell. *Riddley Walker*. Expanded ed. London: Bloomsbury, 2002.
Horace. *Satires, Epistles and Ars Poetica*. Translated and edited by H. R. Fairclough. Loeb Classical Library 194. Cambridge, Mass.: Harvard University Press, 1926.
Horton, Julian. *Bruckner's Symphonies: Analysis, Reception and Cultural Politics*. Cambridge: Cambridge University Press, 2004.
Hurston, Zora Neale. *Dust Tracks on a Road*. London: Virago, 1986.
Jabès, Edmond. *The Little Book of Unsuspected Subversion*. Translated by Rosemary Waldrop. Stanford: Stanford University Press, 1996.
Jahnow, Hedwig. *Das hebräische Leichenlied im Rahmen der Völkerdichter*. Giessen: Töpelmann, 1923.
Janzen, Waldemar. *Mourning Cry and War Oracle*. Berlin: de Gruyter, 1972.
Johnson, Stephen, ed. *Bruckner Remembered*. London: Faber & Faber, 1998.
Jones, Brian C. *Howling Over Moab: Irony and Rhetoric in Isaiah 15–16*. Atlanta: Scholars Press, 1996.
Jones, William. *Sir William Jones: Selected Poetical and Prose Works*. Edited by Michael J. Franklin. Cardiff: University of Wales Press, 1995.
Kierkegaard, Søren. *The Sickness Unto Death: A Christian Psychological Exposition for Upbuilding and Awakening*. Edited and translated by Howard V. Hong and Edna H. Hong. Princeton: Princeton University Press, 1980.
Lao-Tzu, *Te-tao Ching*. Translated by Robert G. Henricks. New York: The Modern Library, 1993.
Lessing, Reed. "Satire in Isaiah's Tyre Oracle." *Journal for the Study of the Old Testament* 28 (2003): 89–112.
Lewis, C. S. *The Magician's Nephew* in *The Complete Chronicles of Narnia*. London: Collins, 2000.

Lipton, Diana. *Longing for Egypt and Other Unexpected Biblical Tales*. Sheffield: Sheffield Phoenix, 2008.
Long, Jason H., Ph.D. *Biblical Nonsense: A Review of the Bible for Doubting Christians*. New York: iUniverse, 2005.
Lucas, Charles P. "The Influence of Science on Empire." Pages 107–41 in *King's College Lectures on Colonial Problems*. Edited by London: G. Bell & Sons, 1913.
Lucian of Samosata (attrib.). *Lucius, Or the Ass* in *Lucian of Samosata*, vol. 8. Loeb Classical Library 432. Translated by M. D. MacLeod. London: Heinemann, 1967.
Macaulay, Thomas B. Review of Leopold von Ranke, *The Ecclesiastical and Political History of the Popes During the Sixteenth and Seventeenth Centuries* [*Die römische Papste*]. Translated by S. Austin (London, 1840). *Edinburgh Review* 72 (October 1840): 227–58.
MacPherson, James. *The Poems of Ossian and Related Works*. Edited by Howard Gaskill. Edinburgh: Edinburgh University Press, 1996.
McCrumb, Sharon. *St Dale*. New York: Kensington, 2006.
McGrath, Alastair. *The Dawkins Delusion? Atheist Fundamentalism and the Denial of the Divine*. London: SPCK, 2007.
McLeod, John. *Postcolonial London: Rewriting the Metropolis*. Abingdon: Routledge, 2004.
Marsh, Jan, ed. *Black Victorians: Black People in British Art 1800–1900*. Aldershot: Lund Humphries, 2006.
Martin, Mark, with Beth Tuschak and Mike Ford. *NASCAR for Dummies*. 3d ed. Hoboken: Wiley, 2009.
Mercier, Pascal. *Night Train to Lisbon*. Translsated by Barbara Harshav. London: Atlantic, 2009.
Miller, William Ian. *The Anatomy of Disgust*. Cambridge, Mass.: Harvard University Press, 1997.
Nead, Linda, *Victorian Babylon: People, Streets and Images in Nineteenth-century London*. New Haven: Yale University Press, 2000.
Newman, J. I., and M. D. Giardina. "NASCAR and the 'Southernization' of America: Spectatorship, Subjectivity and the Confederation of Identity." *Cultural Studies<=> Critical Methodologies* 8 (2008): 479, published online at http://csc.sagepub.com/cgi/content/abstract/8/4/479.
Nietzsche, Friedrich. *Thus Spoke Zarathustra*. Translated by R. J. Hollingdale. London: Penguin, 1969.
Nussbaum, Martha C. *Hiding from Humanity: Disgust, Shame and the Law*. Princeton: Princeton University Press, 2004.
Nuttall, A. D. *Openings: Narrative Beginnings from the Epic to the Novel*. Oxford: Clarendon Press, 1992.
Obenzinger, Hilton. *American Palestine: Melville, Twain and the Holy Land Mania*. Princeton: Princeton University Press, 1999.
Page, Hugh R, ed. *The Africana Bible: Reading Israel's Scripture from Africa and the African Diaspora*. Minneapolis: Fortress Press, 2010.
Pickthall, M. M. *The Meaning of the Glorious Qur'an*. Hyderabad: Government Central, 1938.
Prickett, Stephen. *Origins of Narrative: The Romantic Appropriation of the Bible*. Cambridge: Cambridge University Press, 1996.

Pyper, Hugh S. "Reading Lamentations." *Journal for the Study of the Old Testament* 95 (2001): 55–69.

———. "The Selfish Text: Memetics and the Bible." Pages 71–90 in *Biblical Studies/ Cultural Studies*. Edited by J. C. Exum and S. D. Moore. Sheffield: Sheffield Academic, 1998.

———. "Swallowed by a Song: Jonah and the Jonah Psalm Through the Looking-glass." Pages 337–58 in *Reflection and Refraction: Studies in Biblical History in Honour of A. Graeme Auld*. Edited by R. Rezetko, T. H. Lim and W. B. Aucker. Vetus Testamentum Supplements 113. Leiden: Brill, 2006.

———. *An Unsuitable Book: The Bible as Scandalous Text*. Sheffield: Sheffield Phoenix, 2005.

Rad, Gerhard von. *Genesis*. Old Testament Library. Rev. ed. London: SCM Press, 1972.

Renan, Ernest. *The Life of Jesus*. Amherst, N.Y.: Prometheus, 1991 (1862).

Rose, Gillian. *The Broken Middle: Out of our Ancient Society*. Oxford: Blackwell, 1992.

Rossetti, Dante Gabriel. *Poems*. London: F. S. Ellis, 1870.

Rozin, P., J. Haidt and K. Fincher. "From Oral to Moral." *Science* 323 (2009): 1179–80.

Said, Edward. *Beginnings: Intention and Method*. London: Granta, 1997.

———. *Orientalism*. Rev. ed. London: Penguin, 2003.

Sawyer, John F. A., ed. *The Blackwell Companion to the Bible and Culture*. Oxford: Blackwell, 2006.

Schweitzer, Albert. *The Quest of the Historical Jesus: A Critical Study of Its Progress from Reimarus to Wrede*. Translated by F. C. Burkitt. Baltimore: The Johns Hopkins University Press, 1998.

Scott, Derek B. "Bruckner's Symphonies—A Reinterpretation." Pages 92–107 in Williamson, ed., *The Cambridge Companion to Bruckner*.

Scott, Jamie S., and Paul Simpson-Housley. "Eden, Babylon, New Jerusalem: A Taxonomy for Writing the City." Pages 331–41 in *"Writing the City": Eden, Babylon and New Jerusalem*. Edited by Peter Preston and Paul Simpson-Housley. London: Routledge, 1994.

Self, Will. *The Book of Dave*. London: Viking, 2006.

Sherwood, Yvonne. "Prophetic Scatology: Prophecy and the Art of Sensation." Pages 183–224 in *In Search of the Present: The Bible Through Cultural Studies*. Edited by Stephen D. Moore. Semeia 82. Atlanta: SBL, 2008.

Skilton, David. "Contemplating the Ruins of London: Macaulay's New Zealander and Others." N.p. Online: homepages.gold.ac.uk/london-journal/march2004/skilton.html.

Sugirtharajah, R. S. *The Postcolonial Bible*. Sheffield: Sheffield Academic, 1998.

The Rabbinical Assembly, *Etz Hayim: Torah and Commentary*. New York: The Jewish Publication Society, 2001.

Reventlow, Henning Graf. *The Authority of the Bible and the Rise of the Modern World*. Translated by John Bowden. London: SCM Press, 1980.

Strawn, Brent A. *What Is Stronger Than a Lion? Leonine Image and Metaphor in the Hebrew Bible and the Ancient Near East*. Biblicus et Orientalis 212. Fribourg: Academic Publishing/Göttingen: Vandenhoeck & Ruprecht, 2005.

Thompson, Neal. *Driving with the Devil: Southern Moonshine, Detroit Wheels, and the Birth of NASCAR*. New York: Three Rivers, 2006.

Twain, Mark. *The Innocents Abroad*. London: Penguin, 2003.

Tyler, Tom. "*Quia Ego Nominor Leo*: Barthes, Stereotypes and Aesop's Animals." *Mosaic* 40 (2007): 45–59.
Ueda, Makoto. *Bashō and His Interpreters: Selected Hokku with Commentary*. Stanford Calif.: Stanford University Press, 1992.
Urry, John. *The Tourist Gaze*. 2d ed. London: Sage, 2002.
Walker, Franklin. *Irreverent Pilgrims: Melville, Brown and Mark Twain in the Holy Land*. Seattle: University of Washington Press, 1974.
Watts, John D. W. *Isaiah 1–33*. Word Biblical Commentary 24. Waco: Word Books, 1985.
Way, Kenneth C. *Donkeys in the Bible World*. Winona Lake: Eisenbrauns, 2011.
Williamson, George S. *The Longing for Myth in Germany: Religion and Aesthetic Culture from Romanticism to Nietzsche*. Chicago: University of Chicago Press, 2004.
Williamson, John, ed. *The Cambridge Companion to Bruckner*. Cambridge: Cambridge University Press, 2004.
Wright, Jim. *Fixin' to Git: One Fan's Love Affair with NASCAR's Winston Cup*. Durham, N.C.: Duke University Press, 2002.
Young, Frances. *The Art of Performance: Towards a Theology of Holy Scripture*. London: Darton, Longman & Todd, 1990.
Zizioulas, John D. *Communion and Otherness*. Edited by Paul McPartlan. London: T&T Clark International, 2006.

# Indexes

## Index of References

| Hebrew Bible/ Old Testament | | | | | |
|---|---|---|---|---|---|
| *Genesis* | | *1 Kings* | | *Song of Songs* | |
| 1 | 41, 137, 173 | 13 | 136 | 5:6 | 162 |
| 1:1 | 6, 40, 44 | 20 | 136 | 6:12 | 162 |
| 1:26 | 137 | *2 Kings* | | *Isaiah* | |
| 2 | 137 | 6:24–32 | 27 | 1:11 | 173 |
| 2:19 | 137 | 14 | 117 | 1:13 | 173 |
| 4:10 | 16 | 14:25 | 116 | 1:16–17 | 173 |
| 11:14–15 | 15 | 16 | 70 | 6 | 50 |
| 11:19 | 15 | 17 | 136 | 14:2 | 70 |
| 32 | 153 | 18:13–36 | 50 | 15–16 | 71 |
| 42 | 49 | 20:12–15 | 64 | 22 | 114 |
| 42:23 | 49 | | | 23:1–14 | 71 |
| | | *Nehemiah* | | 28 | 48 |
| *Exodus* | | 8:8 | 50 | 28:3 | 6 |
| 4:10 | 49 | | | 28:10 | 48 |
| 12:2 | 40, 41 | *Psalms* | | 28:13 | 46, 50 |
| 14:11 | 56 | 12 | 114 | 33:19 | 49 |
| 16:4 | 28 | 14 | 114 | 44 | 170 |
| 16:20 | 28 | 37 | 22 | 44:18–20 | 170 |
| | | 73 | 22 | 51 | 171 |
| *Leviticus* | | 74 | 171 | | |
| 20:13 | 22 | 111:6 | 40 | *Jeremiah* | |
| | | | | 27 | 72 |
| *Numbers* | | *Proverbs* | | 29:49 | 72 |
| 14:22 | 56 | 8 | 171 | 30:3 | 151 |
| 22–24 | 145 | | | 50–51 | 72 |
| 22 | 145 | *Ecclesiastes* | | | |
| 22:27 | 145 | 1 | 175 | *Ezekiel* | |
| | | 1:12 | 174 | 3:16 | 49 |
| *Deuteronomy* | | 1:17 | 174 | 4:9–15 | 23 |
| 23:12–14 | 24 | 2:15 | 175 | 4:12 | 23 |
| 28 | 27 | 3 | 176 | 4:14 | 23 |
| 28:53 | 27 | 3:19–20 | 57 | 4:15 | 23 |
| | | 3:19 | 176 | 16 | 23, 143 |
| | | | | 20 | 156 |
| | | | | 23 | 23 |

## Index of References

*Joel*
2:31        151

*Jonah*
4:11        114

*Nahum*
2:4         62

*Zephaniah*
1:8         151

NEW TESTAMENT
*Matthew*
27:25       22

*Mark*
7:18        28

*John*
6:60        27
6:61        27
11:39       28

*Romans*
8:10–21     60

*Acts*
3           119
10:13       26

*Galatians*
2:11–22     26

*Revelation*
16          151

CLASSICAL WORKS
Augustine
*Confessions* XI iii    42

Herodotus
*Histories* 1:4    16
1.5                16

Plato
*Timaeus* 29c    42

Tertullian
*Ad Nationes*
1.11        141

*Apologeticus*
1.16.12     141

# INDEX OF AUTHORS

Adorno, T. 54
Akenson, D. H. 177
Allsen, T. 135, 136
Anderson, M. 111
Arvidsson, S. 107
Ashcroft, B. 62
Auerbach, E. 90

Barnard, F. M. 101
Barrow, J. 37
Barthes, R. 152
Bashō 67
Blaikie, J. 64
Blake, W. 73
Bloch, E. 7, 53–55
Boer, R. 54
Bottigheimer, R. B. 4
Brenner, A. 23
Brüstle, C. 127, 128

Carroll, L. 45
Cixous, H. 4, 11, 146, 147
Compton-Burnett, I. 1, 180

Darwin, C. 18
Dawkins, R. 167, 168
Dennett, D. 167, 168, 174
Derrida, J. 136–38
Dickinson, A. 13
Dillard, A. 3
Dobbs-Allsop, F. W. 70, 71
Doré, G. 66
Dostoevsky, F. 146
Durrant, S. 73, 74

Eça de Queirós, J. M. 8, 79, 82

Fincher, K. 20
Finkelstein, I. 86, 96
Ford, M. 158
Frei, H. 90

Geyer, J. B. 70, 71
Giardina, M. D. 160

Gilhus, I. S. 141, 142
Gray, A. 98
Grayling, A. C. 14, 15
Greene, G. 4
Griffiths, G. 62

Haas, R. 127
Haidt, J. 20
Harris, S. 167
Hayes, M. H. 97
Herder, J. G. 102
Heschel, S. 107
Higgins, K. M. 148
Hill, J. 72, 73
Hitchen, C. 167
Hoban, R. 95
Horton, J. 128
Hurston, Z. N. 3

Jabès, E. 3
Jahnow, H. 71
Janzen, W. 71
Johnson, S. 130
Jones, B. C. 71
Jones, W. 106

Kierkegaard, S. 30

Lao-Tzu 36
Lessing, R. 71
Lewis, C. S. 139
Lipton, D. 69
Long, J. H., Ph.D. 45
Lucas, C. P. 62

Macauley, T. B. 66
MacPherson, J. 104
Marsh, J. 63–65
Martin, M. 158
McCrumb, S. 163
McGrath, A. 167
McLeod, J. 68
Mercier, P. 30
Miller, W. I. 19, 20

## Index of Authors

Nead, L. 66
Newman, J. I. 160
Nietzsche, F. 147
Nussbaum, M. C. 20
Nuttall, A. D. 38, 39

Obenzinger, H. 79, 83
Oberleithner, M. von 130

Page, H. R. 75
Pickthall, M. M. 36
Prickett, S. 87
Pyper, H. S. 5, 71, 116, 169

Rad, G. von 43
Renan, E. 92, 93
Reventlow, H. G. 89
Rose, G. 40
Rossetti, D. G. 67
Rozin, P. 20

Said, E. 44, 80
Sawyer, J. F. A. 123
Schweitzer, A. 87, 92
Scott, D. B. 123
Scott, J. S. 68
Self, W. 8, 94, 95, 97

Sherwood, Y. 24, 25
Silberman, N. A. 86, 96
Simpson-Housley, P. 68
Skilton, D. 66
Strawn, B. A. 134
Sugirtharajah, R. S. 64

Thompson, N. 159
Tiffin, H. 62
Tipler, F. 37
Tuschak, B. 158
Twain, M. 82
Tyler, T. 138

Ueda, M. 67
Urry, J. 80

Walker, F. 82
Watts, J. D. W. 48
Way, K. C. 144
Williamson, G. S. 103
Wright, J. 160

Young, F. 124

Zizioulas, J. D. 58, 59

www.ingramcontent.com/pod-product-compliance
Lightning Source LLC
Chambersburg PA
CBHW061833300426
44115CB00013B/2359